DUENDE

POEMS, 1966–NOW

QUINCY TROUPE

SEVEN STORIES PRESS

NEW YORK · OAKLAND · LONDON

Seven Stories Press
140 Watts Street
New York, NY 10013
www.sevenstories.com

College professors and high school and middle school teachers may order free examination copies of Seven Stories Press titles. Visit https://www.sevenstories.com/pg/resources-academics or email academics@sevenstories.com.

Library of Congress Cataloging-in-Publication Data

Names: Troupe, Quincy, author.
Title: Duende : poems, 1966-now / Quincy Troupe.
Description: New York : Seven Stories Press, 2021.
Identifiers: LCCN 2021020301 (print) | LCCN 2021020302 (ebook) | ISBN
    9781644210468 (trade paperback) | ISBN 9781644210451 (hardcover) | ISBN
    9781644210475 (ebook)
Subjects: LCGFT: Poetry.
Classification: LCC PS3570.R63 D84 2021 (print) | LCC PS3570.R63 (ebook)
    | DDC 811/.54--dc23
LC record available at https://lccn.loc.gov/2021020301
LC ebook record available at https://lccn.loc.gov/2021020302

Printed in the USA.

9 8 7 6 5 4 3 2 1

All artwork © José Bedia:
FRONTIS: *Stillness*, 1994, tempura & charcoal on Stonehenge paper,
    41 1/8 x 51 3/8 inches wide
PAGE 216: *Avalanche*, 1994, tempura & charcoal on Stonehenge paper,
    41 1/8 x 52 3/8 inches wide
PAGE 229: *A Poem for "Magic,"* 1994, acrylic on amate bark paper,
    47 x 94 1/8 inches wide
PAGE 244: *The Old People Speak of Death*, 1994, acrylic on amate bark paper,
    47 x 94 1/8 inches wide
PAGE 246: *Conjuring Against Alien Spirits*, 1994, 41 1/8 x 52 3/8 inches wide
PAGE 251: *Poem for My Father*, 1994, tempura & charcoal on Stonehenge paper,
    41 1/8 x 52 3/8 inches wide
PAGE 254: *Male Springtime Ritual*, 1994, tempura & charcoal on Stonehenge paper, 41 1/8 x 52 3/8 inches wide
PAGE 260: *La Jolla-1 & 2*, 1994, tempura & charcoal on Stonehenge paper
    (diptych), 41 1/8 x 52 3/8 inches wide
PAGE 261: *The Flip Side of Time*, 1994, tempura & charcoal on Stonehenge paper, 41 1/8 x 52 3/8 inches wide

For Margaret

CONTENTS

From *Embryo*
(BARLENMIR HOUSE, 1972)

From *Snake-Back Solos: Selected Poems, 1969–1977*
(I. REED BOOKS, 1978)

From *Skulls along the River*
(I. REED BOOKS, 1984)

From *Weather Reports: New Poems, 1984–1990*
(HARLEM RIVER PRESS / WRITERS AND READERS, 1991)

From *Avalanche*

(COFFEE HOUSE PRESS, 1996)

From *Choruses*

(COFFEE HOUSE PRESS, 1999)

From *Transcircularities: New and Selected Poems*

(COFFEE HOUSE PRESS, 2002)

From *The Architecture of Language*

(COFFEE HOUSE PRESS, 2006)

From *Errançities*
(COFFEE HOUSE PRESS, 2012)

Ghost Voices: A Poem in Prayer

(TRIQUARTERLY BOOKS / NORTHWESTERN UNIVERSITY PRESS, 2019)

From *Seduction: New Poems, 2013–2018*
(TRIQUARTERLY BOOKS / NORTHWESTERN UNIVERSITY PRESS, 2019)

New Poems: 2019–2020

from
EMBRYO

EMBRYO

for my mother, Dorothy Smith Troupe Marshall

I.
We come from earth
mother give us your blood
give us strong love to become

seed of water-spirit
sunbird of love in flight

poetry of birth in motion

strength of cyclic movement
in a family of plane curves

locus of points that move
the ratio
distance of fixed point
to distance
of fixed line

poetry of birth in motion

that is infinite
plane curve formed
in the water-spirit womb

of the axis
the intersected cone
locus of points summing

sunbird of love birth in flight

distances fixing constants
wind/storm   rain   air   water
sun earth   spirit-birth

point of departure
found in beginnings that ripen

germinating embryo
sprung African shades of ancestors
flung from petals of flowers into
bloodstreams of harvesting eyewinds

poetry of birth in motion

& carried to distant planes
that sing not from wombseeds
of Georgia Tennessee & Missouri
where life sometimes begins & ends

in wombs of concrete labyrinths

2.
Life is molten rocks
spilling out from lips of volcanoes
red/orange finger rivers
that destroy to give birth
within wombs of solid black rock

seed of water-spirit
sunbird of love in flight

poetry of birth in motion

fire songs of snake twisting motion
slide   glide   stride of hip dipping motion

sunbird of birth in flight

raising flame prayers to sun gods

offering up sacrifices of trees

animals   reptiles   insects   villages

seeds of water-spirit

sunbird of birth in flight

burning from guitar strings
of Jimi Hendrix   climbing from
saxophone bell of Ohnedaruth
mystical birds high in the water-spirit night

& in hot pitch-dark a black cat
carrying two suns in the eclipse of his head
swallows two fireflies climbing eyes
in the cavern of night

& the fire-ball that is swallowed
by the Pacific Ocean each sunken dusk
& who burns through earth spirit-water

leaps now from tips of devastated cities
leaps now from delicate Chinese finger paintings
leaps now from spitting barrels to coughing volcanoes

leaps now into sunbird of birth in flight

& burns like a one-eyed black cat eclipsed
in hotpitch-dark   in hotpitch-dark
climbs a firefly born in the night

poetry of birth in motion

sunbird of love in flight

seed of water-spirit

RHYTHMS

COME SING A SONG

Come sing a song, Black Man,
sing of Blind Joe Death,
sing a blues,
sing a black-blues song,
sing a Blind Joe Death blues song,
sing a work song,
sing a prison chain gang
southern blues work song
sing jazz, rock, or R & B
sing a song, Black Man
sing a "bad" freedom song

PROFILIN, A RAP/POEM

for Leon Damas

People be profilin.

People be profilin like
stink on shit,
like come/sweat for money,
like toe-jam doodoo smell

barbecue-wine stains
on picnics in july,
people be profilin everyday
                              of their lives

People be profilin.

People be profilin like
slick stylin pimps leanin bent
at forty-five degree angles
behind mink covered steerin wheels
of cold-gold laméd el dorados
with golden brown velvet roofs for tops
wide-brimmed apple hats
pulled rakishly down
slashes their scowling mugs

(& the sun don't melt
the "ice" these frozen nigga
mackmen wear
on their manicured fingers!)

People be profilin.
People be profilin every day
                              of their lives

People be profilin like
whores on midtown Manhattan street corners,
like Wall Street executives in their sterile
                                    looking
dark, conservative suits,
their brains wrapped in green mothballs,
like big time "Media" intellectuals
styled off
behind their gold wire rimmed
expensive clear-lens shades

People be profilin.
People be profilin everyday
                        of their lives

People be profilin.
People be profilin like
Sad media stars who say:
"Oh, no, dear! Don't take that
side of my face.
It's bad for my public image!"

(& can you dig where that
whole thing is coming from?!)

People be profilin.
People be profilin like
when you stick a camera
into someone's face,
be they Kings, or Queens,
or the President of these United Snakes,
watch how they react to the camera!

(unless they be too old or too tired,
or too dead for this daily crazy shit)

People be profilin.
People be profilin everyday
                    of their lives

People be profilin.

MIDTOWN TRAFFIC

Black jazz piano
struttin' across
Central Park
flowing from hidden
Park Avenue radios

& further down
cars jammed down
into mid-town traffic
musicians layin' down their
own original tunes of

toot toot & honk loud horns

Between dissonance of being
screamed on by plenty ugly
lookin', cursin' cold
purple red bastards
pushin'
beat up
growlin' trucks,
beetle-sized,
hog-sized

cars

dartin' & slashin'
feintin' wise
dented
schemin'

cars movin' through

new york city claw of traffic
crowded with the lives
of beautiful, stylin' ladies
odd schizoids,
people talkin' constantly
to themselves
'long side nose runnin'
junkies doin' a
grotesque sag dance
in search of a scratch
for an itch

Fast movin' traffic
black jazz piano struttin'
high, creating blues

anchored breezes
filled with cocaine

& rock guitars

CHICAGO

for Howlin Wolf

I.

the wind/blade cutting in
& out, swinging in over the lake
slicing white foam from the tips
of delicate water fingers
that danced & weaved
under the sunken light/night;
this wind/blade was so sharp & cold
it'd cut a four-legged mosquito into fours
while a hungry lion slept on the wings of some chittlins
slept within the blues of a poem that was formin'

We came in the sulphuric night drinkin' old crow
while a buzzard licked its beak atop the head of tricky nixon
while gluttonous daley ate hundreds of pigs that were his ego
while daddy-o played bop on the box
came to the bituminous breath of chicago
howling three-million voices of pain

& this was the music;
the kids of chicago have eyes that are older
                              than the deepest pain in the world
& they run with bare feet over south/side streets
shimmering with shivers of glass
razors that never seem to cut their feet;
they dance in & out of traffic—
the friday night smells of fish
& hog maws, the scoobedoo
sounds of bo diddley

2.

These streets belong to the dues/payer

to the blues/players/drinking whiskey on satdaynight
muddy waters & the wolfman howlin' smokestack lightnin'
how many more years down in the bottom
no place to go moanin' for my baby
a spoonful   of evil
back door man
all night long   how many more years
down in the bottom   built for comfort

BLOOD RIVERS

THE SYNTAX OF THE MIND GRIPS

the syntax of the mind grips
the geography of letters
the symbol burns, leaves black
ocean bleeds pearls/washing the shore
darkness crawls in alone like a panther
all luminous eyes watching us make
love, under trees the beautiful
woman in the grass curls
her pulling legs
around my shoulders
the old maid weeps in the window
covers her face with blue veined white hands,
her fingernails painted red
gouges out her love-shattered eyes
while the mirror breaks in the bathroom
falls like razors to the floor
where a junkie is sprawled
with a death needle in his arm
a child cuts his feet in the streets
screams for the old maid
who makes the flags
who is weeping in the window
because the stars have fallen from the flags
she does not hear anything
but her own weeping
hanging the flag has become a garrote
choking the breath/love of a people
whose hero is the armless/legless/brainless
vegetable who sits upon his bandaged stump
in a wheel/chair, in a veteran's
hospital in Washington;
he cannot speak—tell the blood
he has swallowed;

he cannot see for the death
his eyes have seen;
he cannot hear for the screams
his ears have heard; but he feels
the sorrow of the old maid
who is weeping because the stars
have fallen from the flag
and because of the love scene
in wet grass beneath her window

WEATHER REPORT IN LINCOLN NEBRASKA 2/8/71

"It is the coldest night in 23 years in Lincoln Nebraska

Outside my see-through mirror
snow was piled in frozen sculpture
grotesque along the bleak streets
of Lincoln Nebraska
while on television, Apollo 14
streaked through unconquered space
after photographing holes
and collecting weird rocks on a moon
that did not welcome them, also on this day
america was invading Laos disguised
as south vietnamese troops (they recruited
a lot of slant eyed american dwarfs and hired
america's best makeup men to pull off
this standard american hat-trick.)

And in Lincoln Nebraska the temperature
was twenty-three degrees below zero
but it was colder than that
within the pentagoned ruled executive tombs
in Washington; it was so cold that nobody
as yet has recorded the temperature,
and this suited
richie just fine
as he walked around naked
took a sauna bath in a tub
filled with Laotian blood while his
handmade, good-old melvin, scrubbed
his brain clean with a redwhiteandblue
soapbar of pure nitroglycerin

WHITE WEEKEND

April 5–8, 1968

They deployed military troops
surrounded the White House
and on the steps of the Senate building
a soldier behind a machine gun

32,000 in Washington & Chicago
1900 in Baltimore Maryland
76 cities in flames on the landscape
and the bearer of peace
lying still in Atlanta

Lamentations! Lamentations! Lamentations!
Worldwide!
But in New York, on Wall Street
the stock market went up 18 points . . .

WOKE UP CRYING THE BLUES

Woke up crying the blues;
bore witness to the sadness of the day;
the peaceful man from Atlanta
was slaughtered yester/day.
Got myself together
drank in the sweetness of sun/shine
wrote three poems to the peace/ful lamb
from Atlanta; made love
to a raging Black woman
drank wine
got high; saw angels
leading the lamb to heaven?
the blues gonna get me
gonna get me for sure!
went to the beach/to forget
if only eye can
about the gentle soul from Georgia;
ate clam chowder soup and fish sandwiches;
made love in the sand
to this same beautiful woman
drank in all her sweetness;
lost future child in the sand,
saw the bloody sun falling
behind weeping, purple clouds;
tears fell in rivers for this gentle lamb
who eye can't forget.
The bloody star sinking
into the purple grave: blackness falls.
Go out into the decay of day;
copped three keys;
the key of happiness,
the key of creative joy,
the key of sadness.

Came back, watched the gloom on the tube
at her house; which was disrupted.
Kissed her went home by the route
of the mad space ways; dropped tears in my lap
for the lamb from Atlanta
Home at last.
Two letters under the door;
a love letter from the past
grips at the root of memory
at last another poem published!
good news during a bad news weekend;
lights out;
drink of grapes;
severed sight closes
another day
in the life.

IN TEXAS GRASS

all along the rail
road tracks of texas
old train cars lay
rusted & overturned
like new african governments
long forgotten by the people
who built & rode them
till they couldn't run no more,
they remind me of old race horses
who've been put out to pasture
amongst the weeds
rain sleet & snow
till they die, rot away,
like photos fading
in grandma's picture book,
of old black men in mississippi/texas
who sit on dilapidated porches,
that fall away
like dead man's skin,
like white people's eyes,
& on the peeling photos,
old men sit sad-eyed
waiting, waiting for
worm dust, thinking of
the master & his long forgotten
promise of 40 acres & a mule,
& even now, if you pass across
this bleeding flesh
changing landscape,
you will see fruited
countryside, stretching, stretching,
old black men & young black men,
sittin' on porches, waiting

waiting, waiting for rusted
trains in texas grass

THREE FOR THE BIAFRAN WAR

1.
the wet eye
of a woman
in love is both
beauti/ful
glorious
sad

2.
a man
is the sun
of his son
& rain most
time falls
where it's
the warmest

3.
a child
is the voice
closest to
the past
& the ancestors
who are pure
African spirits
& love
everyone
& every
thing

BLOOD-RIVERS

for K. Curtis Lyle

as the ancient black rhythm
as the goat-skin drums
seeking life's pure music
hears the deep feeling,
touches the heart-beat source,
probes earth pulsations,
records the river's endless spirit
as by God's elliptical magic
as the clock turns centuries
through the bones falling to dust

as the life keeps whispering
                                through ashes

where summers are reborn
                        blood-rivers always evoking
the heart-bred flames of creation,
as the poem plunges into itself
the goat-skin drum sings
history of freedom,

freedom   freedom drums the goat-
                                skin voice of the drum
as the winds embracing Mt. Kilimanjaro
the sound of Ohnedaruth's horn
drums the goatskin voice of the drum

as an action is the thought
as love keys the keeper
poetic expression is liberation,

& we are sounds of wind-music,

pumping blood into the heart, transforming,
as new rituals

                    paint flames against the night
the changing music liberates itself,
as in blood-felt rhythm
as in heart-felt rhythm
the genius of the singing
as breath falls drum-deep into another
as into clay embrace of the mother
we weld our joys   linking
the intergalactic barrier
the rhythm liberating fire

EMBRYO

IN SEVENTY-FIVE SYLLABLES

we are here in this space,
as life is locked to air,

welding seeds of our singing,
as black day weds the night,

moon plays infinite rituals,
as gold clouds devour the stars

black minotaurs bleed the blues,
eat eggs, white with eclipse,

where music fucks the easel
pure rhythm paints the day

in seventy-seven syllables

IN THE MANNER OF RABEARIVELLO*

on a sea without motion
a man holding a thousand skies
on his black head that has no color
a man on the blue flame of suicides
finger tips & glides/turns/yearns
always to be more
than simple man with anchored thighs

night comes with its leopard hide like counterpoint
wraps around today's wingless promise shipwrecked
at the bottom of scooped out oceans

& the day vomits out without music
where blood drips up from the sky/eye
the earth disappears beyond the edges

& at the bottom of white volcanoes 1000 sharks
struggle to swim free of the grip
of a hundred boneless skeletons
while at high/noon
amongst invisible tree/poems in madagascar
rabearivello hovers amongst the branches
& sings his mournful dirge of mystery

while children crawl out without legs
towards a sea that has no motion
that is washed red by the ink
of the sky
that is filled by a poet's
eye always capsizing

---

* Jean-Joseph Rabearivello (1901–1937) was one of the most remarkable poets of the 20th century. A Madagascarian poet, he was completely original in the last half of his life. He always seemed to write in a dream-like trance, conjuring up remarkable cosmic images, totally contradictory, impossible to believe images. He has been called a pure African/surreal poet. He wrote in French. He died, a suicide, in 1937, in Madagascar.

DREAM POEM/SONG

silence, silence on the roads
blending with wind/song
that is also silent
silent are words though spoken
with microphones amplified through anger,
with flames, silent the sound of four-
string guitars played by sightless donkeys
in the road, in the middle of the road
blind donkeys sit playing
silent four-string guitars,

& silent are the stampeding herds
of butchered headless elephants,
silent the bear trapped raging
in steel-fanged trappers grip,
though the blood gushes out washing the pear
fallen from branches, the earth beneath
receives no storm released blood/drops
that are tears for a grave
of darkness no longer hearing music

not even nature's woodwinds/Coltrane
amongst branches singing love
drowned out by lynch mobs,

though the blood gushes out washing the pear
though the blood gushes out washing the pear

in the streets where an empty junk wagon
with rickety wheels of hunger
rattles soundlessly over cobblestone bricks

the blood stains the wheels stains the pear
bleeding over bells pleading of plunder

soundless the squeals of cancerous hunger
of sin sane voices, silent the proclamations,
theories, revolutionary buttons
replacing substance with rattling voices
of silence, the total noise of absurdity
of hatred-filling the air with their silence,

silence on the roads filled with blood & corpses
silence blending with wind/song, wheeling
across centuries that are also silent
bleeding silences within silences
bleeding silences within silences

though the blood gushes out staining the pear
in the road, in the middle of the road
blind donkeys sit playing
silent four-string guitars,
& silent the stampeding herds of butchered
headless elephants, silent the rage of the bear

RAIN / TIME

In a hurricane of dust morning
this man jumped sideways out of a dream
dressed in black,
jumped right out of his own bleeding thumb,
and standing wide-legged in the middle
of the bone road,
in the middle of a corpse crowded road,
drew a gun that shot out fast
from a fast drooping barrel of flesh,
that reminded me of an old military man's penis
after this daily hecatombs
and after everytime he thinks about
sex shot out
from the eye of that drooping black barrel,
sleeping gristle,
where the moon crawls into hide
everytime the sun bursts spitting down
its lasered sword/shafts of death,
on the deserts at high noon in the fire-time,
shot out into cloud of bleached bone
fang-night
slashing rain-time
in needle rain-time,
a song decree slithering
from fast-drooping black barrel

transformed into hurricane
of dust morning
like a wild-eyed cobra trying to escape
from a red-eyed purple mongoose
who leapt out from a yellow cough
of limping smoke
weeping from the eye

of that invisible cold barrel,
leapt out into the rain-time
dressed in black
serious as a final heart-attack
serious, dead serious as cancer

DREAM / DANCE

seven wingless syllables, dance
peal across blues of chanting rivers
swim within cathedrals grown from bones
huckabuck across electric circus tables
synchronized to unchanging faces of stone
fourteen perfect anachronisms
creep within the bleeding dome of the soul
plunge towards the black/dead face of the sun
eclipsed by a solo of the Bird
eleven soundless syllables wrapped in stone
& dead from overliving, chant of silence
weeping red tears within the temperate zone
between silence, obvious death
thirteen perfect deaths cylindrically
symmetrical hang from fifty bleeding
money trees in Washington
& thirteen perfect deaths dance in stone
unknown/thirteen soundless syllables
wrapped in stone   dream/dance

BIRDS FLY WITHOUT MOTION TO THE SUMMIT

when air freezes into heat
birds fly without motion to the summit

when the flag of despair is planted
death rushes headlong into the blood,
and time rolls, like a tide backwards

the hours run slipping on banana peels
and skeletons rattle night-seeking flesh
where the dead masquerade as the living

the eyes seek heights of the sightless

where birds fly without motion to the summit
the air dressed like a clown freezes into night

BENEATH THE BLUEST SEA

birds flap crumbling wings
beneath tailfire of metal hawks

distance deepens
as the last deep breath
of the fish-man swimming within the falling
dark void
slips away; as

flesh falls away from
bone, as time drops blood
into inkwells
death filled with piranhas & sharks.

all around,
the earth grows cities
upon mountainous sinking brows of edges.

here,
people sink into themselves;
within hours/steps
flesh hangs loose from bones.

from
SNAKE BACK SOLOS
Selected Poems 1969–1977

ASH DOORS & JUJU GUITARS

we have come through doors flaming
ashes the sad written legacy
smoldering bones heaped in pyres behind us

& yet campfire blues people singing
softly still under blue-black moonlight

ash doors & juju guitars conjurin' ancestral flights

sweet memories of shaman juju men
cotton-eyed bands, croonin'
softly the guitar-woman stroked enjoins

blues chanting mantras across throbbing land

at the flight of sun   light
at the flight of sun   light

I.

UP SUN, SOUTH OF ALASKA: A SHORT
AFRICAN-AMERICAN HISTORY SONG

for my son, Quincy Brandon Troupe

I.

slit balls hung in southern/american winds then
when drumheads were slit made mum by rum
& songs hung way down
around our ankles bleeding up sun south of alaska
swinging silhouettes picked clean to bone
by black crows
caw caws razor scars black-winged crows ripping
sunset flights of slashing razors
crows crows
blues caw caws & moans
& blues caw caws & moans

then sunsets dangled voices
crowing blues caw caws black crowing razors streak
silhouettes against a frying skillet
broken necks & sun-gored bodies blistered in eclipse
hung nails rope burned
into sweet black lives

rip of pendulum razors
lays open the quaking earth of flesh/moans
from blue-black dues paying women
dropping embryos into quicksand
african secret songs strapped across blood-stained blades
of glittering american razors
songs of sun/down flesh karintha dusk flesh
drug through spit/ripped
bleeding up sun,south of alaska
bleeding up sun south of Alaska

2.

& crows & razors & ropes & bullets
crows & razors & ropes & bullets
the shared cold legacy
& crazed pale men, lassoing the sun out of the sky
& darkness then bleeding up sun south of alaska
crow wings covering the sky & our eyes & their eyes too
eclipsing the face of the sun
now an invisible clock with laser-beamed hands
that are branding rays burning our flesh
reduced over time to bone/dust
kissing stone but the nature of stone
is not moved by the tongue of heat entering
the mouth of our lives—passionate sweet touch of meaning

but still we move through space towards grace
carrying a sphinx in one eye
a guitar in the other knowing that time is always
in the possession of the keeper

3.

so now son black
roll the pages of your american eyes back son
black son back roll them back black son american
son, way way back son
back before the sun ripped your flesh here
way way back sun
for the pages of your eyes carry the memory son
they are blue-black pages dues pages fingers strumming
music of oral history songs griot songs
african songs
strong black strumming fingers son
american black lives as humming caw caws

black crows transformed into eagles

no matter ripping suns son
no matter slit drums/tongues
we are here son
are sun music spirit son
caw caw blues razors

keepers of secret guitars

THESE CROSSINGS, THESE WORDS

for Pablo Neruda

where will they take us to
these crossings
over rivers of blood-stained words
syllables haphazardly thrown together
as marriages that fall apart
in one day

we have come this far in space
to know nothing of time
of the imprisoning distance travelled
the scab-fleshed hobos passed
we have most times asked nothing

of the mirrors of our own shattered reflections
passing as lava smoldering in the streets

in our eyes the guillotine
smile of the hangman
a time-bomb ticking for our hearts
the brain an item bought like so much gooey candy
the laugh a razor's flash
the party time juba
of My Lai's sickening ritual

as american as elvis presley's dead days

& the blood-scarred wind
whipped rag blue squared off with stars
that are silver bullets
& pin-striped with bones of mythologized peppermint
will not hide the corpse-lynched history
hanging there twisting slowly

as a black man's body
screaming through soft magnolia air
over a tear-stained bride's veil
breeze blown & fluttering
as a flopping fish
in a gesture of surrender

we have come all this distance in darkness
bomb-flashes guiding our way
speaking of love/of passions instantly eclipsed
to find this corpse of freedom hung & machine-gunned
for the blood of a name beneath a simple word
(& what do we know who have not gone there in truth
of the roots of these flames burning at river-crossings
of the crossbones of our names connecting rivers
of blood beautiful as a fusing coltrane solo?)

& there are times when we see
celluloid phantoms of mediarized lovers
crawling from sockets of cracking up skeletons
posing as cameras & t.v. screens

times still when we stand here
anchored to silence by terror
of our own voice & of the face revealed
in the unclean mirror shattering
our sad-faced, children
dragging anchors of this gluttonous
debauchery & of this madness
that continues to last

NEW YORK CITY BEGGAR

his body held the continence
of a protruding tongue
of a hanged man twisting & turning
in sweltering, needle-sharp heat
held the continence
of a jet plane's high propulsion saliva
his body swollen tight as a toilet stool
packed full of two-day-old shit
warts crawling like frenzied roaches
over his skin of yellow fever
the texture of quivering pus
bloated as the graves of earth
or jammed as rivers full
of lynched black bodies—
sores popping open through ventilated
clothing like hungry termites
devouring flesh
the texture of quivering pus

& he looked at me
with the look of a wrung-necked chicken
with that of a somnambulist
blasted, by poison of thunderbird wine
storms his eyes streaked red
with crow-wings raking corners
of his peppermint moons
like claws of a rooster

& his fingernails, the color of tadpoles
sought the origin of a 400-year-old itch
which held the history
& secret of crushed indian bones
& of clamoring, moaning voices

of unborn black children who were
screaming semen of castrated nigga dicks
& his look held the origin of ashes
the blood-stained legacy of sawdust on the floor
of a butcher
               & his rasping sawblade voice cutting
held the unmistakable calligraphy of lepers
who with elephantiasis feet drag themselves across
sword blades of murderous pentagon juntas

(which is the history of reared-back cobra snakes
which is the truth of the cold game we're in)

& when he spoke to me
his maggot-swarming words reeking of outhouses
"brother, can you spare a dime?"
his spirit low as coal dust
his energy drained as transparent shells
of sunstricken roaches his breath
smelling of rotten fish markets
his teeth looking like chipped tombstones
nicked away in a hurricane of razors
eye heard a fork-tongued capitalist
on wall street, fart & croak

(which is the history of reared-back king cobras
which is the truth of the game we're in)

& when eye walked away with my dime
still chattering in my pocket
he put a halloween leer on me & said "thank you
boss"gave the V for victory/peace sign
cursed under his breath
& left, like an apparition flapping
his raggedy black coat
like giant crow wings in the wind

AFTER HEARING A RADIO ANNOUNCEMENT:
A COMMENT ON SOME CONDITIONS: 1978

yesterday in new york city
the gravediggers went on strike
& today the undertakers went on strike
because they said of the overwhelming
amount of corpses
(unnecessarily they said, because
of wars & stupid killings in the streets
& etcetera & etcetera)

sweating up the world   corpses
propped up straight in living room chairs
clogging up rivers, jamming up freeways
stopping up elevators   in the gutters   corpses
everywhere you turn
& the undertakers said they were
being overworked with all this goddamned killing
going on   said they couldn't even enjoy
all the money they was making
said that this shit has got to stop

& today eye just heard, on the radio, that
the coffin-makers are waiting, in the wings
for their chance to do the same thing
& tomorrow & if things keep going this way
eye expect to hear of the corpses
themselves boycotting death
until things get better
or at least getting themselves
together in some sort of union espousing
self-determination
for better funerals &
burial conditions
or something extraordinarily
heavy like that

STEEL POLES GIVE BACK NO SWEAT

after Waring Cuney

in new york city people
cop their own posts
underground waiting on subway platforms
lean up against them
claim them as their own
ground & space

while up over ground
winds scrape the back of skies piercing
poles of concrete laced with laughing quicksilver
mirrors square phallic symbols
in their glint
of limp-dick capitalism
stone repositories for fallen
pigeon shit

below them stoned bums
scrape their lives into asphalt sleep
on sidewalks slow shuffle scabby bruised feet towards terrors
only they know
leaning underground
against graffitied steel subway poles
alone carrying their own feverish frenzy
that needed bathing long ago

& so each day here where we pass
each other waiting for love to speak
to us to everyone so slow in coming here
to cleanse our needs of these terrible wounds
scraped raw by these clawing days
leaning forward into one another
our lives touching here

these underground steel poles
propping up our bodies
flawed by breath
& anointed with scents
from wherever it is we are coming from

& can feel our flesh rubbing steel
& think the steel flesh
& tell ourselves we are not lonely here
couldn't be lonely
here in this gargantuan city
where steel poles
give back no sweat

SNOW & ICE

ice sheets sweep this slick mirrored darkness
as keys that turn tight trigger brains
of situations
where we move ever so slowly
         so gently into time-traced agony
bright turning of imagination
so slowly
through revolving doors opening up to enter mountains
where spirits walk voices so slowly swept
by cold breathing fire
         as these elliptical moments of illusion
fragile loves sunk deep in snows as footprints
weak chained black gesticulations
bone bared voices
         chewed skeletal choices
in fangs of vampirish gales
these silver slivers of raucous laughter
glinting bright as hard polished nails

A SURREALISTIC POEM TO EVERYONE
& NO ONE IN PARTICULAR

high above the ceiling of imagination
crescendo thunderclaps of silence
before lightning, a tongue of pearls slashing
the tapestry of God's eye
totemic gong-ringer of cocaine spells
consummate tapdancer on the holy rings
around saturn
        hydraulic wingbeater
of a dehydrated eagle
laid back soothsayer
who sees the world as one grain of sand
cosmic mindsmoker of the seven skies of dewdrops & doowops
righteous deep sea diver
of the hot sucking womb

this tomb-headed chronicler of the dark
secrets of the vatican
omnipotent court jester
        of the kingdom of novocaine
stomp down choreographer of the nod & stumble
junkie ballets
scientific finder of collapsed river veins
molecular rhesus monkey of the ultimate trip of battery acid
peyote sky tripper, eater of jagged sharp tin cans
fire swallowing termite of esoteric books
bringer of hot-ice seasons of unknown climates
gri-gri stone eater of broken lightbulbs
bubonic trigger man of no hesitation

out here your test-tube children wearing
uniforms full of worthless medals wearing tight-fitting suits

with buttons popping club-footed dancers
of wet dream midnights

totemic gong ringer of cocaine spells
all these desert-fried faces
of sandstorms/chopped iguanas
rattlesnaking eyeballs swarming with garbage
flies sweating speech as buzzsaws of termites
cutting through redwood trees
night-trippers of onion & garlic kisses
toe-tappers of naked nose rubbing eskimos
bellringer of sandpaper pussies
sardine flesh rappers of cat-shit breath

whose eyes gleam sharp as piranha teeth
whose skunk smelling sword blade words reek
of no consequence & nixonian intentions blubberous
jellyfishes of short legs knobby knees
& long flat-footed premonitions

no doubt about it gong-ringer
the brain of mankind is sometimes a piss
of swiss cheese on the plate of a begger

FROM RICHMOND COLLEGE
POSTMARKED—MANHATTAN

from this plate-glass window
high above staten island
night closes in on the jugular vein of day
as black paint spreads down over space
of white canvas
squeezing out the life
cycle of day

artificial lights shimmer/dance
bojangle out of focus
tap-dance across the sound stuffed with slow moving ships
as the verranzano bridge strings out its chainlink
of stars/glittering notions
blurs of flashing carlights
rippling motions

& from here across the sound's
waters the shore of brooklyn comes alive with yellow
lights that glow
like eyes of panthers

headlights shutter/blink
down freeways carved from blood & stolen gold
while the american flag shivers/whips back
hung up there atop staten island's
city hall tower
alone in the face of ice
cold winds
black hands on the white face
of the luminous tower clock
move methodically

while under the bridge
the strung-out motion red
lights pulsate like heartbeats
of a rebreathing bag/dreams
rise & fall against the darkness
blood colors
bloodshot eyes in flight
feverish eyes of countless rodents
impressionistic images swirling
penetrate the dark rhythms

while down at the ferry landing
cars move like monstrous bugs
down long curving rampways
headlight tongues for eyes probe/open up
the darkness with their bone bright keys of light
crawl up the snaking asphalt pavement
while people move in slow
fast shuffling motion as in old homemade
silent movies in black & white dragging
their day behind them
anchored to tired drooping shoulders

now across the sound
in the other direction towards manhattan
the eye locates the oxidized green french
woman carved from stone lighting her torch
in the harbor
while manhattan looms up behind her
a gigantic electric circus
of sizzling lights

now night closes finally
its walls of mystery like dracula
enfolding himself in his black sweeping cape

while all around staten island supper smells
tantalize the nostrils

now as eye am leaving
the wind dies
down up on the flagpole the flag hangs limply
while black hands on the white face of the clock
turn around the hours fast as jessie owens
winning the olympic dashes
in hitler's germany in 1936

now panther against the dark
eye enter the ferry
slip down through the womb of its doors
like a letter being slid into
an envelope

slide back into the night
postmarked: manhattan

II.

LEGON, GHANA, AFTER DARK

soft voices invisible serenade
from roadways, courtyards,
laughing trees & serene ponds palming
flat wide green leaves
holding incredibly loud bullfrogs
croaking over motion
of silent goldfish

Ga language sings over
darkening shadows mixing Akan where
English is pushed back into corners
of language gumbo style

crickets orchestrate
their deafening oracular melodies
blend high-life rhythms & C. K. Mann
with afro-sound of Fela Ransome Kuti
rumbling ground & a lonely
car horn

music, life's music
punctuates the sweetness
of this beautiful modal cadence
lifts the spirit into rare ecstasy

now listening to sculptors
of ancestral root music arranging
& rearranging their perfect chords
& octaves of discord & accord, dissonant
counterpoint eye begin my fall back into the black
inkwell that leads to the egg-yoke
on the blue plate of God's table

fall into deep & untroubled sleep
at Akuafo Hall, at the university of Ghana
under rare dark incense showers under
rare deep dark incense showers

GHANAIAN SONG-IMAGE

after rain
dark trees &
ghost shadows
sit upon
shoulders of
cotton mist

IGBOBI, NIGERIAN NIGHT

for Ron & Ellen Pulleyblank & Seyi Bajilayia

dark fall
african masks
martell bottle
shadows
the wall   spider
in the corner
of the cognac
bottle a lone candle
burns on the table
invisible sounds
hum from imagbon
street climbs through
the open window
& love in
the heart will last
beyond distance
& time beyond
separation
of the graves

MEMORY

a lone candle
burning penetrating
the dark deepening
memory—pain
only a finger
thought away

OUT HERE WHERE

out here where
the sky grows wings
the land is broad
& everywhere eye go
space holds me
within

III.

IT IS NOT

it is not who or what
you see
but how you see
it. the night.

the woman. the rhythm
of night lights going on.
off. in her face.
the smile of neon.
jewels on fingers.

the sound of ash
colliding with cotton.
the sound tears make falling
through blues. the voices.
guitar strings strummed
by silence. echoes.

echoes. gold-capped
dues of a mississippi black
man's grin. is. not who or what.
you see. but how.
you see it. thin.
or otherwise. deep.

this life is.
what you make of it. not
what you hope it to be. but
what it is. right or wrong.
what it is what you make it
to be it is right
or wrong. thin.
or otherwise. deep.

a blues. or its absence.
it is. a lyrical
rhythm. dissonant.
painting the night. the sound
of ashes. colliding with cotton.
is. how you hear it. feel it.
is. not what or who.
you either hear. or. you do
not hear. but how you hear
is the question here.

this poem. that gold-
capped blues. of that. black
man's grin. mississippi. is.
the sound tears make falling
through guitar strings.
colliding with cotton.

echoing bones
that lay screaming under-
water. under earth. is
the feeling you hear. chains.
is not what you see
but how you see it. death.
this life. is how you
make it. see it.

feeling, see it. hear
this life wedded to death.
see it. feeling. see it.

feeling. see it.
see. it.
hear. it.

IN A SILENCE OF BELLS

in a silence of bells
& cardboard mackmen
round midnight
a screaming riot of trumpets
fork the suffocating hours

bones stretch here
& are hands time-clocks
beating hearts with no bodies
surrounding them stall
an absence of rhythms

but eye come in on time
with no outside help from metronomes
picking bass strings of the night
but have forgotten
my subway token

so have to walk
the music all
the way home

IN MEMORY OF BUNCHY CARTER

in this quick breath
of water spray airy
eye see your face
of light so darkly lit
through knifing
rain long gone friend
shadow of your tracking
tongue still moving
this pin of lost friend-
ship to call out your name
so distant now
so night grown green
under avalanches
of sunlight
& flowers

THE OTHER NIGHT

the other brandy
sweetened night we was
kissin' so hard & good
you sucked my tongue
right on out
my tremblin' mouth
& eye had to
sew it back in
in order to tell
you about it

FLYING KITES

for Nathan Dixon, friend & poet

1.

we used to fly kites
across skull-caps of hours
holes on blue wings
canvas of sinking suns eclipsed
winged eyes locked to wind
we'd cut the kite string away
then run them down blue tapestry
up the sky down again the sin-
king sun over
again the sinking sun

2.

now we fly words as kites
on winds through skies
as poems;
holy bloody sounds
ringing like eclipse
the sun's tongues

TRANSFORMATION

catch the blues song
of wind in your bleeding
black hand, (w)rap it around
your strong bony fingers
then turn it into a soft-nosed pen
& sit down & write the love
poem of your life

FIREFLIES

fireflies on night canvas
cat eyes glowing like moonbeams
climbing now towards hidden places
they speak to the language
of darkness & of their own lives torn
from roots in flux & of their sub-
stance forming the core
substantially transparent they
swim through ethereal darkness
where silence can be wisdom
searching for open doors

IV.

THE DAY DUKE RAISED: MAY 24TH,1984

for Duke Ellington

1.

that day began with a shower
of darkness calling lightning rains
home to stone language
of thunderclaps shattering the high
blue elegance of space & time
where a broken-down riderless, horse
with frayed wings
rode a sheer bone sunbeam
road, down into the clouds

2.

spoke wheels of lightning
spun around the hours high up
above those clouds duke wheeled
his chariot of piano keys
his spirit now levitated from flesh
& hovering over the music of most high
spoke to the silence
of a griot-shaman/man
who knew the wisdom of God

3.

at high noon the sun cracked
through the darkness like a rifle shot
grew a beard of clouds on its livid bald
face hung down noon, sky high
pivotal time being a five in the nine
numbers of numerology
as his music was the crossroads
the cosmic mirror of rhythmic gri-gri

4.

so get on up & fly away duke bebop
slant & fade on in strut dance swing riff
float & stroke those tickling gri-gri keys
those satin ladies taking the A train up
to harlem those gri-gri keys of birmingham
breakdown sophisticated
ladies mood indigo
get on up & strut across gri-gri
raise on up your band's waiting

5.

thunderclapping music somersaulting
clouds racing across the deep blue wisdom
of God listen it is time for your intro
duke into that other place where the all-time
great band is waiting for your intro duke
it is time for the Sacred Concert, duke
it is time to make the music of God
duke we are listening for your intro
duke let the sacred music begin

FOUR, AND MORE

for Miles Davis

1.

a carrier of incandescent dreams this
blade-thin shadowman stabbed by lightning
crystal silhouette
crawling over blues-stained pavements his life
lean he drapes himself his music across edges
his blood held tight within
staccato flights

clean as darkness & bright as lightning
reversed moments where the sound is two cat eyes
penetrating the midnight hours of moon pearl lacing
the broken mirrored waters
mississippi mean as a sun-drenched trumpet/man
holding dreams held high on any wind/light

voice walking on eggshells

2.

& time comes as the wrinkles
of your mother's skin shrinks inward
fly towards that compelling voice
light calling since time began
on the flip-side of spirit
you shed placentas at each stage of your music
then go down river exploring new blues

the drum skin of young years wearing down

the enigmatic search of your music
now your autumn years of shadows creeping twilight
dancers wrapped tight in cobwebs held on
to one another

beneath fractured lights cracking the floor
their lives now prismatic poems at the point where the sun
disappears with every turning of the clock hands
spinning towards the death of light
there in the diamond point
of the river beyond the edges

the light glows smaller
grows inward becomes a seed to grow
another light illuminating the shadows
crystalline as this trumpetman

voice walking on eggshells

phosphorous as truth or blue
as luminescent water beneath the sun's eye

3.
Oh Silent Keeper of Shadows
of these gutted roads filled with the gloomy ticking
of time-clocks/razor-bladed turnings of hairpin corners
of these irreducible moments of love found
when love was sought
iridescent keeper of rainbow laughter
arching out of broken-off gold-capped teeth

blues man holding the sun between his teeth

soothsayer of chewed-up moments
shaker-re-man at the crossroads of cardinal points
talisman hanging from dewdrops singing deep
sea diver of transparent rhythmic poems

trumpet voice walking on eggshells

your shadow is as the river snake-thin
man at flood time blood lengthening in the veins
coursing through the earth's flesh
shaman man gone beyond the sky's limit

music sleeps there in the riverbed
mississippi where those calcified shining bones sleep
deep reminding us of the journey from then to now
& from now to wherever it is we have to go

so pack your bags boy
the future is right around the corner
only a stone's throws from yesterday's/light

as is this carrier of afternoon dream music
trumpet voice walking on eggshells

this eggshell-walking trumpetman
voice hauntingly beautiful lyrical music man
gold as two cat eyes penetrating the midnight hours
as blood blackening the pavement mean music man
shadowman holding the night in the bell
of his trumpet singing

mississippi river pouring from roots of his eyes

4.
shadowman holding the night in his music
shaker-re-man at the crossroads of cardinal points
elliptical talisman hanging from dewdrops singing
deep sea diver of haunting magical tones

trumpetman walking on eggshells

your shadow as the river at flood-time
snake-thin shaman man blade-sharp gone beyond
the sky's limit music sleeps there in your coursing
river veins curl around the bones
clear as diamond points on waters of sunsets
there where light grows inward
your genius moving out from that source
trumpetman walking on eggshells

afternoon dreamcarrier of blues in flight
steep night climber of haunting magical poems

juju hoodooman conjuring illuminating darkness

SNAKE-BACK SOLO

for Louis Armstrong, Steve Cannon, Miles Davis,
& Eugene Redmond

with the music up high
boogalooin' bass down way way low
up & under eye come slidin' on in mojoin'
on in, spacin' on in on a riff
full of rain
riffin' on in full of rain & pain
spacin' on in on a sound like coltrane

my metaphor is a blues
hot pain dealin' blues is a blues axin'
guitar voices whiskey broken niggah deep
in the heart is a blues in a glass filled with rain
is a blues in the dark
slurred voices of straight bourbon
is a blues dagger stuck off in the heart
of night, moanin' like bessie smith
is a blues filling up the wings
of darkness is a blues

& looking through the heart
a dream can become a raindrop window to see through
can become a window to see through this moment
to see yourself hanging around the dark
to see through
can become a river catching rain
feeding time can become a window
to see through

while outside windows flames trigger
the deep explosion
time steals rivers that go on & stay where they are

inside yourself moving soon there will be daylight
breaking the darkness

to show the way soon there will be voices breaking music
to come on home by down & up river breaking darkness
to come on home by stroking with the music
swimming up river the sound of louie armstrong
carrying river boats upstream on vibratos
climbing the rain filling the rain
swimming up river
up the river of rain satchmo breaking the darkness
his trumpet & grin polished over pain speaking
to the light flaming off the river's back
at sunset snake river's back
river mississippi big muddy up from new
orleans to alton & east st. louis illinois
cross river from st. louis to come on home by
up river the music swims breaking silence of miles
flesh leaping off itself into space
creating music creating poems

now inside myself eye solo of rivers
catching rains & dreams & sunsets solo
of trane tracks screaming through night stark
a dagger in the heart solo
of bird spreading wings for the wind
solo of miles pied piper prince of darkness
river rain voice now eye solo
at the root of the flower solo leaning voices
against promises of shadows soloing of bones
beneath the river's snake-back solo
of trees cut down by double-bladed axes
river rain voice now eye solo of the human condition
as blues solo of the matrix mojoin' new blues solo
river rain voice now, eye solo   solo

& looking through the heart a dream
can become a raindrop window to see through
can become this moment this frame to see through
to see yourself hanging
around the dark to see through this pain
can become even more painful as the meaning of bones
crawling mississippi river bottoms snakepits beneath
the snake-back solo catching rain catching time
& dreams washed clean by ajax

but looking through the dream can be
like looking through a clean window crystal
prism the night where eye solo now to be-
come the wings of night
to see through this darkness
eye solo now to become wings & colors
to become a simple skybreak shattering darkness
to become lightning's jagged sword-like thunder
eye solo to become to become
eye solo now to become to become

with the music up high
up way way high boogalooin' bass down
way way low
up & under eye come slidin' on in mojoin' on in
spacin' on in on a riff full of rain
river riff full of rain & trains & dreams
come slidin' on in another riff
full of flames
leanin' & glidin' eye solo   solo
loopin' & slidin' eye solo now solo

V.

POEM FOR SKUNDER BOGHOSSIAN, PAINTER

music drumming skies
of your paintings of poetry
miles cooking there
with long gone trane leaping
canopies of distance

& space can be canvas
or bark negotiated by brushstrokes of silence

ghosts evoking myth in illusions
wind-voice gongs
shaping shadows from mist

signatures that echo

COLLAGE

wings of snow sweep
disintegrate
slow fall chimney ashes
belch through gray night
silently screaming

voices thick as molasses

blanket fluttering pavements
slide into one another
below moments
faces
ringing like bells

MY POEMS HAVE HOLES SEWN INTO THEM

my poems have holes sewn into them
& they run searching for light
at the end of tunnels they become trains
or at the bottom of pits they become blackness
or in the broad winging daylight
they are words that fly

& the holes are these words
letters or syllables with feathered wings
that leave their marks on white pages
then fly off like footprints tracked in snow
& only God knows where they go

this poem has holes stitched into it
as our speech which created poetry in the first place
lacerated wounded words that strike out original
meaning bleeding into language
hemorrhaging out of thick or thin mouths
has empty spaces & silences sewn into it

my poems have holes sewn into them
& their voices are like different keyholes
through which dumb men search for speech blind
men search for sight
words like drills penetrating sleep
keys turning in the keyholes of language
like knives of sunrays stabbing blind eyes

my poems have holes sewn into them
& they are spaces between words
are the words themselves
falling off into one another/colliding
like people gone mad and they space out

fall into bottomless pits
which are the words

like silent space between chords of a piano
or black eyes of a figure in any painting
they fall back, into themselves
into time/ sleep
bottom out on the far side of consciousness
where words of all the world's poets go
& whisper in absolute silence

this poem has deep holes stitched into it
& their meanings have the deadly suck of quicksand
the irreversible pull of earth to any skydiver
the tortured pus-holes tracking arms of junkies

my poems have holes sewn into them
& they run searching for light at the end
of tunnels or at the bottom of yawning pits
or in the broad daylight where
the words flapping like wings of birds
fly whispering in absolute silence

from
SKULLS ALONG THE RIVER

I.

SKULLS ALONG THE RIVER

for my mother, Dorothy Marshall, and my father,
Quincy Trouppe, Sr.

1.

up from new orleans, on riverboats
from the gulf of mexico, memory carries
sweet legacy of niggerland speech, brown tongue, bluesing
muddy water
underbottomed spirits, crawling, nightmares
of shipwrecked bones, bones gone home to stone, to stone
bones gone home to stone, to stone
riverbottomed, underbellied spirits

bones gone home to stone, eye say
bones gone home to stone, eye say

skulls along the river

2.

& the faces of these faceless bones unknown
screaming arpeggios of stitched memory in cold light
cadences of blues
shrinking sun sprays, shrieking with every turning
of black bone armed clocks

& it is the collected face of memory that wears
the metaphor of collected dust
the collected mathematics of lamenting calibrations
hieroglyphics
crackling & peeling & curling in stone, dust storms swirling
around edges
bones white as chiclet teeth in memory cloning
the images come locked in whatever
time gives them

death there forever, forever locked in time
death there forever & forever locked
in time, in time

we suffer because we must
there is no other way to find beauty
there is no other way to find love
we suffer because we must
there is no other way home
to find the memory

& O the skeletons that have passed
my cracking eyeballs seeking true cadence
within the lamenting calibrations of music
history rattling dice bones
on their worn out knees
the already dead scraping earth, breath
for an even deeper death

the ultimate transmissioning migration

& O you midnight men of peppermint moons
rooster claw soliloquies raking at vision's corner
heroes emerging from sandblasted history books
grant me leather flesh of your weather worn wisdom
O blood-drenched gravediggers
anthracitic soothsayers
O mellow prophets of crushed grapes & stomped berries
grant me holy syllables of your blues laced tongues
perfect eardrums
O grant me sacred light of your blues
doowopping mackmen
grant me holy flight of your eagle-
winged life, O grant me the tongue of your blues
perfect eardrums, grant me holy flight
of your eagle-winged life

O grant me the tongue
of your blues perfect eardrums

3.
beginning now with the formless mystery of love
informing it all, cadences, its ritualized celebration
of birth as death as drama
its copacetic language of blues
inside the journey back under buzzard wings of parody
textures realized & lost & found & lost once again
the slitting, definitive answer
of a pearl handled razor hissing through
the dark's wailing wall mystery, of flesh
wallowing in its own gluttony inside the breath of death

now hear the hieroglyphics of space & time forming
sculpting in winds from great distances, voices
shapes down way way low, voices
taking on colors, turning around & taking on shape
voices spinning into blurring faces swimming
trying to breach this calligraphy
of space & time & distance

voices, down way way low, spinning themselves
into memory phono-discs, voices as faces
down way way low, way way low
voices spinning & turning into faces in memory
phono-discs, down way way low, down
way, way low

send back now the memory further back than bone
see there, now, the polished stones lifted
& singing, singing

becoming birds that are words
their wings being the holy myths that fill up our lives

with movement, movement
now, listen to the blood burning song breaking
through & into our rivervoiced veins
climbing towards the plateau
of the heart

listen to the rains
beating against the underbelly of those stones
marking worm deep earth bottoms where
the narcissus of flesh

rests

listen to windtongues
drums breaking now into flames & wind trumpet songs
opening up doorways to rivers, listen now
to hearts, listen
to rhythms of stones, beating hearts climbing
towards the dark, listen to rhythms
your soon to be calcified
worm eaten heart
listen now

listen now, to the dark

4.
we are the dark
are dark stitched voices climbing
memories from the heart, are secret
arpeggios of spirit
scaling towards the light
voices of weeping rains, teardrops
hanging from history's eyelids
of that toad squatting
city by the mississippi river

wide spread arms of slippery catfish
deep inside skulls of mississippi
river nights born of savage flights
are dark, hip voices stitched
into fabric of those razor
bladed nights
blues kneeling down
eye say blues kneeling down
before that packing house city
wide spread arms slippery as cat
fish, spirits climbing towards
the cracks of moonbeams
slashed light, blues
kneeling down, moonbeams
climbing towards cracks
slashed light

5.
O sweet lovers of no faces

of all races with desert bone dry eyes
of no reception
pain knee deep in quicksand
who give sandpaper tongues of no sweetness
kisses cold as piranha teeth
eyes digging scaly reflections in dirty mirrors
cracked & fading
become, now a confluence of rivers, blood
a confluence of musical faces, blood swimming through
sundown, dusk, blood, the sonorous magic of elliptical
calibrations spinning inside
memory discs, blood
stitched into music

sing, now, of windprints, birds
climbing cadences, stitched memory

sing now of rapture swimming through river-veins
spirit of bones bright as lightning in blood
deep mud bed of mississippi river bottoms
where the ancestors sing now in sleep
sing now a bone deep rhapsody
a memory of skulls
blues steeped

sing, now stone-sculpted
legacy, of blues, chiseled mornings
sing now, sing now
sing a blues

6.

but this road back long gone,again long
gone, back again blues
long gone eye went back forward again, to this
river Mississippi, to this toad squatting city
catfish arms widespread in slippery welcome
come back home again
                              to these dry-bone kisses
of formaldehyde memories, eyes death ridden
as forty-five bullets

come back home again carrying my age strapped
on my side like a revolver
all my young quicksilver years running into this river
mississippi river, snake-back carrier of dreams
& home is wherever ancestor bones are
buried, kneedeep memories live as dreams
become ribcages of miracles
built from death
as a man holding the sun between his teeth

his smile a dazzling daybreak, a blue-black blues man

sun man caught the sun between his gapped teeth
sprouted wings & flew away into the music
now his spirit holds up the sky
his smile the golden eye
torching high, mornings skies

snake-back carrier of dreams, mississippi
seven throw eleven to win at the game of dice
eye carry snake-back river of dreams on my back
river mississippi, where the spirits climb out
of now, move beneath the arch's
parabolic flight
upside down question mark
razor's edge of a stationary pendulum slashing
the blue throat of the sky turning now
a skillet fried-yellow now

snake-back carrier of dreams, the song climbs
out of itself now, shaking riverweeds that turn
into faces familiar on memory discs, spinning
faces familiar as crushed coal
dust, greets me here
with outspread arms filigreeing cobwebbed drapes
old streets where familiar buildings have been
removed, like abscessed teeth from the mouth
of old fisherman ghoul
who used to tell me all those great stories
of the heydays of st. louis, before the scars came
before the mumbles came & he lost his peg-legged teeth
like those abscessed buildings
before he fell into senility & was pulverized
by the pendulum wrecking ball of progress
that is time, which is history's
consuming fire, which is death
& life at the same time

7.

but this road that has been so long gone now
is here again, back again blues
long gone eye have come back to this muddy river
again, to this toad squatting city of catfish arms
widespread in slippery welcome
come back home again
to all my quicksilver memories running
into this river, mississippi river
snake-back carrier of dreams

river mississippi

snake-back carrier of dreams
seven throw eleven eye win
at the game of dice
seven throw eleven eye win whatever
the game holds for me, now
whatever this catfish armed city
holds for me now, eye win if only
eye can come back & go forward again
at the same time, seven throw eleven
eye win at the game
of dice & the blues

snake-back carrier of dreams

seven throw eleven eye win
the blues, seven throw eleven

eye win the blues

SOUTH CENTRAL VANDEVENTER STREET RUNDOWN

to leave any house
was to smell the scent,
burnt flesh scent hanging
noxious in the air
& to leave any house
was to know the odor
burnt flesh hanging
like death in the air,
burnt flesh hanging
like death in the air

& to know the odor
was to know
where death came from
packin' house, slaughter house
burnin' flesh blues
spreadin' the news 'bout death

& can smell it in springtime,
can smell it in summertime
can smell it
seven days a week singeing air,
in autumntime, in wintertime
all the time anytime

burnt flesh, hanging
as death, in the air
burnt flesh hanging
as death in the air

RIVER TOWN PACKIN HOUSE BLUES

for Sterling Brown

Big Tom was a black nigguh man,
cold & black,
eye say Big tom was a black nigguh man,
black steel flesh,
standin' like a gladiator, soaked in
animal blood, bits of flesh,
wringin' wet,
standin' at the center of death,
buzzards hoverin',
swingin' his hammer called death,
260 workdays,
swingin' his hammer named death

Big Tom was a black packin' houseman,
thirty years,
eye say Big Tom was a black packin' houseman,
loved them years,
& swang his hammer like ol John Henry
poundin' nails,
swang that hammer twenty years
crushin' skulls
of cows & pigs screamin' fear
the man underneath slit their throats,
twenty years,
the man underneath slit their throats

Big Tom was a 'prentice for ten long years,
watchin' death,
eye say Big Tom was 'prentice for ten long years,
smellin' death,
was helper to a fat white man
who got slow,

was helper to a fat white man
who swang a hammer
till he couldn't do it no mo',
so he taught Big Tom how to kill
with a hammer,
he taught Big Tom how to kill

& twenty years of killin'
is a lot to bring home,
eye say twenty years of killin'
is a lot to bring home,
& drinkin' too much gin & whiskey
can make a gentle/man blow
don't chu know
eye say drinkin' too much
gin & whiskey
can make a good man
sho nuff blow,
don't chu know

Big Tom beat his wife after killin' all day,
his six chillun too,
eye say Tom beat his wife after killin' all day,
his young chillun too,
beat 'em so awful bad, he beat 'em right out they shoes,
screamin' blues,
eye say he beat 'em so awful bad
he made a red-eyed hungry alley rat spread the news
'bout dues
these black/blues people was payin', couldn't even bite 'em,
cause of the dues
these black/blues people was payin'

Big Tom killed six men, maimed a couple a hundred,
& never served a day,

eye say Big Tom killed six men, maimed a couple a
hundred,
never in jail one day,
the figures coulda been higher, but the smart ones,
they ran away
eye say the number that was maimed, or dead, coulda
been higher,
but the smart ones,
they ran away, swallowin' pride, saved from the graveyard,
another day,
the smart ones,
they ran away

Big Tom, workin' all day, thirty years,
uh huh, sweatin' heavy
Big Tom swingin his hammer, all right, twenty summers
outta love
Big Tom killin' for pay,
uh huh, twenty autumns, outta need,
Big Tom dealin' out murders, like a houseman, all night,
in the painyards, outta false pride,
Big Tom drinkin' heavy, uh huh,
laughin' loose in taverns,
Big Tom loose
in Black communities, death fights cancel light,
& Big Tom keeps on, stumblin'

& twenty years of killin'
is too much to bring home to love,
eye say twenty years of killin'
is too much to bring home to love,
& drinkin' heavy gin & whiskey
can make a strong man fall in mud,
eye say drinkin' too much gin & whiskey
can make a good man have bad blood

don't chu know
can make a strong
man have
bad blood

Big Black Tom was a cold, nigguh man,
strong & black
eye say Big Black Tom was a cold nigguh man,
hard steel flesh,
& stood like a gladiator, soaked in blood,
bits of flesh,
soakin' wet,
stood at the center, in the middle of death,
sweatin' vultures,
swingin his hammer called death, 260 workdays,
for twenty years,
like ol John Henry,
eye say swingin' his hammer named death

POEM FOR MY BROTHER TIMMY

for Timothy Troupe

we walked streets
of river-rhythm town counting
cars that passed
for nothing else better to do
warm cold days now packed
away in straw

& when at home on Delmar
& Leonard Streets, living over Joe's
supermaket, on weekends
would repeat from our window
the same ritual
all over again

this counting of passing cars
(you took the Fords
eye took the Chevrolets
but the Cadillacs would win).

& from our window, on saturday nights
we would watch the drunken fights
across the street
at Meyer's Tavern
where people died with
ridiculous ease from street surgeons' knives

summers brought picnics & barbecues
baseball games & hot, funky parties
where we styled hard laid off
in bad summer rags

& on warm idle days
on concrete, playground courts
eye would beat the hell out of you
playing basketball, until it got dark

in winter, we would bundle up tight
in fast shrinking clothes
bought three years before
when daddy was making money playing baseball
in Batista's Cuba, before Castro,
or when mother was working downtown
as a deskclerk at Sonnenfeld's

& on frozen winter nights
we would fight like two vicious alley cats
over who pulled the cover off of who
afterwards, we would sleep side by side
in the dark in our own spilt blood

& if someone was ever foolish enough
to mess with either one of us
they had to contend with the both
of us sho-nuff righteously stomping
eleven thousand corns on their
                    sorry asses

but time has worn away those days
as water rubs smooth, in time
                    a rough & jagged stone

you took the blues of those days
filled with sun dues & blood & turned them
into rhythms you played
superbly on your talking drums
before you heard the calling of your Lord sanctified

eye took that beautiful song
you gave to me & turned it into poetry
this poem eye give to you now

with a brother's deep, love

OLD BLACK LADIES ON BUS STOP CORNERS

for my grandmother, Leona Smith

Blue black and bow bent under beautiful
Blue black and bow bent under beautiful
Blue black and bow bent under beautiful

& it never did matter
whether the weather
was flame tongue licked
or as cold as a well digger's asshole
in late december when santa claus
was working his cold money bullshit
that made financiers grin
all the way to secret bank vaults
overflowing with marble eyes
of third world children

Blue black and bow bent under beautiful
Blue black and bow bent under beautiful
Blue black and bow bent under beautiful

never did matter
whether the days were storm raked
with lightning streaked clouds
tornados skipping crazy
to their own savage beat
shooting hailstone death
at the skulled sunken eyes
of tired old ladies
tired old black ladies
standing on bus stop corners
pain wrapped as shawls around their necks

Blue black and bow bent under beautiful
Blue black and bow bent under beautiful

Blue black and bow bent under beautiful

& "Mama" it didn't matter
that pained scarred feet overworked
numb legs bow bent under beautiful
grew down out of old worn dresses
seemingly fragile   gauntly skeletal frail
as two old mop sticks   scarecrow legs
didn't matter because you stood there anyway
defying nature's chameleon weather—
defying all reason
stood there testifying over 400 years
of madness & treason

Blue black and bow bent under, beautiful

no, it didn't matter
because the beauty of your heroic dimensions
grown lovely in twisted swamps
grown lovely from desolate land
grown pure & full from wombs
of concrete blood & bones
of concrete blood & bones & death
of death & sweat chained to breath
didn't matter dark proud flower
scrubbed by age & cold & rain
the foreign name given your father
swaying body high up there in the burning breeze

Blue black and bow bent under, beautiful

because you stood there anyway
unforgettably silent in your standing
work scarred black lady
numb legs & bow bent under beautiful
stood there on pain scarred feet overworked
numb legs and bow bent under beautiful

under the image of your father
swaying high up there in the burning breeze
now sweet music   love sings calm
soft beauty from your washed aging windows—
giving us strength
                during the mad, bizarre days

no, it didn't matter
whether the weather was flame tongue
licked or as cold as a well digger's asshole
in late December
because you stood there anyway
in full bloom
of your strength and rare beauty
& we have learned to love your life
& will vindicate the pain of your life
the memory of your father
who is also our great grandfather
with the foreign name & who sways high up there over your legs
blue black & bow bent under beautiful
the weight of 400 years carried
of blood and bones and death in mud
of breath & sweat chained to death
        numb legs & bow bent under beautiful
the image of your father swaying high
up there in the burning breeze

        didn't matter whether the weather was flame-tongue-licked
or as cold as a well digger's asshole in late december
because you stood there anyway
flowering in full beautiful
& made us strong

Blue black and bow bent under, beautiful
Blue black and bow bent under, beautiful
Blue black and bow bent under, beautiful

RIVER RHYTHM TOWN

River rhythm town
under sun/moon laughter,
river blues town filled
with blues people
doin' blues dues thangs

cycles of shinin' laughter

listenin' to dues sounds, everyday
of Chuck Berry   Miles Davis
Little Richard   The Dells
Thelonious Monk
yardbird parker,
& John Coltrane

Walkin' the hip walk
wearin' the hip new thangs
laid off clean as a broke-dick dog
in the cut,
chasin' hot black girls down
rhythm & blues,
doin' the belly grind in corners
of smoke filled red lighted
funky parties

music risin' hot
between cold funk
of wall to wall
partyin' black shadows

weavin' spinnin' dancin'
drinkin' in the beauty of sensuous
black foxy ladies

yeah!
rubbin' thrills against the pain
of imprisoned skin screamin' for release
from over-worn tight-fittin' fabrics
& eye remember smiles
dazzling as daybreak,
& soft as mother's
warm embracing eyes

& eye remember love
in the grass sweating as rivers
from our fused flesh

eye remember thrills
eye remember smiles
eye remember love
in the grass sweating rivers

from our fused flesh

eye remember sadness

eye remember St. Louis
river rhythm town under
sun/moon laughter,
river blues town, filled
with blues people
doin' blues dues thangs

& eye remember death
shattering as daybreak

II.

WHOSE DEATH IS THIS WALKING TOWARDS ME NOW

whose death is this walking towards me now
eye know it's not mine, eye left mine
behind, back at the undertaker's

so who belongs to this corpse that just passed
me now, wagging a st. james version of the bible
or was it the readers digest version

look, his eyes are black & flat as crushed
shadows, deep as hot tar pits
whose corpse is this walking towards me

now, eye know it's not mine—
eye left mine behind
back at the cemetery

ODE TO JOHN COLTRANE

With soaring fingers of flame
you descended from Black Olympus
to blow about truth and pain: yeah,

just to tell a story about Black experience.
then the flames left your fingers and soul,
came winter you lay down
in cold snow
and was cool.

But during the bebop-filled avant-garde summers
you weaved slashing thunderclaps of sound
weaved spells of hypnotic beauty,
blew searing extensions of sublimation.

Trane Trane runaway train smashing all known dimensions
Trane Trane runaway train smashing all known dimensions

Hurtling thru spacelanes of jazz
a Black Phoenix of Third World redemption.

eye say Trane Trane runaway train smashing all known dimensions
Trane Trane runaway train smashing all known dimensions

With immortal pure sounds of brotherhood
turning and churning inside you,
boiling and steaming and exploding,
until reaching a stratified piety
whose deity was universal truth

eye say Trane Trane runaway train smashing all known dimensions
Trane Trane runaway train smashing all known dimensions

In sheets of sounds of injustice
you poured forth the bitter truth, the agony,
the pain, but making even that
seem beautiful too

J.C. J.C. John Coltrane, J.C. J.C. John Coltrane

You blew your fingers to smoking cinders
preparing for the "Ascension,"
blew beautiful sad death songs
on "Kind of Blue" mornings,
blew love on "A Love Supreme,"
now the ages await you,
beyond the infinite darkness,
where the "Bird" of bebop slumbers.

But rage rage rage Coltrane!
Rage against the taking of a vision
Rage rage rage Coltrane!
Rage against the taking of Life!
For after Life eye know of no other vision.

And there is no guarantee
that one will follow bringing sight
to the place beyond my perception.

But eye concede to time/scarred myth of grand possibility.
eye concede to this, but to no more;
cause my life been filled with grand possibilities
but most have shut their doors.
But this be no mere cry of self/pity.
Naw, eye don't look at life that way.

Eye am the pessimistic realist
who sees death as final and ugly;

waxed faces, unreal smells in mortuaries;
and flowers that rot upon mounded clay.

If Ojenke or Curtis Lyle were to die
eye would cry. Eye would remember times
that we ate and drank and laughed and chased
beauti/ful Black Women thru streets of Watts together.

Eye would remember new poetry
read in back rooms;
eloquent statements on the pig's inevitable doom:
bringing restoration of the waste of the people,
and that was resurrected from the dance
upon smoking cinders of love.

Eye see death—as only eye can—
as a hushed kind of deep vast silence,
where roosters never crow
to herald the leaving of deadness,
where the clanking of chains is soundless
when dragged across the bottomless floor;
death is the infinite vigil beyond the door of Life;
death is the lengthening ocean of night
where there shines no light.

Yeah!—eye admit it!—death to me seems forbidding!
Descending into unexplored pits all alone;
pits of inescapable gloom where the air is heavy and dank,
where all flesh has fallen away leaving bones,
and soon the bones are no more,
only the crumbling grave/stone remains
to tell about who you were.

Death is weekends where great hornmen remain silent;
the "Bird" Lester Young Eric Dolphy Clifford Brown
except on ancient scratched-up records

on phonographs of old/timers
who lounge speaking of the good/old days
of dilapi/dated or polished rooms.

Those who followed you thru spring
thru summer thru autumn into winter,
those who watched you scatter the phalanx of jazz
and send them reeling and searching for cover,
those who remember your cry from "Round Midnight"
beauti/ful, esoteric, searing, when it flamed over
the entire sky, prelude to earth shaking thunder and fire
of "Equinox," these friends
who acknowledged your greatness quite early
will weep the hardest and the earliest.

Those who were familiar with your agony.
Those who were familiar with your pain.
Those who felt the hotness of manhood
surge like flames thru their veins, yeah!
These are the ones fear will not claim: they will cry;

"Kulu Se Mama" "Kulu Se Mama" "Ole" "Ole" Coltrane!
"Kulu Se Mama" "Kulu Se Mama" "Ole" "Ole" Coltrane!

Those who felt the prick of hypodermic death needles
hung off loaded in some shabby dark room,
who drinking wine and dying chased america's illusions
thru cold rank streets steeped in delusion
garbed in the evil mantle of white doom,

who sucked and fucked and jived and shucked
in strait-jacket tombs of insanity,
who came to the game in hopeless pain
and thought his mangled body to be the cobra's fangs;
who died just to be doing something different.

Who were witch doctors of intrigue.
Who were voodoo/men of death.
Who were ghosts called hunger.
Who were men called sweat;
not men of "SEN-SEN" smelling death,
but men of halitosis smelling death!

Who shot "smack" to ease the pain
of rapes by savages of innocent Black Mothers,
who shot "smack" to ease the torture
of lynchings by white savages
of noble Black Fathers,
who shot morphine to ease the agony
of "Blondes have more fun" type Black spinsters.
These ebony maidens who are prostitutes of the soul
who hoped and groped thru the "Jackie" mystique
went plunging an decadent into the "Twiggy" mystique'
lost Black beauti/ful Women: chasing images of impossibility

while dancin' and swingin' to the down blues beat
of the philosopher of the Black masses, yeah!
James Brown James Brown Black Brown James Brown!
splendid rhythm of hips that sway
sing you not a song for the Trane?
sing you not a tune of lamentation
for this sacred bard, this jujuman—like you
whose song was about pain and love
and whose heart was very gentle with love?

And you Johnny Mathis, nightingale with the clearest chime,
will you not croon the Trane a line
of love and enduring admiration?

And what of you conceited weavers of rhyme?
You Poets, spilling unfinished drinks
upon the carpet of these times

sitting mesmerized by cheap wine
writing: "It's time it's time to write those lines
but I'm too drunk to do it now,
I'll wait until tomorrow to do it,
but it's time, it's time."

And tomorrow coming and going
leaving unquenchable footprints of yesterday
and you the fearless warrior-poet
lying stone cold dead in your lead head
gripping an unfinished poem to Trane in your head.

Death has no sympathy for the unfinished.
And genius and greatness? It feels
not one way or the other.
It simply comes like the exalted thing that it is:
Alone, and unescorted into any room—the room perhaps!
bringing news of dimensionless wandering.

Yeah, Trane! I'm gonna weep for you!
As will Miles blowing sad songs of style!
As will Poets writing wondrously sad elegies cry!

Yeah! I'm gonna weep for lost and pain Coltrane!
But during moments of future clarity
eye will see you as Black John the jujuman,
Black Phoenix who soared sky high! and even beyond!
Breathing love fire light upon a dark vast night
speaking about years of monumental human agony!

Trane Trane John the Baptist, Ohnedaruth,
immortal burning flame of Black jazz,
jujuman running wild over galloping Black Music,
eye give you this poem of remembrance,
the most sacred gift this poor Black man has.

Trane Trane John Coltrane, you came and while here
breathed light love upon cold red sky
dripping with blood death and ire
so that Black music love
would not falter and die,

eye say rest rest rest Coltrane
Trane Trane John Coltrane
and sleep the deep sleep
of all the ages. . . .

THE SKY EMPTIES DOWN ICE

the sky empties down ice
winter grows quickly in your face
of crowded ashtrays

you say
you have come this far for cigarettes
fun & a warm adventure
in bed
but your razor nails
clawing my back
tell me

another story

meanwhile   the sea whispers
rapture on the other side of time
pigeons drop slimy
shit into
your vanilla ice cream cone

but don't get angry
just yet

just because this moment defies
gravity takes off & lands
just there
where a fart just left

all eye know is this:

the sky is emptying down ice
& winter is growing quickly in your face
of crowded ashtrays

in your butt-end face

of crowded ashtrays

HALLOWEEN PARADE IN GREENWICH VILLAGE, 1978

it was the night of your funeral mama
the ritualized mourning night of your death
& at the head of the affair
a black man selling luminous green bracelets of light
then a space man   plastic arrows flashing on & off
a richard nixon double stalks in clown costume
rubber face   long curled-up harlequin
shoes   juggles silver balls
as dracula bites a young girl's neck
on bleecker street   eggheads bobbing up & down
skeletons grinning gyrating bones   saxophones
wailing deep in the unreal noise
conga drums underneath the muffled night
pulsating tight runs as tambourines
rattle the drunk & staggering night

now fabulous masks pop out of the crowd
like champagne powered corks   cold-cock eyeballs
of people   sequins waving cat-tails   funny witches
rake long silver fingernails   transmit light
dance up & down fire
escapes up side walls of buildings drowning
& saturated in rainbowed flights of color
sight octopus like twenty-foot gondolas
of silk jitterbugging the night
as a pig in a red satin dress switches
her oversized rubber-packed poontang quivers
a trembling tall wolfman on stilts shivers
two styrofoam black gloves
hold moon faces of two uptight men-girls
framed like twin sunflowers in their plucking fingers
a flute choir floats rhythms over space & sights
two screaming homos swapping spit

crossing seventh avenue south the parade claws
traffic packed ten blocks back in the night
honking its whining anger

slide now down greenwich street
hook a left on west tenth   pass patchin place
(time keeping the heart of the energy) moving
pass jefferson market library
which used to be a church & before that on the other
side of time   the old women's clocked high tower
of detention   where angela davis once looked out
& down from on molasses cheering crowds—
old-time ritualized masturbations—
but where now   mama
& on the night of your funeral   mama
the ritualized hour of your death
a gigantic spider waves its eight legs
then folds them back over its abdomen   mama
beneath the cheese-faced dial of the high
tower clock   mama   where black hands still turn
around time but where now this gigantic gyrating spider
mama is gripping its eight legs around the church spire
mama   appears to make love   shivers in climax
mama   turns voices into agitated flights

now the drums move away carrying the spirit
hubbub of the thing unrecognized that holds us here
past peter's backyard charcoal room
in front of which
a two-headed pig holds titties of a possessed dracula girl—
cackling like that clawing hissing girl thing in *The Exorcist*—
while the two-headed pig thing mounts& begins humping her
with a four-foot rubber penis
a sing-song man with a t.v. for a head screams:
give me your money

give me all your dreams & money
eye sell sleeks cars guaranteed to fall apart in three years
sell sewing machines   poison eye stitch into your ears
& eyes   sell bona-fide illusions   packaged mannerisms
just for your use give me money
give me all of your dreams & money
1984 has arrived

now the drums up ahead call us to turn   mama
at fifth avenue   rip van winkle on roller skates
& dressed in orange black & purple   cruises by
sashaying   the parade laid now dead up in the cut of its own rhythm
moves past feathers now
(above which the fine lady from mississippi lived over once
before she moved in with yours truly & blew her final chance of staying
a swinging young bachelorette)
comes to washington square park   on top of whose   spotlighted
    lookalike   champs-élysées gateway perches a red-suited devil waving
    blessings
like the pope welcoming everybody to the final destruction
of this american bacchanalia

now television cameras roll their shadow-catching eyes
prop lights splash darkness to the bone with light

a beggar drags by pre-arranged rags
two more fags in rock drag fall out with one another
scream at each other over whose tongue tastes the sweetest
while a latin band warms up the square with salsa
languaging the park
spirit runners slip in & out the dark
mounting rhythms lovers themselves to flesh
richard nixon's double-take juggles silver balls
bad as rubber checks
the band leaps into burning salsa

sways the people   cooks & turns passion
into joy on the very edge of frenzy
rockets go off in the sky of margaret's eyes
whose smile is a kiss
as a ten-foot high silk dragon with people for legs
rides by stunning night air above rhythms the crowd is dancing
holy inside salsa spirits moving away inside themselves
while outside the park a pale man in white lace
directs traffic with jeweled conductor's baton
rollers under his hairnet yawn open
their gulping mouths looping
bleached blond arrogance

now at the end of this strange affair   mama
the black man still jaw-jacking selling green bracelets
of light   ringing corded necks   as the weird man
with the t.v. for a head is still screaming
we fall out of the dying confusion into the restaurant
volare which in italian means *to fly*
eye ease on up next to margaret
climb through the love she carries in her eyes
leave the strange evening behind
enter *volare*'s soft candlelit rhythms
simmer the magic down mama with a kiss
on the night of your funeral   mama
on this halloween night you were laid to rest

EIGHTH AVENUE POEM

on eighth avenue
between 116th and
121st streets
some of the junkies
have feet so bad
they could step
on a dime
and tell you
whether it's
heads or tails

POEM FOR LADY DAY & DINAH WASHINGTON

there is nothing but yawning space between
us now, lady day, dinah washington
queens of the blues, your memories breaking stillness
the octaves of your genius voices razing where
silence reconstructs itself
is pregnant punctuation of absence between chords
a hesitation of sound, arrested like speech
of a revolutionary nailed to a star
your memories of eyes & slurs
bending around your sicknesses fill us with omens
we know is nothing but indigo-blues stabbed
with light deepening between us now
like sorrow, your voices of broken necks twisting
black men lynched, slurs through your muddy syllables
flowing like the mississippi river over bright
bones black flesh use to wrap itself around once
your voices of highways & night trains
blues with dead men & heroin
secret as the voice in the moon of gin bottles
filling this awesome stillness of empty rooms
the octaves of your memories scaling—
silence reconstructing itself, stillborn—
in this indigo new absence, your voices
punctuating between chords, becoming syllables
the image of your voices in memory
full of omens, like your sad, beautiful
faces rooted in this american apocalypse of blues
rooted in this american apocalypse of blues

IMAGE

within the murmuring of darkness
silence grows wings of shadows
locked between cued spaces of syllables
the moon contemplates its own distance
from itself, yawns from the breath
of God, nails itself
deep in black, shimmering velvet—
a rune-pearl replacing the sun
after trembling sundown runs
after trembling sundown runs

RIFF

may days bring an explosion of music
bouncing off edges, walls, polyrhythms
nodding sad junkies seducing daddy death
swinging around corners, cool breezes
floating, touching everything
love left whispering now, new shadows
crisscrossing connections tucked away
in memory, winter yielding, spring
resurrects all things possible
& the sun laughing always on the run

IMPRESSIONS 8

american lawrence welk
saturdays
football games
hot dogs & falstaff beer
chased by fire
of bourbon

mcdonalds & a&p
sears   bank of america
crackers
in chicken noodle soup
ivory snow liquid
miss america   kentucky fried
Palmolive   dove
commercials

madison avenue
cowboys
hillbilly black
militant japtalians
niggindians hungericans
mestizos mulattoes
quadroons

slick hip styling spirits
of the greased way highsign
give high of speech
step the low road
strut bojangle
their words in motion
prancing say "gimme some skin
lay a fin on me" confront
soda crackers

in this gumbo soup
chaos of conflicting
dreams this
american gumbo
soup of chaos
& conflicting dreams

IMPRESSIONS 12

buck dance antlers frozen
in the still air
like fingers gripping death
by the side of the crooked road
a young deer dropped down
in its tracks
assumes a praying position
a bullet hole in the middle
of its shocked
forehead

IMPRESSIONS 15

bright day in pennsylvania
steel blue
    the mountains clear
from here & out hear cold
the naked sky
soft at duskglow, when the sun
sinks clear down

through winter trees bare
skin leaves shake down

    snow mounds cover
the ground & footprints
like inked words on white pages
print themselves
into snow

stretch themselves around
& into the dark, awesome
silence, grows
into worlds

JUST CRUISIN' & WRITIN'

writin' poems
while cruisin
at seventy miles
per hour
on the pennsylvania
turnpike
can be spiritual
fun
if you don't
run into
anyone

IV.

HARLEM LATE NIGHT LYRIC

trucks growl these iced empty streets
as do voices fleet silence punctuates in flight
stabbing screams of death
pharoah blows through his saxophone light
some carry as lodes of memory the language of tradition replaced
by catastrophic absences
the awesome muted hush of talking drums

where then the machinery of benevolence predicted
where the infant rose of new breath opening as a fertile womb
was promised once somewhere back in all those doctored scriptures
a seeding sun disguised perhaps
is what was promised us in autumn

now winter reminds spring is just off-stage
recharging love perhaps then will arrive—enter rooms—
lovelier than the fragrance of fresh-cut roses
the swelling of sweet tongues lathered in saliva

the cooing of birds skying through eyes

THE DAY STRIDES THERE ON THE WIND

for Leo Maitland

the day strides there on the wind
its wings are the people's thoughts
breath contains
& finally it is the speech of God
that shapes everything

that brash shouting trumpet
leaping out of a window somewhere
that lonely saxophone woman walking
there in your erotic imagination
the books opened & closed
that tell us nothing
but what they are

these smells from hidden kitchens
emerging from other smells
surround our nostrils with incense
show & tell everything that you are
is most things but standing up naked

so we wrap ourselves in illusions
wear the mask that dunbar spoke of,
wrap our dreams in dreams
of others who never know
what to do with their own
so we sit watching patches of light
falling through the hairdos of trees

still the day strides there on the wind
& its wings are the people's thoughts
that it contains
& finally it is the speech of God
that shapes everything

V.

MEMOS & BUTTONS

he couldn't even spell albuquerque
had tuna fish garlic breath
mixed in with cigarette blues & a job way beyond
his capacity
he was a bona-fide ten martini man over lunch
same exact thing during rush hours
walking around
with a copper wire for a brain
someone was sending
morse code to

he was a modern man of technology
read the wall street journal & forbes
religiously every day
commuting on suburban trains with spittin'
images cloning himself, locked in
& gigging for xerox, texas instruments,
ibm, hadn't read a deep book
in God knows when
computer printouts being his bible

found himself thinking one day
of murdering his invalid wife, widowed
mother & three teenaged children

he was a modern, western man of technology
who carried his mind around locked up
in a leather brief case

liked to push memos & buttons

LAS CRUCES, NEW MEXICO

For Keith Wilson, Donna Epps Ramsey, Andrew Wall, Charles Thomas & Thomas Hocksema

the high, great mesas, flat as vegas gambling tables
rock-hard, as red dust swirls into miniature tornadoes
dancing down roads red with silence as these
faces of solitary Indians, here where white men quick-tricked
their way to power with houdini bibles, hidden agendas
of bullets & schemes of false treaties

& black men alone here, in this stark high place of mesquite
bushes, white sand mountains, colors snapped in incredible
beauty, eyes walking down vivid sunsets, livid purple scars slashing
volcanic rock, tomahawking language scalping this ruptured space
of forgotten teepees so eye listen to a coyote wind
howling & yapping across the cactused dry high vistas
kicking up skirts of red dirt at the rear end of quiet houses

squatting like dark frogs& crows, etched silhouettes high on live
wire popping speech, caw-cawing, in the sand-blasted wind
stroked-trees caw-cawing all over the mesilla valley

& here along the rio grande river, dry, parched tongue bed, snaking
mud, cracked & dammed north in the throat of albuquerque
mescalara, zuni, apache & navaho live here,
scratch out their firewater breath, peyote
secret eyes roaming up & down these gaming table mesas
their memory dragging chains through these red breathing streets

while geronimo's raging ghost haunts their lives with what they did
not do, stretching this death strewn history back to promises
& hope a hole in the sky, a red omen moon
where death ran through
like water whirlpooling down a sink

& this shaman moon blown here a red target of light at the end

of a tunnel of blackness, where a train speeds through now
towing breaknecking flights of light, where daybreak sits wrapped around
a quiet, ancient navaho, wrapped in cosmic, american colors, sits
meditating, these scorched, white sands, flat
distant high mesas, shaped like royal Basotho hats, chili peppers, churls
pecan groves, roadrunner, chaparral birds, salt cedars, sprouting
parasitic, along bone white ditches bordering
riverbeds thirsting for water
meditates these flat, wide black, lava rocks
holding strange imprints of fossilized speech that died
before they knew what hit them, as did those silent
clay faced ancestors of this solitary navaho sitting in breaking
colors, bursting sunlight, meditating the lay of this enchanting
blues land, changing its face every mile or so

& in their faces indians carry the sadness of ancestors
who wished they had listened to those long gone
flaming words—battlecries!—of geronimo, whose screaming ghost
prowls these bloody, muddy streets, baked dry now by the flaming eye
torching the sky, they wished they had listened to instead of chaining
his message in these coyote, howling winds
kicking up skirts of dirt
whose language yaps like toothless old men & women
at the rear-end of quiet houses, whose lights dance slack
at midnight, grow black & silent as death's worn-out breath
beneath these pipe-organ mountains, bishops peaked
caps holding incredible silence, here
in the mesilla valley

where the rio grande river runs dry
its thirsty spirit dammed north in the throat of albuquerque
at the crossroads of fusion & silence in the red gush swirls—
whispering litanies sawblading through ribcages, dust memory—
snaking winds all over the mesilla valley brings
long-gone words of geronimo,
haunting las cruces, new mexico
long-gone wind whispering, geronimo, geronimo

IT ALL BOILS DOWN

it all boils down to a question of what
anything is being done for, in the first place
a reason, perhaps, stronger than the pull of any
magnet, perhaps, the first recognition
of clouds cruising through seas of blue
breath, shaped like battleships

on the other hand, it could be a fascination wearing
rings on sweating, claw-like fingers
something we have forgotten, knew nothing about ever
like the future of a question only time holds answers to
such as the exact moment death puts a lean on flesh, perhaps
& the thin suit vanity wears collapses
in on itself as the spirit takes leave of breath
& voices swell into a cacophonous blues, mother

somewhere in all of this there are connections fusing
something perhaps, in the mellifluous
nodding of crazed junkies—that sad colony of leprous, popeye feet & hands—
is a dance, a catatonic premonition of unheeded weather reports
like the knowing somewhere deep
eclipsed suns will perhaps experience joy
in the shaved light—

a shopping list of syllables is what poets carry
when confronting the winds of language
beyond that only the wind knows what it is doing—
like evil laughter gleaming machetes swing under streetlamps
slicing quick words that cut a man too short to shit sometimes, perhaps
a concertino stream of blue ragas when
breath flies suddenly back here, mysterious, as in those moon glinting
eyes, fixed in silence, the dime-polished speech of felines
in a midnight moment of celebration

a bone dry, squawking hawk talking away up there
suddenly, beyond dues, disappearing into blue quicksand
flapping wings of unanswered questions

down here, it all boils down to questions
ribcages pose & leave scattered under terrifying suns
on desert floors, the timeless, miraging sands holding
light, the steaming, seamless language
in flight & flowing into midnight

moons climbing between me & you

116TH STREET & PARK AVENUE

for Pedro Pietri & Victor Hernandez Cruz

116th street fish smells, pinpoint la marqueta
up under the park avenue, filigreed viaduct
elevated tracks
where graffied trains run over language
there is a pandemonium of gumbo colors stirring up
jumbalaya rhythms
spanish harlem, erupting
street vendors on timbale sidewalks
where the truth of things is what's happening now
que pasas on the move, andale
worlds removed from downtown, park avenue gentry luxury co-ops
where latino doorman just arrived, smile their *tip me good*
tip me good, tip me good, greetings
opening doors
carry their antediluvian, rice & bean villages, old world
style, dripping from zapata moustaches
shaped perfect as boleros
their memories singing images underneath shakepearean
cervantes balconies, new world don juans
smelling of cubano cigars, two broken tongues
lacing spanglish up into don q syllables, cuba libre
thick over sidewalks, voices
lifted & carried up into dance
into mambo, cha cha slick steps out
on the ballroom floor imagine themselves
rumbling car horns, palmieri fused
machito fired, pacheco tuned, barretto drums
bolero guitars wiring morse code puns, root
themselves back in villages
of don juan, romeo,
zapata, marti in cuba, writing poetic
briefs, under cigar trees the lingua-franca

of nicolas guillen, morejon, cruz & pietri
laying down expressions of what's happening now
& weaved through this pandemonium of gumbo
colors up under
the park avenue, filigreed viaduct
criss-crossing 116th street fish smells pinpointing
la marqueta
where elevated trains track over language
run over syllables up on elevated tracks, fuse words
together, (w)rap lyrical que pasas on the move,
andale, spanglish harlem
nuyorican sidewalks, exploding fried bananas
timbale shopping carts up into salsa
sweat new borinquen slick steps
buzzard winged, moustached, newyorican muchachas
in a new world black latin groove, where the truth
of things is what's happening now
the truth of things is what's happening, now

LEON THOMAS AT THE TIN PALACE

eye thought it was the music when
in fact it was a blender
grinding down ice
making stuffings for drinks, but then
you jumped right on in on the downbeat, leon
stroking rhythm inside time
inside the bar, then

people flew deeper into themselves
became the very air sweeping language to crescendo
between feathers of touch looping chord changes
your voice blued down, blues cries, field hollas
mississippi river flooded guttural
stitches through your space
images of collective recall, leon

your voice strokes scattin' octaves—
ice grinding down still inside the blender
making stuffings for pina coladas—then
you scooped up our feelings again
in the shovel of your john henry doowops, leon
jazzed through ellington, count & bird
yodeling coltrane, blues cries
the history of joe williams
sewn into the eyes of our eardrums
transmitted to the space between
the eyes where memory lies

your scatting licks brings us back dancing
in our seats, you kick swelling language, inside
your lungs, voice stroking colors painting
the Creator's Masterplan
as pharoah explodes inside the tone blender of his horn

the ice grinds down the bar jumps out of itself
scooped up in the shovel of your john henry doowops
blue as a mississippi gutteral river flooded
octaves kicking back black scattin'
rhythms loop busting your chops

feather stroking phrasing, leon thomas
yodeling octaves, sewn back black

where they came from

VI.

UNTITLED 3

birds ski down the day's inscrutable smile
wheeling, banking their diaphanous
sawblading voices, their sword-like sleek feathers
cutting through the day's upper reaches of silence
their convoluted language cacophonous
& raucous, as a lynch mob
in old georgia, the rope-rasping burning of their syllables
hanging their twisting meanings around us & these blooming
dark hours stormy with chaos april brings—
spring leaping suddenly upon us
like a black panther clawing our breath
but is filled with so rare & mysterious
a beauty, it thrills us to death

EYE THROW MY ROPE TONGUE INTO THE SKY

eye throw my rope tongue into the sky
send out words of love lassoing to you cross
blue valleys of distance
fight off swirling tornadoes, desert fried
fools who want to intercept this message for you
only for you, rain-swept cooing lady, wooing
tongue of cool rain
my voice, a wing of stroking feathers
riffing & riding the hot wires, comes tickling
your eardrums, my sweet tongue looping
lyrical melodies of fire
rope tongue looping melodies cross skies
comes tickling, sweetly, your eardrums

A THOUGHT FOR YOU, MARGARET

for Margaret Porter

eye stretch my lips, 3000 miles
cross telephone wires, sucking silence
of wings beating down breath, space
a hemorrhage of distance

& you there singing, as dusktones
rainbow feathers, sleeping, as loveliness
peace, we have come to this magic, apart
with ourselves, alone
serene, inside this g music

muted trumpet kissing fabled dusk song
skin of scarred history, long distant embraces
in dreams, memory easing out of breath, rhythms
gliding in & out, over & under
like birds—footprints in white snow—
banking down sunset skies

& now your love call coming through
clear, the night wind's sucking deep mystery
through space, black distance collapsing in
on itself, screaming, the grip
of your sonorous name, soothing

soothing, tongue touch, your sonorous name

A POEM FOR OJENKE & K. CURTIS LYLE

if in a comatose instant of deep listening
you should come across a syllable
wide as the sky of pure hearing & sleep
as whenever anytime your eyes carry themselves
to their limits of recognition, crystal
as on a steel blue day of bright clear winter
at the moment of that rare clarity
as in the listening to a black, blues band there
steeped in the bone & blood utterance of gut-bucket
bucket of blood tradition, if in the stop-action
freezing of that negative
snapped image heard & fashioned there
from that sound you just perceived now in the knowing
of that terror, just now, there, guttural
as in the whiskey-broken voice life of ma rainey
chained to microscopic grooving of a vinyl instance
recorded then full of all things considered
meaningful there—then, as now—
what it all means when everything is left
hanging out there in the cold, like blood-splattered
sheets billowing under a lolling blue morning
cool rinse that now switches up
under a chameleon sun's heat, now, like cynical
laughter, sweating down rivers of gold light
beamed there, & if in the rifle sighting
focusing of that clearly cold instant,
comatosed, you should happen across a syllable
wide as the sky of new hearing & blue deep
blue deep, as where anytime your vision carries
itself to the limits of recognition
if you should hear a crystal song ringing out
there, & during that moment of rare clarity
a voice, perhaps, a note, like a breeze fluting over

informing this moment, perhaps, like a cool blue morning
rinsed, folding over a beginning poem there
& in the crystal clear hearing of that moment
& in the bone & blood spirit of gut-bucket blues
tradition, & if you should hear a new crystal image
there, call me with a poem, good brothers
call me & singing, call me through a poem

SOUTHERN LYRIC; RITUAL

evenings rise here with voices of old people
whispering up sky, a cat-eyed moon riding
wings of bat syllables rising
brushing up against mystery, eyelids of language
winking their hushing rhythms through serenading trees
xylophones carrying cooling winds to memory
couch their soothing sounds in magic of primeval wisdom
the orchestration of harmony between ensembles of birds
whose voices whisper riffings up steep skies
carrying history a lynx-eyed moon rides up on
rising, like muted tongues of old people
ventriloquists of southern nights
whispering, there on porches
cobwebbed in filigreed shadows
half light, the old peoples' voices
yeasting with wisdom in their sundown
eyes, riding up sky, longside a lynx-
eyed moon, wings of bat syllables
soothing, a xylophone, a tune

PASSING ON THE LEGACY

for my son Quincy Brandon Troupe & Henry Dumas

we stand within these bones
of ourselves within
flesh of these years melting
like ice cubes in drinks
within stone these thoughts
this miracles of roots inside
our folklore the link
stretching four hundred years
back to villages eaten black
by euro-american halloween flames
eating up the dark rhythms rhythms
eating up the dark rhythms, rhythms

here, weaving shadows dance
through leaves stretch to hear
across salt water the boogieman high
in trees the drummers harden hands

& time breaks wind & bone
stone juxtaposed next to feathers

& there aren't too many secrets
these days that are not known we speak
through our eyes
& see through our ears & hear
through our tongues

we stand within tone of these bones
inside these years ringing like bells
a coltrane solo solo
& so eye reach out the smile
of my tongue blue-black with blues rhythms

a jazz-riff born of dues payments
to you a love gong
chiming from my eyes
hand over to you this signature
born in blood & fire
& baptized in river-bottoms

a sun toned hardness
a guitar full of lives

so take the vision brandon
& run up sun with it
look back into your own eyes

you are the memory
carrying the future

NEW YORK CITY STREAM POEM

sounds sounds of crushed traffic
wind sounds   sounds
symphonic voices of multi-lingual people
of new york city people   moving
through space   pace
of kinetic energy

                              energy of space/place

of new york city space/place
a pickpocket of energy new york giving energy

                                        city space/place

space/place of music   colors
energy of music   colors & sounds weaving motion
rhythm guitar   dancers of sound

                              motion

& faces odd   cold beautiful faces
& legs & figures that burst out of colors
races
traces of races that move beyond races colors that
fuse & blues the only language we know hear
faces sensuous faces
faces with lips that invite   sounds
they are succulent
they are very very succulent
these sounds   these colors
these lips that invite

colors   traces of races
in the fused shadow world leaping
from faces   lips that invite
sounds colors of sound

color me soundcolor me motion color me
wind sound motion
                            color me poem
color me African wind poem
color me music
color me African freedom music
                        color me black

color me traces of races
bursting from colors moving beyond races
color me faces   sensuous faces
lips that invite
          color me energy
color me voodoo/hoodoo
space/place of energy
color me motion moving

color me love color me love
color me hoodoo/voodoo
traces of races in love

color me love

AT THE END

at the end
of every sentence
a period
occupying space
as molecular energy

a point to make
another point
in space the end is
the beginning
of another end

recurring cycles
occupying space

& death being
only a period at the
end of a sentence

earth

a point
that starts
another point

& at the end
there is space
to begin again

always space
at the end to

begin again

from

WEATHER REPORTS

NEW POEMS 1984–1990

PERENNIAL RITUAL

for all the dictators in Haiti & anywhere else

they are killing the joy of laughter once again
they're slaughtering the smiles of children
they're banning the music from language once again
they are marching in goose-steps to rhythm of bullets
they're putting cyanide in people's drinks of hope again
they are trading back their freedom for strings of puppet money
they're digging mass graves for the innocent once more
they're cutting down trees that hold back the floods
they're macheteing roots of their bloodlines once again
they're smearing blood on their mother' faces dead as moats
they're ripping out the tongues from their history again
they're butchering all love like they would a goat

what is it that they hate in themselves, in clear, new mirrors
what is the dry as bone spit of their snake-eyed fear, their terror
of bloodlines, running deep as the secrets of voodoo
what is the future they want everyone to dance through
where did the poison come from that is flowing through their puffer-fish
hearts & where do their thoughts turn to after uzis shoot joy from the dark
& the eerie silent roads hold only the shadows of murderers

bufo marinus namphy, sweating beneath his tunics medalled with skulls
his henchmen sitting black stone-faced behind him with their slit cobra eyes
cool & evil prosper avril & william regala, lafontant & old bossman, duvalier
what is the is the suicidal urge they pick up from other scumbags
licking out their lizard tongues cancerous with warts
their dum-dum, bazooka eyes of mamba snakes
deadly as a fart at a republican party, whose american president keeps them
stumbling here with his famous soft shoe, his chicken neck flapping clues
his glued hair plastered in place, embodying what they will sink to
what they will kill for to become

O, they're shooting out the lights of port-au-prince once again
they're turning people into zombies with their snake-eye guns
they're trying to kill the moon in a dreamer's eyes once more
they're feeding the vacant-eyed poor with teaspoons half-filled with garbage
they're lining up beggars & killing their hunger again
they are goose-stepping to the rhythm of bullets

BOOMERANG: A BLATANTLY POLITICAL POEM

eye use to write poems about burning
down the motherfucking country for crazy
horse, geronimo & malcolm king
x, use to (w)rite about stabbing white folks
in their air-conditioned eyeballs with ice picks
cracking their sagging balls with sledgehammer blows
now, poems leap from the snake-tip of my tongue
bluesing a language twisted tighter than braided hope
hanging like a limp-noosed rope down the question mark
back of some coal miner's squaw, her razor slanted
killer shark eyes swollen shut with taboos
she thought she heard & knew
the sun in a voice looking like bessie smith's severed arm
on that mississippi back road, screaming, like a dead man's son
who had to watch his old man eat his own pleading heart
& sometimes eye wonder if it's worth the bother
of it all, these poems eye (w)rite holding
language percolating & shaped
into metaphoric rage
underneath, say
a gentle simile, like a warm
spring day, soft as balm or talcum
on the edge of a tornado that hits quicker
than the flick of a bat's wing nicking the eye
eye use to write poems about killing fools like ronald reagan
duffy duck grinning off 30 million sucked down
the whirlpooling black holes of cia space
director casey taking a lobotomy
hit, slash to protect
the gipper
dumb
motherfuckers
everywhere tying bombs

to their own tongues, lighting fuses
of staged events that lye of peace & saving
money in the s & l pirateering, like president gipper
they are metaphors for all that's wrong in america right now, all this
cloning, brouhaha, paid mouthpieces on wall street & the gipper
giving frying skillet speeches, others that ray gun reagan
ray gunning america, now, cannibalizing airwaves
with mouthpieces fronting slimy churches
building up humongous bank accounts
in the name of the holy bones
of jesus christ, long gone
& dead
& it is a metaphor
boomeranging jimmy
& tammy bakker, sleazy swaggert
vacuuming pocketbooks of the old & the dead
like medusa meese heads nicked off & sluicing like bad faith
they dangle heads from "freedom fighter" mouths
tell the black bird press herded up on a wire
that it's okay, it's okay, it's okay
& them believing it
eye use to write poems about burning
down the motherfucking country for crazy
horse, geronino & malcolm king
x marks the spot where "coons" signed away
their lives on dotted lines, black holes
sucking away their breath
for a sack of cotton
full of woe
eye
sit here
now, (w)riting
poems of the soft
calm beauty welling
in my son's innocent 4 year

old eyes, thinking, perhaps of the time
when this rage will strike him, driving him towards madness
knowing all the while it will come quick
sooner than expected
& nothing
absolutely nothing
will have been undone

LES CAYES, HAITI & RELIGIONS ON PARADE: 1984

1. VOODOO

on good friday, fronting the square
rara called the few old faithful here through
bamboo, the drum masters stroking their signatures
rooted clues deep beneath the surface, voodoo
found its medium in lulu
the lithe, loa dancer
baton twirlers, beyond the blues
that lightning spoke in a mojo hand
a mojo hand, a sequined loa called through
sluicing, bamboo clues, voice deep
in voodoo, a mojo hand, calling
somewhere, somehow, old
lightning hopkins knew
came close to playing
what this was all about

2. CATHOLICISM

the catholic parade hustled many through
droves moved through the dark streets of les cayes
mixed bloods & pure bloods walking shoulder to shoulder
the crucifiction myth nailed in all their heads
nailed in their hearts, bloods
bearing up the cross through the dark
the hymns of jesus christ's blood running
through their voices up ahead, pulling
blood of three nails hammered down
through centuries of His blood
running like ribbons through these streets
reining ropes pulling His invisible image, here
through these litanies of blood
& bloody all these bodies snaking through
les cayes, full of nails driven through

open palms & feet, screaming
their bloody, burdened, invisible voices
of mythical blood flowing invisible through
these dark, narrow streets
the many faithful meet, shoulder to shoulder
mixed bloods & pure bloods, carrying
their crosses in their voices
shoulder to shoulder, snaking through les cayes
les cayes, spirit to spirit, on this good friday
evening, & all of them deep in voodoo, too

3. THE PROTESTANTS
the protestants were silent on this day
& perhaps their silence spoke for them, too
whatever their numbers
silence spoke this evening for them, too
who were not there

IN MEMORIAM

for James Baldwin (1924–1987)

it's like a gray dreary day, wet with tears & mourning
when someone you love ups & goes away
leaving behind a hole in your laughter, an empty space
following you around like an echo you always hear & never see
high up in the mountains
the spirit gone & left, circling there its diminishing sound
a song looking for a place inside this gray day of tears
to lay down its earthly load,
to drop down its weary voice among the many blue ones missing
there, who are elbowing their clacking bones rattling like false teeth
loose in a jelly jar up against each other, their voices
dead as lead & silence yawning
with the indifference final breaths acheive
& the open mouths are black holes framing endless space
words fall through like stars sprinkled through the breath
of your holy sentences, jimmy,
up there now with the glorious voice of bessie
the glory hallelujah shouting gospel
you loved so deeply, wrote it out in your blood
running like dazzling rivers of volcanic lava blood
so dazzling your words blooming van gogh sunflowers
you planted as sacred breaths inside our minds & hearts
the image of the real deal going down funky & hard

& so we celebrate you, holy witness, celebrate
your skybreaking smile infectious laughter
hear your glory hallelujah warnings everywhere we look
see clearly the all-american scrubbed down button down
greed rampant in these "yet to be united states"
& so we take heed, beg for your forgiveness that you might
forgive us for our smallness for not rising up with you
for being less than our awesome pitiful needs

forgive us now in your silence, jimmy,
forgive us all who knew & were silent & fearful
& forgive us all, O wordsaint, who never even listened
forgive us for all the torture, for all the pain

AVALANCHE AFTERMATH

for Earl Maxie

outside lake tahoe we see scorched white bones
of stake-like trees, felled (they remind of crude war
weapons, sharpened & hidden & pointing up from pits)
cutting a wide swath through murmuring green
pines, pointing their branches accusingly up at a steel blue
spring sky, crystal clear above our voices, where the highway once
loped & looped back, winding down from echo summit
the year before half the mountain walked clean across the american river
intact, to the other side of the road, thrown there after an avalanche
triggered abrupt & permanent change in the way things were
like a track of train rails, switching up directions, after
the juice is thrown at the main power station: & it reminds
us that destinations are always in the hands of God

PORTER, AT 18 MONTHS

for Porter Troupe

you slipped down into this world, porter
during the dead hours of night
slipped down in a form already perfect
kicking & screaming & bursting
from your new ballooning lungs
older than time though young
in this miraculous moment of celebration

& you are the mysterious meaning of magic, porter
the fused dialectic of passion alchemized
a sweet miracle beyond all words

& now already you speak
in a strange tongue to birds & ants
now already terrorize the cat from its sun-nap
& draw your imagination exploding
over all the clean walls
reject all helping hands you go about
your own business in your own way
full of wonder we watch you
grow into yourself charting your own course
like an explorer discovering new worlds
opening up like flowers before you

& we are both amazed & afraid, knowing the way
in front of you will be treacherously beautiful
having travelled this road before
so now, we teach you bonding
principles absent of miracles but soon
very soon we will stand aside & let you go

CHANGE

for Margaret & Porter

use to be eye would be lying there
in margaret's lap, longside her sweet
soft thighs on sunday mornings, sipping
champagne, sucking on her soft open lips,
drinking in the love from her moist brown eyes
now, porter's there giggling twenty month old
squirming squeals—a tiny spitting image of me
his eyes kissing everyone including me, & me?
well, eye'm sitting here apart from them
hungry, alone in my favorite chair
watching television & listening to them
& watching them, watching me

EYE WALK

eye walk liquid footsteps of my words
across tongue bridge to where you stand
just now, offer you these bittersweet syllables
pregnant with history of what
we have seen together, metaphors,
as in the color of sea breezes & wind, rustling
hairdos of trees tossing & turning in the ebb & flow
of meaning between us, the rhythms of your seduction
flowing into sound of your body breathing
just outside my ears where your licking
tongue—a breeze, blowing softly—teases
your voice a mere whisper & your pouting lips
shaping a kiss succulent as a plum, bursting

TOUT DE MÊME—NICE & MALIBU

the cote d'azur is
like the coast of malibu
a necklace of lights

21 LINES TO CARNOT, GUADELOUPEAN MASTER DRUMMER

his wood & zinc house hard by the bay in goyave
carnot, master of traditional guadeloupean le woz
drumming, six other palm to skin rhythms, he of the flying
hands cracking thunder, he splits the silent speech of night
machete fingers cleaving a passageway
voices flowing through ancestral
cadences pulsating lyrical voodoo sewing breezes
painting pastel music from deep inside itself
a secret language swells the way to magic, ritual,
whose ears have heard the mystery of love unfolding

holding the history of doves, a sea crab scuttles over
the stone floor cold & hard as poverty, carnot leans strong
his body an exclamation mark—
& sharp as a honed sword's blade the edges torn & jagged
as starpoints screwed into his peasant catfish eyes
the electric boring up deep simmering coals burning from within
the steady gaze hawk-like holds the sky
cruising through his two brown lagoons—
leans into the sea salted wind where he goes,
a fisherman drumming his life, the last of his kind here—

african roots dropping secret notes from his palms

POEM FOR THE ROOT DOCTOR OF ROCK N ROLL

for Chuck Berry

& it all came together on the mississippi river
chuck, you there riding the rocking-blue sound wave
duck-walking the poetry of hoodoo down
      & you were the mojo-hand
of juju crowing, the gut-bucket news—running it down
for two records sold to make a penny
back then in those first days "majoring in mouth"—
a long gone, lean lightning rod
       picking the edge, charging the wires
      of songs, huckle-bucking "roll over
beethoven" playing "devil music" till white devils stole it from you
& called it their own "rock n roll"
      devils like elvis & pat boone
who never duck-walked back in the alley with you
& bo diddley, little richard & the fatman from new orleans
all y'all slapping down songs meaner than the smell
of toejam & rot-gut whiskey breath
back there in them back rooms
     of throw down

back there where your song lyrics grew like fresh corn
you, chuck berry, an authentic american genius of barbecue sauce
& deep fried catfish licks, jack-salmon guitar
      honky-tonk rhythms
jangling warm, vibrating sounds choo-chooing train
whistles fiddling & smoking down the tracks of the blues
motivating through "little queenie," "maybelline"
decked out in red on sarah & finney
alarms rolling off your whipping tongue
in the words of "johnny b good"

you clued us in, back to the magical hookup of ancestors

their seamless souls threading your breath
                         their blood in your sluicing strut
& too much "monkey business" the reason for their deaths cold & searing
your spirit reaching down to the bones of your roots
deep in the "show me" blood of missouri soil
                         your pruned hawk-look profiling
where you rode your white cadillac of words cruising
the highways of language (what we speak & hear even now)
breathing inside your cadences
                         you shaped & wheeled the music
duck-walking the length of the stage
duck-walked your zinging metaphors of everyday
slip-slide & strut, vibrating your hummingbird wings
your strumming style the cutting edge
you were what was to come

so hail, hail, chuck berry, root doctor of "rock n roll"
authentic american genius
                         tonguing deep in river syllables
hail, hail, chuck berry, laying down the motivating juju
you great american mojo hand

root doctor, spirit of american "rock n roll"

REFLECTIONS ON GROWING OLDER

eye sit here now inside my fast thickening breath
the whites of my catfish eyes muddy with drink
my roped, rasta hair snaking down in coiled salt & pepper
vines twisted from the march of years, pen & ink lines etching
my swollen face, the collected weight of years swelling
around my middle, the fear of it all overloading circuits
here & now with the weariness of tears coming in storms
the bounce drained out of my once liquid strut
a stork-like gimpiness there now, stiff, as death
my legs climbing steep stairs in protest now, the power gone
slack from when eye helicoptered through cheers
hung around rims threaded rainbowing jumpshots
that ripped popping chords & envious peers
gone now the arrogance and the belief that hard-ons would swell
here forever, smoldering fire in a gristle's desire
drooping limp now like wet spaghetti the hammer-head
that once shot ramrod straight into the sweet
kiss of a wondrous woman's sucking heat
wears a lugubrious melancholy now like an old frog wears
its knobby head croaking like a lonely malcontent
& so eye sit here now, inside my own gathering flesh
thickening into an image of humpty-dumpty
at the edge of a fall, the white of my hubris gone
muddy as mississippi river water
& eye feel now the assault of shot-gunned years shortening
breath, charlie horses throbbing through cold tired muscles
slack & loose as frayed old ropes slipping from round necks of executed
memories see, now these signals of irreversible breakdowns
the ruination of my once, perfect flesh as medals earned
fighting through holy wars of passage, see them as miracles
of the glory of living breath, pulsating music through my poetry
syncopating metaphors turned inside out
see it all now as the paths taken, the choices made

the loves lost & broken, the loves retained
& the poems lost & found in the dark
beating like drumbeats through the heart

FALLING DOWN ROADS OF SLEEP

we are falling down roads into sleep
falling into sleep from blues
posing as the sky, the eye of the Creator moves
black cataracts of clouds around pointillist as clues
wet as when a bad knee tells us that rain is coming
before night floods down the streets
sleep is seducing, as the light
slips from the night, slips from our eyes
& slides across the sky like feet over ice
the lances of our intentions glancing off moons
slicing the edge of noon
we remember a sky blue & deep with light
remember the wings of birds turning around hours
burning off suns, flights of music diving toward night
like warring elements, our speech thunder-clapping
down streets lugubrious with sleep
deep down we leap back into sleep so steep
then fall back into blues
we forget the fading of night coming,
begin climbing up ladders of song rung by rung
sleep falling between our language, now lifting
toward flight, rain clouds like circling crows
cruise under light, under the bold
gold polished coin of the sun, holding

FOLLOWING THE NORTH STAR BOOGALOO

for Miguel Algarin

following the north star boogaloo
the rhythm takes
back to where music began
to percolate language like coffee in another form
back before frederick douglass laid it down
heavy on abe lincoln
when music was breakdancing old hottentots
throwing down mean as bojangles as did
now jump forward through history's dice game
pick up the steps of james brown
michael jackson moonwalking
the old blues talking about yo mama
now fast forward down the lane
pick up the dance of five brothers
skateboarding the court
out in the open, one closes the break
doing a 180 degree phi slamma jamma dunk
stamping their footprints all up in the paint
up in this poet's word dribble
a drummer's paradiddle
word up, yo bro, hip hop, rappers
skateboarding the go go out in the open
court of macking the holy ghost down

hey, you diddle-diddle voodoo griot, take me
back to when eye was black & hitting proud
out on the slick bop thoroughfares
back before the mean homeboys rolled snarling
duckwaddle down the middle, eyes empty with death
before the alley-oops wore their lives as chips on shoulders
in stratospheric attitudes, hung hip from wall to wall
chained gold, caps on heads quaking sideways

muscling up bold masterblasters
checking out reeboks
chillin' dead up in the cut "fresh as death"
after "mo money," "mo money," "mo money"
check it out, bro, pharmaceutical wizards
making seven figure bank accounts do somersaults, no sweat
it's rolling in so fast for crack—("& it ain't nothing
but a hole in the wall") for homeboys
cash 'n carry, cold 16 year olds
who can't count nothing but greenbacks
sliding off the screen & roll they helicopter
after dipping & rolling down the middle
high up above the paint, their footprints walking on space
up over your face hang-gliding to the basket like praying mantises
so fresh they make poot butts faint slamming
faster than high fiving glory—
180 degrees of schoolboy legends, saints
unfolding in prime time memory

so roll it back, kojak, before magic's knees go permanently
south for the winter & leave air jordan footprints
in yo face game as the baddest one in town
before they change up the shake & bake jam off the sky again with a new
phenom, double clutching up there in space like a ferrari stretching out
flat out burning up german autobahns, changing up the guard quicker
than fear brings down doodoo
but hey, young bro, flash the dice roll back through shit
to when the big O was jack knifing through all them bodies
out on the court, to when goose tatum was shimmying magic
down in the middle, down in the paint
as roy haynes jitterbugged like a magician
hoola hoopin' the ball around him, before fast forwarding to dr. j
    —Julius Erving!
& did we ever think we'd lose these hoodoo gods
to old age homes for roundball royalty
new age homeboys not even knowing who they are

& do they even know about jonestown, all them
bloated bodies cracking beneath the sun
& did they ever hear about the north carolina
astronaut david skywalking thompson
jamming out in the open off the fly
helicoptering to roundball heaven
off the motherfucking coast to coast
before he took the fall for all that shit
he snorted up his nose, before hitting the pipe
that took him right on out like a blown lightbulb
way back before kenny anderson was even
a glint in his parents' pick 'n roll eyes

before he skateboarded off the juju fake
picked up his dribble, like magic
than rose up in space like hallelujah 4th of july
glory, before dropping a deuce or a trey quick
as a pickpocket off the slide by
sleight of hand trick, eased on by like mojo with his yoyo
pitter patter, now you see me, now you don't, yo bro
whodunit, poor guy got caught in kenny's school yard
voodoo, jump back in the alley
say what? did you see that motherfucking bad-boy sky?
past where it all started somewhere back before
language followed the north star boogaloo
dancing back when they was hamboning the black
bottom for fun, back then in the language
when homeboys picked cotton
played the dozens; "eye hate to talk about yo mama
she was a good old soul, but she got a two-ton pussy
& an iron ass hole, & yo daddy got a dick
big as a motherfucking toothpick!"

say what chu say, say what chu say? say what?

word, when we knew ourselves through songs
through what we saw alive in homeboys eyes
through love, through what it was we were before
commercials told us how to move & groove, who to love
when we did it all & had fun & knew the heroes
new & old & never confused dope for the bomb
back before we fast forwarded to integration
entered the 60s on a bullshit tip
lost ourselves in the fast forwarding
70s & 80s in the cloning xerox machines
before kenny anderson skateboarded
his prince of a hip hop, roundball game
breakrapping all the way to roundball legend

up north, south of the voodoo connection
north of where we entered from africa

from
AVALANCHE

THE SOUND, BREAKING AWAY

finger touching breeze there gentle in air   almost silent
save voices of birds   winging in midair banking
down & over mountains
                                        when suddenly there is
movement in the craning upwards of necks of animals
startled glances pop fear around & around
suddenly
                        above it all is the beginning of a sound

crip   crip   carip   crip
                                                crip crip carip crip
crip crip carip crip crip carip crack crack carip

crack

the sound in crevices under rock high up in the mountains
the sound now in the air is of a pulling away
a crack in the plate of rock breaking

                    caaa-rack   crack caaa-rack
                        crack   crack   caaa-rack   crack
                                                caaa-rack

the assonance of sound breaking from ground
breaking away from itself & is found in the bounding syllables of snow
moving now   beginning to roar above the cracking
                                                separation
        crack   crack   caaa-racking rocks breaking

away from themselves   a movement   as if raising rock
hands skyward in prayer toward the creator
& is a breaking away of syllables   a breaking & tumbling & shattering

                  language flaking
off verbs shaking off original meaning & swirling in a white storm
            of words that resemble
snowflakes roaring down a mountain
of words mounting other words creating their own wind
storms of flatted fifths & drumrolls snarling down & around & around
& the maelstrom is a piranha of sound eating up ears with verbs
sounds building into a blizzard of metaphors spread round & around
as eyes spread wide in disbelief as words rain down
in hurricane fury   up inside a giant snowball of verbs
rocks & severed arms & tree limbs
pinwheeling & roiling in a boiling white statement of adjectives & nouns

& the verbs   voom   vooming galoom   galoom voodun galoom
galoom voom   vooming galoom   galoom galoom   doom doom

& then it's over suddenly as it began

only clouds of white words swirl around the new eddying
white doves swirling up in cold air
as if they were white lace floating skyward torn off wedding dresses
cold as snow crystals here   the air prickling
the once shattering roar quiet
now above the whispering

wind

& the birds   mute witnesses   gliding in to view
as new life settles   after verbs blew
the color of snow as metaphor through this poem—
the theme of renewal evoked—
as winter becomes spring becomes
summer becomes autumn
becomes ad infinitum
in continuous cycles of seeding

growing & mending
breaking away everywhere

as avalanches of sound
& words create new language

everywhere

I.

WATCH OUT FOR SOUND BITES & SPIN DOCTORS

the silliness of it all rushing like cartoons into black holes drilled
inside our heads & once there became instant throwaway images
wrapped in plastic, like our hunger for fast foods & zippered smiles
glued to faces blow-dried hair politicians wear decked out in shiny
suits everywhere, their hands all wet & clammy with bile
greed & indifference, spinning their sordid messages through sound bites
as they puppet doll-dance through sold air all strung-up flashing snake eyes
pulsating images of bulging gold nuggets watch out as they bore openings
into our heads, pore themselves sporting wire-attached halos
the wind all funky hot around them, as television cameras—hand operated
from shoulders of men scurrying around like roaches apprehended
in broad daylight—glint their bug-like-roving glass eyeballs, shadow stealing
everyone around them on cellulose strips of emulsion, better watch out
when floodlights glance off electric teeth of senators, mayors, or anybody else
wired for sound, in this moment when the cameras spin frenzy around
their shutters opening & closing like mouths of beached fish
gulping for air (so dance, now, you odd figments created by our own
imaginations, dance when the spin doctors of print & celluloid start
    waving their batons,
orchestrating you—& me—like some cold-blooded conductor
director of the slant & angle of this well-rehearsed, scripted & staged photo
opportunity, grin & wave a hand, kiss some motherless child on the cheek,
wear all kinds of silly caps & hats, but always grin & skin some scheme
we all will see and hear later on, & after the rush dies down, you sap
gushing, silly rhetoric, cheap, invented image wrapped in plastic
throwaway grins some spin doctor taught you always to wear)
so we'd better watch out, better learn to click off these fuzzy blinking
blizzard-snow screens blocking out the dreams we will never imagine again
rolling through these moments of sound bites & spin doctors—as we do—
waving batons that control our lives through manipulation
of zippered grins in suits spouting linguistic novocaine that disappears
like thruway images sucked down black holes of fastfood brains

A RESPONSE TO ALL YOU "ANGRY WHITE MALES"

eye mean please, already, give me a break, can we agree to disagree
about who stole all them greenbacks from all them s & l's,
owns all the major corporations in red white & blue america, who
closed all those military bases,
fired all you "angry white males" in the first place, who
was it, some out-of-work black jigaboo, some poor illegal immigrant,
who stole what job from who, or was it your good-old-boy neighbor who
looks just like you that broke your balls—no foolin?—& calls himself buddy

tell me, who runs all the big banks & movie studios in this country, who
owns all the powerful daily newspapers, writes most of the major stories,
shoots us with all this song & dance rapid fire over god's airwaves
who sits on benches in judgment of everybody, who
brings most of the dope that destroys our children
into this country, who planted the hatred in the KKK, the white aryan nation
in the first place, who sent all those jews to ovens back in world war two,
who wins the title hands down for being the champion serial killer
on the planet, who lynched all those black & american indian people
just because they could, who's polluting & destroying the ecology of the planet
just for money & property, who wiped out all those american plains indians,
gave them all those doctored-up blankets laced with disease
who bloomed a mushroom cloud over nagasaki & hiroshima, who
unleased AIDS in central africa & gave us tarzan as king of the jungle,
like elvis got to be "king of rock 'n' roll" after he chained all those black
blues singers to his voice, who complains all the time about this or that
about not getting a fair shake if things don't go their way,
like petulant two-year-olds with their mouths stuck out in a pout,
wearing some cheapo rug toupee on their shiny, bald pates, who do

you do, white boys, that's who, eye mean, is it anybody's fault you can't sky
walk like MJ through space, what do you want, for christ's sake, everything
you done created, all the test-tube heroes as white boys in the first place—
batman, superman, spiderman, john wayne, indiana jones—

inside your media laboratories
eye mean, whose fault is it you don't believe you've got any flesh-
&-blood "real" live heroes anymore—do tell, shut my mouth wide open–
walking on the planet, eye mean, is that my fault, too

what's the problem here, when you can go right out & make a hero up,
invent all the ones you like with a flick of the TV teleprompter, movie camera
switch &, *voilà,*
there you are, all of a sudden you've got a short sylvester
stallone invented bigger to idolize & immortalize forever
as "rocky" through "tricknology"—which elijah muhammad told us once
was your game—who beats up on any man twice his size that comes along,
but especially large black men, when everybody & their mama knows
white men haven't had a real great boxing champion for years,
& you talking about being disadvantaged in everything
because of affirmative action, which you've had all along in the first place,
talking about some myth of a level playing field that's been tilted now
to favor me when everyone & their mama knows
it's been tilted all along to favor you, anyhow,
go tell that simple-simon bullshit to someone else

"eenie meanie miney moe, catch a nigga by his toe, if he hollers let him go,
                                eenie meanie miney mo"

eye mean, please, gimme a break, already
eye can't take too much more of this bullshit

eye mean

who bankrupted orange county, passed proposition thirteen—
now all you guys don't speak at once answering these tough, complicated
questions, please, take your time, get it right—who invented computers
creating all the paper-pushing service empires
that put all you rust-belt blue-collar "angry white male" workers—
& black & brown & yellow & red & female workers too—out of work

in the first place, though "those people" are not entitled to anger
because they don't count in america these days
now let's see, was it "eenie meanie miney moe"
who let the genie out of his bottle so he could grow some more into, say
a jigaboo-niggra-scalawag, who took the whole nine yards & everything else
that wasn't tied down, maybe it was some indian chief, sioux perhaps,
some ghost returned from the grave disguised as sitting bull,
or a ching-chong-slick-charlie-chan chinaman
& his nefarious gang of thieves, maybe a mexican "wetback" perhaps,
or some inscrutable slant-eyed japanese kamikaze businessman
who took away all your sweat, all your life's savings, but it wasn't buddy,
no, it couldn't have been buddy, your next-door neighbor,
who looks just like you, & is you,

                    could it
was it–eye mean, who lied about just about everything imaginable
in this century, & before this century, anyway, back in time to whenever,
christopher columbus lied about discovering america—he didn't
because you can't discover anything that was already here
& accounted for in the first place—so please, get serious
for once, give me a break, will ya, just cool it, lighten up
don't be so uptight, go out & get yourselves a good lay, grow up

the world isn't going to continue to be your own private
oyster bed for only you to feed on anymore, you two-year-old
spoiled brat
get a move on, "straighten up & fly right"
stop all your goddam complaining & whining
just shut the fuck up, will ya

just shut the fuck up

EYE CHANGE DREAMS

for Joe Overstreet, Corrine Jennings & George Lewis

eye change dreams at 42nd street, times square
as swirling people wearing technicolor attitudes speed
through packed days, carrying speech that machine-guns out
in rhythms equaling movement of averted stares
squares even sashay by quick in flip
mimicking motions, as slick street hustlers roll their eyes around
like marbles searching for hits, lick their chops after clicking in onto
some slow-witted hicks dribbling spit down their lips
eating hot dogs paid with fifty-dollar bills
in broad daylight—

                              yeah, tell me about it, trick

escalator sidewalks moving everything along
so swiftly everyone thinks it's their own feet carrying
            their bodies, grooving to a different song
                            than say, in gloster, mississippi,

where time is a turtle moving after a flood has crawled back
into the space it came out of in the first place
hear no beepers here
in gloster, no portable telephones panicking anywhere
only the constant slow humming glide of bloated mosquitos
as they slide through air & bank in for fresh blood-kills
                  wind-tongue guiding them into the target
                        wobbling on their zigzag ride above bearded

irises waving sword shaped leaves in the breeze
as if preparing to do righteous battle with anyone or something
like people living in the big apple (their game faces constantly in place—
& they even wear them into bathrooms, so scared to death they are
of running into some cold-blooded rat there

staking out their own notion of territorial space)

try keeping their fluctuating dreams up to speed
switching up each & every moment, in midtown manhattan
         manic chameleons
everywhere, here, changing faces at high noon, say,
on 42nd street & 8th claustrophobic
heat-drenching crowds packed in, in august, locks in on flesh cold
as a triple life sentences served out at comstock—
people here switching up gears, trying to sidestep panic
                    in the middle of slapstick dreams
                              in the center of it all

a con man who looks like a swifty lazar, the late hollywood agent,
tools around inside a white rolls royce car, peddling gimmicks for
         false tooth legends
who look so bizarre in public, devoid of heavy makeup—
comic, even—outside their dream machines, illusions—
tattered memorabilia the coon man peddles at some tacky bazaar
inside a rundown building in a cobwebbed room where he hawks
         fading photographs of
zsa zsa gabor, back in her prime, before she started breaking down
in front of our eyes, wearing all that weird graphic white
pancake makeup over her ever-changing face-lifts, masking the dreams
we wear ourselves, inside our switching, ballistic imaginations
bewitching us here as we move through times square
popping with the charge of electrical currents

energy eye imagined this poem having when eye first started writing it
then having to deal with how it slowed down midway through
when eye hit that part about gloster, a third of the way down
& tried to avoid all those zigzagging mosquitoes
dive-bombing in for fresh blood-kills—
my direction moving all over the place after that, changing up the focus,
the rhythm, the way my dipstick lines started composing themselves—

at that point in time, they began making it all up
as they went along, as if they were different musicians improvising
this poem—like the swifty lazar look-alike peddling old hollywood
wonders before the fall, before they became toothless legends,
before they became zsa zsa gabor
this sputnik verbal drumstick—a thing to be eaten
after all—promises way more than it could ever deliver
traveling at the speed of complete bullshit, as it were—

a technicolored times-square attitude, without rhyme,
riding in on a broomstick, heartsick & caustic

homesick for that good old big-apple charge

SLIPPIN' & SLIDIN' OVER SYLLABLES FOR FUN

WITH SOME POLITICS THROWN IN ON THE SIDE

slippin' up on syllables, digital flipflops
on the masterblaster waves, ridin' hip hop rays
spacin' through miles's deebop grown up from bebop
underneath echoes of who popped that lyin' brotha
up side his head on a way out trippin' chronic
skyride, movin' against the tide
of soul sista number one—whoever that is
these days, though for me it's always been aretha
by a ton of mouth—so hiphop hooray for days
after scottie pippen sank all them treys
in that 1994 all-star game, frontin' off the media blitz
of shaq o'neal's put-the-funk-on-the-nasty dunk attack
yo, so get back, brotha, with that ton of gold hanging
around yo linebacker's neck, gold rings stranglin' all yo fingers
gold cappin' all the front teeth in your cartoon character's mouth
eye mean, you look like some kind of new age monster grinnin'
bodacious as some of those cold mean doorags useta look
back in them way-gone days before time changed them up
into a zillion handkerchief-head clarence thomases—
or as amiri baraka once said, "tom ass clarence"—radiating
themselves in the microwave oven of the good old conservative
u s of a, grinnin' & skinnin' like old chalk-lip stanley grouch
sweatin' & scratchin' with the heat turned way up under his ass
playing "hanging judge" on black progressives for right-wing zealots
helpin' to blow out the lights in a lot of young brothas' brains—
whose murders, too, are as fractricidal as crack in pipes—
while blow-dried hair clones reading running teleprompters—
copy for network commercials—crack down
hard over TV air waves on misogynistic gangsta rap,
which is OK, if they'd just do the same thing to good old corny arnie
schwartzenegger, bruce willis or sylvester stallone—all wrapped up

in the flag as they tell us they are—
& don't even mention steven segal for uzi-ing all them white policemen—
for real deep-sixed up there on them big silver screens & rakin' in tons
of fresh lettuce greenbacks to stash away in numbered swiss bank accounts—
so, say, yo, what've all you boot-lickin' house knee-grows gotta show
for all that ass-scratchin' liver-lipped talk you shamin' on everyone—
your gas-swollen bellies hanging down over your hangman belts
like blown-up balloons—you torpedo-mouth brigades—
neo-negro conservative correct nests—you are, at best
panting jack-in-the-box pop ups, clowns appearing in murder
mouthing black pathology talk-show soap operas—
so crank it up high as a crack attack on a coon coppin' a plea
bustin' a nut plea on TV, cut it loose, juice, & pump up for new word
neologists of death mac attacks, new-jack hip slidin' from the mouths
of homeboys sportin' short nappy dreads, cropped on top & shaved around
edges—a lone pigtail drooping down backs—& they look like drooping snakes
atop side-trimmed california Mexican fan palm trees & bounce up like giggles
when they walk, like mac daddies scammin' on fly hoochies
clockin' dead presidents, while some were laid back, kickin' it up
gaffled by a one-time okie, from knee-jerk muskogee—
"cut me loose," someone screams—a blue-suited badge
messin' with the low-ridin' jean-wearin' cross-cultural homey
with his quack-quack cap turned backward, unlaced
black nike, reebok, hightops, shufflin as they dipped & jiggled def
chillin, some lean, gliding moonwalk, clean for the shake down
walkin tough with their syndicates while the five-o's cruise by
in the hood, slamdunkin high fivin jack, mind fuckin the words
is what their macks are all about jimmying the groves of cadences
is what this poem is all about, slippin & slidin over syllables
for fun, break dancin with verbs & nouns this poem's on the run
from juba to mozart, from beebop to hiphop, this poem's
on the run, slippin & slidin on syllables & digital flipflops
this poem's on the run, on the run, on the run, these words
slippin' & slidin', runnin' off new jack, from the mouth

A POEM FOR "MAGIC"

for Earvin "Magic" Johnson, Donnell Reid
and Richard Franklin

take it to the hoop, "magic" Johnson,
take the ball dazzling down the open lane
herk & jerk & raise your six feet nine inch
frame into air sweating screams of your neon name
"magic" johnson, nicknamed "windex" way back in high school
'cause you wiped glass backboards so clean
where you first juked & shook
wiled your way to glory
a new style fusion of shake & bake energy
using everything possible you created your own space
to fly through—any moment now, we expect your wings
to spread feathers for that spooky take-off of yours
then shake & glide till you hammer home
a clotheslining deuce off glass
now, come back down with a reverse hoodoo gem
off the spin & stick it in sweet, popping nets
clean from twenty feet right-side

put the ball on the floor, "magic"
slide the dribble behind your back, ease it deftly
between your bony stork legs, head bobbing everwhichaway
up & down, you see everything on the court off the high
yo-yo patter, stop & go dribble, you shoot
a threading needle rope pass sweet home to kareem
cutting through the lane, his skyhook pops cords
now lead the fast-break, hit jamaal on the fly
now blindside a behind the back pinpointpass for two more
off the fake, looking the other way
you raise off balance into tense space
sweating chants of your name, turn, 360 degrees
on the move your legs scissoring space like a swimmer's
yo-yoing motion in deep water, stretching out now
toward free flight, you double pump through human trees
hang in place, slip the ball into your left hand
then deal it like a las vegas card dealer off squared glass
into nets living up to your singular nickname, so "bad"
you cartwheel the crowd towards frenzy
wearing now your electric smile, neon as your name

in victory we suddenly sense your glorious uplift
your urgent need to be champion
& so we cheer, rejoicing with you for this quicksilver, quicksilver, quicksilver
moment of fame, so put the ball on the floor again, "magic"
juke & dazzle, shaking & baking down the lane
take the sucker to the hoop, "magic" Johnson
recreate reverse hoodoo gems off the spin
deal alley-oop-dunk-a-thon-magician passes, now
double-pump, scissor, vamp through space, hang in place
& put it all up in the sucker's face, "magic" johnson
& deal the roundball, like the juju man that you am
like the sho-nuff shaman man that you am
"magic', like the sho-nuff spaceman you am

& SYLLABLES GROW WINGS THERE

a blackboard in my mind holds words eye dream—
& blessed are the words that fly like birds into poetry—
& syllables attach wings to breath & fly away there
through music, my language springing round from where
a bright polished sound, burnished as a new copper penny
shines in the air like the quick, jabbing glint of a trumpet
lick flicking images through voices there pulsating like strobe lights
the partying dark understands, as heartbeats pumping rhythms hip-
hopping through footsteps, tick-tocking like clocks with stop-gap
measures of caesuras breaking breath, like california earth
quakes trying to shake enjambed fault lines of mini-malls
freeways & houses off their backs, rocks being pushed up there
by edges of colliding plates, rivers sliding down through yawning
cracks, pool underneath speech, where worlds collide & sound cuts
deep fissures into language, underneath earth the mystery of it all,
seeded within the voodoo magic of that secret place, at the center
of boiling sound & is where poetry springs from now
with its heat of eruption, carrying volcanic lava flows of word
sound cadences, a sluiced up voice flowing into the poem's
mysterious tongue, like magic, or fingers of fire dancing
gaseous stick figures curling off the sun's back
& is where sweet music comes from, too, to improvise
like choirs of birds in springtime, when the wind's breath
turns warm & their voices riff off songs, a capella

ONE FOR CHARLIE MINGUS

into space time walks bass strings of charlie mingus
jambalaya rhythms deepening our ears, hear
voices springing from tongues of mingus riding sweet bass strings
deep stepping through sound, through light & shadows of blood
cut out into the leaping night walking music swings the wind
as tongues of evening caress the flying darkness, there
inside rhythms, tight embraces of sound-thump bass grooves
lengthening the graceful flights of cadences shading chords of voodoo
who doing who there, juicing mean watts boys sluicing, shimmy down
mean streets of the city of angels, when mingus played a strange, disquieting
beauty, turned it on, believed in whatever he thought he was back then
played it all the way here, where eye am dreaming now, listening
within this moment of musical amazement, walking in
his voice riding in through vibrating strings thumping & humping
like naked lovers inside musky hot steaming rumpled backwater bedrooms
in the afterglow of undercover of damplight, in the nighttime of their dreams
mingus skybreaking his bass through steep blue
lifetimes of urban screams, who doing what to who here
inside the city of lights, raining tears, raining blood & blue showers
electrifying nights where mingus walked music through voodoo
flying all the way home, thumping the rhythms, mingus stalks
the music tone after magical tone, walks the mysterious
music all the way home, tone after magisterial tone

AVALANCHE

for K. Curtis Lyle & the memory of Richard Wright

within an avalanche of glory hallelujah skybreaks
spraying syllables on the run, spreading
sheets, waving holy sounds, solos sluicing african bound
transformed here in america from voodoo into hoodoo
inside tonguing blues, snaking horns, where juju grounds down sacred
up in chords, up in the gritty foofoo
magical, where fleet rounds of cadences whirlpool
as in rivers, where memory spins down foaming into dances
like storms swallowed here in a burst of suns
up in the yeasting blue voodoo, holding
the secret clues mum, inside the mystery, unfolding
up in the caking dishrag of daybreak, miracles
shaking out earthquakes of light
like mojo hands luminous with spangling
& are the vamping blood songs of call & response
are the vamping blood songs of call & response

as in the pulpit, when a preacher becomes his words
his rhythms those of a sacred bluesman, dead outside his door
his gospel intersecting with antiphonal guitars, a congregation of amens
as in the slurred riffs blues strings run back echoing themselves
answering the call, the voice cracked open like an egg, the yoke running out
the lungs imitating collapsed drums & he
is the rainbowing confluence of sacred tongues, the griot
the devotion of rivers all up in his hands, all up in his fingers
his call both invocation & quaking sermon
running true & holy as drumming cadences
brewed in black church choirs, glory hallelujah vowels
spreading from their mouths like wolfman's mojo
all up in mahalia jackson's lungs
howling vowels rolled off hoodoo consonants, brewing
magic all up in the preacher's run, of muddy water

strung all up in the form drenched with coltrane
riffin' all up in miles of lightning hopkins mojo songs
blues yeasting lungs of bird
when music is raised up as prayer & lives
healing as june's sun quilted into black babies
tongues, sewn deep in their lungs as power
& blueprinted here in breath of rappers

& this is a poem in praise of continuity
is a poem about blood coursing through tongues
is a praise song for drowned voices lost in middle passage
is a praise song for the slashed drums of obatala
is a construct of orikis linking antiphonal bridges
is a praise song tonguing deep in the mojo secrets of damballah
in praise of the great god's blessings of oshun
in praise of healing songs sewn into tongues
inflating sweet lungs into a cacaphony of singing
praise songs tonguing deep mojo secrets

& this poem is about music, when music is what it believes
it is, holy, when voices harmonize, somersaulting colors
in flight, & glory is the miracle poetry sings to in that great getting-up
morning, within the vortex of wonder, confluencing rivers, light
glory in the rainbows arching like eyebrows across suns
glory in the moonlight staring from a one-eyed cat's head
& eye want to be glory & flow in that light
want to be coltrane's solos living in me
want to become wonder of birds in flight of my lines
want the glory of song healing in me as sunlight
want it tongued through leaves
metaphoring trees, transformed where they seed & stand up here
as people, in this soil, everything rooted here in blood of mother's flesh
& is the poetry of god in deep forest time, singing & listening
& the music there is green, as it also is purple
as it also is orange brown & mind-blowing electric banana

as it is red cinnamon & also again, green
sound ground up against lavender
beneath sunsets fusing crisp blue light
& night here stitched with fireflies flicking
gold up against bold midnight & once again, yes
green, as shimmering caribbean palm fronds
are green in the center of apocalyptic chaos

& my poem here is reaching for that greeness
is reaching for holy luminosity shimmering in gold-
flecked light, where the mojo hand is seaming through
high blue mornings, waving like a sequined glove up in the glory
of hallelujahs, calling through the inner tube lips of the great god
singing, up in the blues root doctors, jacklegging sermons
up in the condolences mourning death
up in the sunburst of god's glory
& eye want this poem to kneel down itself before healing
want it to be magic there beneath the crucifixion of light
want it to be praise song, juju rooted
want it to be mojo hand raised up to powers of flight
want it to be tongue of gritty foofoo, feeding
want it to be a congregation slurring amen riffs
running back through me to you
the voice raised up here, guitar blues licks, holy
want it to be glory hallelujah, call & response, glory
want it to be yam song rooted in the bloody river, holy
want it to be ground earth of resurrection, in you, in me
the bridge tongue of healing is the drum of this song
& it is reaching out to you to cross over
to the sun, is reaching out to touch your heartbeat
there, to become one in the glory
to feel the healing touch
to become one with the glory
this poem waits for you to cross over
to cross over the heartbeat touch of your healing

hands, touching hands, touching hearts
this poem waits for you to cross over
to cross over love, this poem waits for you
to cross over, to cross over love
this poem waits for you to crossover
too crossover, too, love

II.

POEM FOR FRIENDS

for Calvin Hernton

I.
the earth is a wonderful
yet morbid place
crisscrossing reaping complexities
of living

                    seeking death

we go
with foot/steps
that are either heavy or light
(depending upon your weight

your substance)

go into light, or darkness
(depending upon the perception
of your vision)

we flounder, we climb
we trip

                    we fall
                        we call upon dead prophets
to help us

                        yet
they do not answer

(we hear instead the singing in the leaves
the waves of oceans, pounding)

we see sheer cliffs
of mountains polished by storms
sculptured to god's perfection

we see the advancing age of technology
see soulless monsters

eating up nature's perfections

hear wails & screams

& sirens howling

but hear no human voices calling

we sit at the brink of chaos laughing
we idle away time
when there is no time
left us

we jump out of air/planes with no parachutes
we praise the foul mad/men of war
we are pygmalions

in love with cold, bleak stones

& aphrodite is not here

to save us

seeking death

we come to origins
forks in the road of indecision
shaped like wishbones
& we go down unknown roads
seeking light in an ocean
of pure darkness

2.

journey if you can
to the far poles of the world
there you will find flocks
of sick birds
dying in the blue sea that is sky
you will find herds of animals
huddled together in the snow
against the cold
with no feeling or touch
of each other, no knowledge
no love, dying in the fierce
blowtorching cold
yet they graze eagerly
into seas of light
meeting darkness

3.

& the mind is so wide
& wide again
   so broad and deep
& deep again
   far down we go so slow
to find knowledge
sad songs of who we are
but go slow from here
from everywhere, effendi
go slow into sadness
     of who we are
     where we are
go slow into slow dance of what
you are
   go slow into beauty
of space & time & distance
measure

every breath that you breathe
for it is precious
                    holy
                              go free into sun/lit days
fly free like old african ibises
confronting the wind
swim long in the currents of these times
like the dolphin
                    plunging through blue waves
for time is holy

& the faces that we see
upon the curl of the foam
                    of the fingered blue waters
are the faces of the world, sandstones
falling through hourglasses
& deposited upon these shores
& they are seeds
in need of nourishment
in need of beauty, requesting wisdom
are children of the universe, glissando falling
upon these death-littered shores
that are reefs breaking rabid waves
seaweeds that remind of varicose veins
peeping up through the skin of these transparent
shallows—churning red waters beating up against
savage rocks, spiked with bones—
surrounding these islands
where all life buries itself
under rocks & sand

4.
we must investigate our bodies
we must investigate our sources of beauty
we must investigate our exalted images

the parade of decayed heroes that we cheer
that we help invent
we must probe & descend into life/styles
like surgeons seeking cancer
we must cut away with truth's scalpel
all verbose flesh, all diseased portions
we must fly free & weightless
as a summer breeze
to nests in truth's sanctuary

5.
& the shell is bursting
from within
from without

& in order to go out
we must come in, again
so come in, come in, again
go out, go out, again
go out there now, effendi
          to the sweet places

where the good folks gather
                talk to everyone
for everyone is someone whose life is important to someone
to everyone
                whose flesh is a/part of your own

universe

so come in, come in, again
go out, go out, again

be beautiful for all people of the world

walk back into streets that are ours, effendi
walk back into hours & years carrying joy

go now, go now, go now
                              effendi
do your thang
do the righteous thang
for the world
for the world
to save the world
to save our children

to save yourself.

"MINNESOTA NICE"

for Dawn Renee Jones, who taught it to me by her actions

the sky here deep with questions of heat in summer–no matter
ice-cold blue freeze can pounce at any second–the eyes hold
within themselves dead of winter in an instant–only softer here
when the air hums clues of mosquitoes hovering in their search for blood
after humidity wraps itself around our every movement in august–
each moment draining sweat that pools around a tradition of politeness–
disturbed here now by swarms of gnats–some natives call "minnesota nice"
in Minneapolis/St. Paul peoples' dispositions seems almost sweet
though they can change as fast as weather switches up here–
as the quick green breath of summer ablaze with rainbowing light swims
the long river wail of saxophone solos, running the length of mississippi
river, ending up here, close by, closing out its song into the stillness of a lake
after climbing & and winding up from the gulf of mexico–
the sky up here always changing its clothes
reflecting off the mirrored back of the big river
reminding us of the skin on the back of a rattlesnake–
after running between the twin cities, the nordic blood flow mixing
whatever is real there & out in front–whenever the love jones comes down
hard, integrating mulatto sweat of white & black lovers
here where the test of understanding is always duplicitous,
at best, in the knowing that what you see & hear–to you–is as confusing
as it also is to natives–the sky here cobalt blue now as the feelings
in one lady day's songs–mixed with perplexing questions of heat
& cold–attitudes, as they are, will in a blinking switch become subzero
weather, chilling the surface of whatever passes before us, summers
passing seamlessly into winter, what's called here "minnesota nice"

LET'S SAY YOU ARE WHO YOU BELIEVE YOU ARE

let's say you are who you believe you are—yellow light
burning delirium in your cat quick eyes—
& you have imagined yourself more than one time
spreadeagled across the rifle sight of a man's
crosshairs, in the line of fire
so to speak
& that man is aiming
    to erase the blackboard
        of your memory with one true shot
            right between the eyes

& let's say, on the other hand, you're some sad sack dancing
ghost blabberthoning around some bleached old language
filled with creepy metaphors of werewolves
you sing starring in some opera
& where you see & recognize your true self for the first time in the stunned
faces gathered at the opening night's party
after you skunked up the air
with the blooming storm-clouds of poots
            you oozed & leaked out of your fat

derriere, boxcar, you know
what some might call your caboose

        anyway

& let's say you are some fly homeboy who likes to count
dead presidents, stacked up high on some cocaine dusted table
while all around you sound tracks pulsate
to the time of dancing bones anchored to puppeteer's strings you pull
& the overriding melodies stitching through the music is one of cracking
gunfire, spitting bullets that reminds you of the pungent, full smell
of gladiolas & carnations blooming in the air you inhaled

just last week, at another funeral—how many this year, homey?—
the face there cushioned in a bed of white satin
looks waxed & unreal, the life-force gone somewhere
you won't know about until you get there

& let's say perhaps you are someone else who is always lifting up
fluted champagne glasses—full & bubbly—to the memory of himself
standing in the middle of a sentence of history
let's say perhaps it is a saga of the bloody march of cherokees
that one of your ancestor's penned, back when those syllables were strange
sounding—when heard by our ears now full of british accents as they were
back then—& desperate to please as say those feathers
swirling around that beautiful round ass of josephine baker's were back then
in the closer to now nineteen-twenties, over in paris—
(& she couldn't do what she did over there over here
because of some god forsaken reasons of some two-faced religious zealots
pushing christian words around while killing & fucking over everyone else
on the planet who didn't look like them—& even some of those who did look like
them—god, some people are so pious & sanctimonious—
& they seem more so today than they were back then—
well, as they say, "some things never seem to change")
what do the words mean you salute yourself with, lifting that glass
so high up into that poisoned air, what does the gesture mean, my friend
after mushroom clouds have evaporated—like the words your ancestor
pinned on the cherokee nation—remind me of those yellow badges
nazi germany pinned on jews on their way to auschwitz—
what does it all mean when the light is fading fast from that place
where you stand alone—despite all those grinning fools genuflecting
around you—saluting yourself behind glass topped walls
a sumptuously set table heaped with food—piled high as stacks
of that homeboy's money on that cocaine dusted table—
laid out next to where you stand in the wet, poisoned air
as the sad sack opera star with werewolf metaphors in his voice
spreads around his oozing farts thick as marmalade—
stuffing himself like the pig that he is as he goes—

a sniper spread-eagles your head across his crosshairs
for no reason at all except his random anger

& in the silence of the moment, just before the explosion
let's say you are who you believe you are—yellow
light burning delirium in your cat quick eyes—
& let's say that—for all intents & purposes
    & for the sake of argument—
        we're all in this thing here together—
            watching each other swarming around
                swerving & colliding like bats in a cave—

can we stop that assassin's bullet aimed at your head
my friend, the sniper crouched high up in a tree somewhere
in sarejevo, the red pouting lipped
woman poured like a perfect ten into her tight new jeans styled by
gucci, can we stop her from strutting her sweet rolling doobop switching
slick fucking inner city hip hop quick with her snapping pussy licking clean
some quivering dick, can we stop her from passing that deep seduction on
for a little taste of money
        my friend
homeboys stacking paper on their tables
everywhere, people dreaming as they fall screaming
through the burning holes bored into their imaginations
by some random bullet, like the one that is just
about to greet you, my friend

like the one just about to greet you

THE OLD PEOPLE SPEAK OF DEATH

for Grandmother Leona Smith

the old people speak of death
frequently now
my grandmother speaks of those now
gone to spirit
now less than bone

they speak of shadows
that graced their days made lovelier
by their wings of light speak of years
& of corpses of years of darkness
& of relationships buried
deeper even than residue of bone
gone now beyond hardness
gone now beyond form

they smile now from ingrown roots
of beginnings, those who have left us
& climbed back through holes the old folks left
inside their turnstile eyes
for them to pass through

eye walk back now with this poem
through holes the old folks left in their eyes
eye see them there
the ones who have gone beyond hardness
the ones who have gone beyond form
see them there
darker than where roots began
& lighter than where they go
with their spirits
heavier than stone their memories
sometimes brighter than the flash
of sudden lightning
but the green branches will grow
from these roots darker than time
& blacker than even the ashes of nations
sweet flowers will sprout
& wave petals their love-stroked language
in sun-tongued morning's shadow
the spirit in all our eyes

they have gone now back
to shadow as eye climb back out
from the holes of these old folks' eyes
those spirits who sing through this poem
gone now back with their spirits
to fuse with greenness
enter stones & glue their invisible
faces upon the transmigration of earth
nailing winds singing guitar blues
voices through ribcages
of these days
gone now to where the years run
darker than where roots begin
greener than what they bring

the old people speak of death
frequently now
my grandmother speaks of those now
gone to spirit
now less than bone

CONJURING AGAINST ALIEN SPIRITS

for Ishmael Reed

if there is something that takes you
to the brink of terror
turn your pockets inside out, like a lolling dog's
tongue, salivating, in heat, make a screech-
owl's death cry go away, go away
make a screech-owl's death
cry go away, go away

turn shoes upside down at your own
front door, tie a knot in your apron string, mama
sister, throw fire on salt
talk to raw head & bloody bones
make a hoot owl screaming death
go home, take it away
make a hoot owl take it away on home

turn your pillowcase inside out
see a cross-eyed devilish fool, cross

your fingers—drop goobadust in your mind medicine
eat a root doctor's magic root—spit on them
make a cross in the road
where you met yourself going
& coming, spit on it

that same spot where you passed over
in the road, spit on it, to soften up enemies
walk backwards along any road you have passed over
before, a red moon, like a one-eyed
wino's stare,stuck in bone
shadowed trees, throw dirt over
your left shoulder, spit down on it
in the road, on that same spot where your terror
locked itself into another enigma

where someone's footprints leave their signatures
of weight, define shapes of worn soles
speak to raw head & bloody bones
great-great-great grandmama
make a hoot owl screaming death

take his case all the way home
screaming, all the way home
make a hoot owl screaming death

take your death slip all the way home

THE ABSOLUTENESS OF SECONDS

there is time still to consider the absoluteness of seconds
time still even to hear time bombs ticking within words
the metaphors of power swollen
fat behind chewed-up ends of smoldering cigars
the bogus ten of surgically repaired apple-pie white women playing
jane in ever more stupid tarzan movies, red omens circling overhead
like bloodshot moons cocked behind scopes of rifles
zeroing in on stars & bright eyes of babies
time still to recognize those who swear their computerized egos dance
for art instead of money & who sing of cloning as a sacred religion
in place of passion in the wet, sucking bloom
& whose art springs from legacies of crosses & ashes
& whose prophecies produce wars & chains & even more bullets

time, still, even to reconsider the trip upriver
from new orleans to st. paul, Mississippi-ing the lynched history
passing natchez, st. louis to lacrosse, rolling vowels sewn deep
within voices, invisible ghosts whispering along bottoms of the big muddy
the sky above full of blue rhythms & catfish hanging from hooks
barracudas sleeking through the slippery wash underneath the river
time still to listen to those africans
who came here singing
learned here to gut-bucket, fuse bloody syllables into mysterious
hambones, learned here to shape a sho-nuff american blues
into a song full of genius, into a song that embraces love

FOR MALCOLM, WHO WALKS IN THE EYES
OF OUR CHILDREN

for Porter, Solomon, Neruda & Assiatou

he had been coming a very long time
had been here many times before
malcolm, in the flesh of other persons, malcolm
in the flesh of flying gods

his eyes had seen the flesh turned to stone
had seen stone turned to flesh
had swam within the minds of a billion great heroes
had walked amongst builders of nations
of the sphinx, had built with his own hands

those nations, had come flying across time
a cosmic spirit, a notion, an idea
a thought wave transcending flesh fusion of all
centuries, had come soaring like a sky break

above ominous clouds of sulfur, wearing
a wingspan so enormous it spanned the breath
of a people's bloodshed, had come singing

like coltrane, breathing life into miles
into stone-cold statues formed from earthworms & lies

malcolm, cosmic spirit who still walks back-straight
tall among us, here, in the words of nelson mandela
in the rap of public enemy number one, ourselves
deep down, we hear your lancing voice splitting wide open still
the pus-filled sores of self-hatred covering our bodies here
like scabs infested with AIDS—the poisoned
blood running out of us still stains the ground here, malcolm

creates bright red flowers of art everywhere—we stand up
our love for you & are counted in the in open air—

hear your trumpet voice breaking here, like miles
zigzagging through the open prairie of our minds
in the form of a thunderbolt splitting the sky—& just before
your tornado words dip down inside an elephant trunk
conveying winds carrying the meaning of your words
shattering all notions of bullshit here—

we see your vision still in the life force of men & women
see you now in the high-flying confidence of our children, malcolm
who spread their enormous wingspans & fly through their minds
with confidence, mirroring the beauty you stood for, brother—

your spirit, malcolm, burning in the suns of their eyes

POEM FOR MY FATHER

for Quincy T. Trouppe, Sr.

father, it was an honor to be there in the dugout with you
the glory of great black men swinging their lives as bats
at tiny white balls burning in at unbelievable speeds
riding up & in & out
a curve breaking down wicked like a ball falling off a high table
moving away snaking down screwing its stitched magic
into chitling circuit air, its comma seams spinning
towards breakdown, dipping like a hipster
bebopping a knee-dip stride in the charlie parker forties
wrist curling like a swan's neck
behind a slick black back
cupping an invisible ball of dreams

& you there, father, regal as an african obeah man
sculpted out of wood from a sacred tree of no name no place origin
thick roots branching down into cherokee & some place else lost
way back in africa, the sap running dry crossing
from north carolina into georgia inside grandmother mary's womb
who was your mother & had you there in the violence of that red soil
ink blotter news gone now into blood & bone graves
of american blues sponging rococo
truth long gone as dinosaurs
the agent-orange landscape of former names
absent of african polysyllables dry husk consonants there now
in their place, names flat as polluted rivers
& that guitar string smile always snaking across
some virulent american redneck's face
scorching like atomic heat mushrooming over nagasaki
& hiroshima, the fever blistered shadows of it all
inked as body etchings into sizzled concrete

but you there, father, through it all a yardbird solo

riffing on bat & ball glory breaking down all fabricated myths
of white major league legends of who was better than who
beating them at their own crap game with killer bats
as bud powell swung his silence into beauty

of a josh gibson home-run skittering across piano keys of bleachers
shattering all manufactured legends up there in lights struck out
white knights on the risky edge of amazement
the miraculous truth slipping through
steeped & disguised in the blues confluencing
like the point at the cross
when a fastball hides itself up in a shimmying slider
curve breaking down & away in a wicked sly grin
curved & broke-down like the back of an ass-scratching uncle tom
who like old satchel paige delivering his famed hesitation pitch,
before coming back with a hard high fast one rising
is sometimes slicker, slipping & sliding,
& quicker than a professional hitman—
the deadliness of it all, the sudden strike
like that of the "brown bomber's" short crossing right
or the hook of sugar ray robinson's lightning cobra bite

& you there, father, through it all catching rhythms of chono
pozo balls drumming like cuban conga beats into your catcher's mitt
hard & fast as "cool papa" bell jumping into bed
before the lights went out

of the old negro baseball league, a promise you were,
father, a harbinger of shock waves soon come

MALE SPRINGTIME RITUAL

for Hugh Masekela

it's hard on male eyeballs walking new york streets
in springtime, all the fine, flamingo ladies
peeling off everything the cold winter forced them to
put on, now breasts shook loose from strait-jacketed overcoats
tease invitations of nipples
peek-a-boo through see through clinging blouses
reveal most things imagination needs to know about
mystery; they jelly-roll, seduce through silk
short-circuit connections of dirty old men
mind in their you-know-what
young men too, fog up eye glasses, contact lens, shades—
& most of these sho-nuff hope to die lovers
always get caught without
their portable windex cleaner bottles
& so have to go blind throughout the rest of the day
contemplating what they thought they saw

eye mean, it can drive you crazy walking behind one of those
sweet memorable asses, in springtime, when the wind gets cocky
& licks up one of those breeze-blown slit wraparounds revealing

that grade A sweet rump of flesh moving like those old black
african ladies taught it to do & do
eye mean, it's maybe too much
for a good old boy, staid Episcopalian, christian chauvinist
with a bad heart & a pacer
eye mean, what can you expect him to do—
carrying that kind of heavy baggage around—
but vote for bras to be worn everyday
& to abolish any cocky wind whose tongue gets completely out
of hand, lifting up skirts of fine, young, sweet thangs
eye mean, there ought to be a law against some things
eye'm sure he would say, "reckless eyeballin,"
eye'm sure he would say

anyway, it's hard on menfolk streetwalkers in springtime
liable to find your eyeballs roaming around dazed
in some filthy new york city gutter
knocked there by some dazzling sweet beauty who happened along
your field of vision—who knows, next thing you know
they'll be making pacers for eyeballs—
who cares if you go down for the whole ten count
& never pull your act back together again, & so become
a bowery street, babbling idiot, going on & on
about some fine, flamingo lady you thought
you saw, an invitation, perhaps
who cares if her teasing breasts shook you
everwhichaway but loose

it's springtime in the old big apple
& all the fine flamingo ladies are peeling off
    everything the cold forced them to put on
their breasts shake loose from overcoats
tease invitations of nipples
it's all a part of the springtime ritual

& only the strongest eyeballs, survive

III.

UNTITLED

speed is time clocking itself
birth to death
      seconds beating quick
as heartbeats thumping

drums in cadences
imitating breath

SAN JUAN ISLAND IMAGE

ride chuckanut drive
through mist rolling off Puget
sound, san juan islands
pushng through fog, humpback whales
rocks sat down on a mirror

LA JOLLA

living out here, calm, on the edge of the streaking western whirl
where most sunsets leave vivid stains on the thin black line
separating the pacific from the plunging ocean of flight

above it, time stretching as a peacock's tail feather
through a landscape crisscrossed with colors of bright rainbows
stitched & weaved through green light luminous with complexions

where kite strings split in half a swallowing blue sky leaping
as blue music heard anywhere, voices buried deep in hushed distances
beneath windswept pines whose leaves serenade throughout valleys

& dipping hillsides, as overhead hot air balloons cruise
like great bowhead whales swimming underneath serrated edges
of bouffant gray-white clouds that look like huge battleships

& where the eye locates on the brow of some precipice a glass
house, that is an atrium—& wondrous beyond all comprehension—
where the sky is a roof, the pacific a glittering blue veranda

swelled with surfers & salt waves terracing in one foaming wave
after another, swimmers bobbing up there like red apples in a tub
at a halloween party, just offshore, while up verdant hills

golden with light, runners jog up & down streets as nervous people
behind walls & signs reading "armed response," sit fingering triggers
of shotguns, their eyes boring in tight as two just-fired bullets

THE FLIP SIDE OF TIME

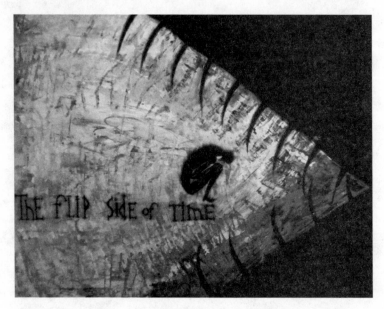

there is nothing on the flip side of time but more time
yawning, like a cat's wide open mouth of space
above us, around us, dilating like our mother's womb

just before we came out screaming catching our breath
& found ourselves breathless, bent out of shape with rage
after being cooped up asleep for so long & now all this light

searing here where before all was darkness & now this slap
that wakes us up with such a start, as if it were necessary
since most of us sleepwalk all our lives until death

anyway & sometimes we find ourselves somewhere
hanging from the spur of the moment, barely awake, caught
between twilight & pitch black, perhaps hanging there

from the spur of some island somewhere off the cowboy boot
of italy, looking at a full moon submerged beneath crystal blue
green waters of the mediterranean, ionian seas & the moon

laughing there, like an alka-seltzer tablet winkling at the bottom
of a clear glass of water, our eyes telescoping from above
trying to decipher the mystery smiling from that magical face

but mystery & magic is what pulls our lives towards meaning—
beauty & wisdom discovered inside all heartfelt joy
what journeys reveal, poetry there inside every moment

BIRTH FORM: TERCETINA

underneath a still life snapshot of grass & rocks, probing light
reveals layer after layer of buried history, there, under beds
of earth's terraced graves, skulls & bones out of sight

in darkness, where a symphony of silence echoes the dead
after sonorous beauty of their voices took flight
after the DNA of their flesh melted away, after all speech was said

& done, the drumscript light fingers played on skinheads pulled tight—
as music improvised anywhere—faded away old rhythms inside our heads
as drums insinuated on the other side of this circular moment, right

here, underneath this place, where a choir of trees stand now & lead
is a soft vein of gray & blue beneath & inside the earth's hot night
where history can be an echo of itself after fleeing time bled

throughout the concave dome breath lost to the great sheer height
of night, where now a new form is being born, this tercetina that sheds
light & birthskin in the process of being torn from this slight

moment time gives us, the uncertainty of creation here, form wedded
inside the blood of ancestral language, this terror of shape, this fight
to keep alive a memory, before sweet tenderness bled

itself to death, staining this concrete modern place of blight
& ice, here where music filling skies is thunder & gunshots played
all around our children, their eyes wide open in fear, but bright

THE VIEW FROM SKATES IN BERKELEY

for Oliver Jackson, homeboy & painter

the clouds were mountains that day, behind the real mountains,
sideways, from san francisco, across the tossed bay, the beauty we saw
from skates, in berkeley, was real there, stretched out, behind sailboats
the wind-driven waves buckling, like rodeo horses carrying cowboys
breaking across the frothing, gray water, like sand dunes

rippling across an empty expanse of desert, mirrored & beautiful
here, near sunset, we looked out through the wide, open windows & took in
the view, unbroken from here, under sinking sunlight, the hills breasts,
the gulls resembling small planes, banked over the waves, searching for fish
they snapped up in their beaks, under fleecing clouds

streaming up high, crossing the jet stream, the pricking mist hung low
over angel island, like the day after too many drinks fogged up your head
in an afternoon sunlight, on a day far back in cobwebs than you care
to remember, but there anyway, as a still life you clung to once
deep in a long-gone memory, the skyline changing now

behind the tumbling clouds, the architecture trembling through the mist
of the "shining pearl by the bay," grown up from split-open gums of the land
like chipped shark teeth, or tombstones leaning white & bright
into the light, shimmering, like the friendship of this meeting is shimmering
here, because we knew we were what we always thought we were

homeboys on top of our games laughing like joyous paint in sprayed mist
the fog overhead hung low, over oakland, thick as a mattress
where you laid down your head full of dreams & painted images in full view
of the bay bridge, stretching, like one of your elegant lines through our view
here, outside skates window, the sun plunging like one of your painted

faces into the rabid wash of gray waves, the wind slapping salt tears across
our faces, creased, as the american flag is streaked with a rainbow of colors

here, where we were what we always thought we were, on this day
when the moment heaved up the water surging, like our dreams
& we were riding these bucking horse waves breaking across

the duned, kicking waters, mirrored & beautiful, we were strong
as we always knew we would be, our view unbroken from here, in skates
under the dazzling sunlight of our dreams, streaming across the jet stream
high up in the turbulent afternoon of our heads, light & luminous
we were homeboys, oliver, on this rare shimmering day filled with flight

homeboys, oliver, on this rare shimmering day filled with light

from
CHORUSES

I.

SONG

words & sounds that build bridges toward a new tongue
within the vortex of cadences, magic weaves there
a mystery, syncopating music rising from breath of the young

the syllables spraying forward like some cloud or mist hung
around the day, evening, under street lamps, yeasting air, where
words & sounds that build bridges toward a new tongue

gather, lace the language like fireflies stitching the night's lungs,
the rhythms of new speech reinventing themselves with a flair
a mystery, syncopating music, rising from breath of the young,

where the need for invention at the tongue's edge, high-strung,
at the edge of the cliff, becomes a risk-taking poet who shares
words & sounds that build bridges toward a new tongue,

full of wind & sun, sweet breath feeds poetry as from art's aqualungs
under the blue sea that is sky, language threads itself through air,
a mystery, syncopating music, rising from breath of the young,

is a solo snatched from the throat of pure utterance, sung,
are wordsmiths blues-ing cadences, weaving lines into prayers,
words & sounds that build bridges toward a new tongue—
a mystery, syncopating music, rising from breath of the young

SESTINA FOR 39 SILENT ANGELS

there was no screaming to announce hale-bopp's comet's second tail
no screaming when those 39 people left their bodies—
their containers—behind, covered their faces with purple
silk shrouds, folded triangles, lay down smiling & fell into the steep sleep
marshall applewhite had prescribed for them, deep inside that death
mansion in rancho santa fe, they knew themselves as angels,

sleuths at creating web sites, cruising internet, space angels
flying on wings of ancient dreams upward to hale-bopp's comet tail,
(& the only way to get there through the invisible doorway of death)
launched through skies of their minds, they willed their bodies
on earth, as people of jonestown did, to be recycled through sleep
bodies board-stiff & bloated, looking for peace, skin purple

going black as the clothes they wore, covered 39 faces with purple
symbols the color of lenten holy week when jesus rose up to join angels,
39 travelers wore black nike shoes, weaved through 39 catacombs of sleep,
dreamed themselves up like 39 shooting stars to hale-bopp comet's tail
of silver ice, where they would transform their—
18 buzz-haired castrated males, 21 females surfing death's

internet—to pass through heaven's gate's needle eye—& death
not even a stopover here for these souls to rest dressed in black & purple,
quarters for phone calls, 5 dollar bills for whatever urges their bodies
needed—before flying through space 39 dreams, they would be truly angels
rendezvousing with the mothership hidden inside hale-bopp's comet's tail
live with extraterrestrials there in a sleeve of silver ice after sleep

cuts them loose to flow through steep mystery above as sleep
like rocket fuel fell over stages, left them asphyxiated in death
after phenobarbital, apple sauce, & vodka, they knew the silver ice tail
as the sign they were waiting for to cover themselves with shrouds of purple,
leave behind computer screens—skies—they flew purely as angels
now towards a higher source than conflicting urges of their bodies—

a tangle of websites, conquered & controlled, their bodies—
surrendering the improvisation of living, they swam in sleep
drifting slowly as motorless boats on the sea—were homeless angels-
took 39 pot pies & cheesecakes for their journey, they kissed death
hard with dry mouths, 39 people down from 1000, pursed lips of purple
open in wonder, they flew up to enter hale-bobb comet's tail

of silver ice particles, gaseous bodies grinning there like death
skulls flashing inside sleep, inside where eye am dreaming now of purple,
faith flashing bright as new angels inside hale-bopp's comet's third tail

FORTY-ONE SECONDS ON A SUNDAY IN JUNE,
IN SALT LAKE CITY, UTAH

for Michael Jordan

rising up in time, michael jordan hangs like an icon, suspended in space,
cocks his right arm, fires a jump shot for two, the title game on the line,
his eyes two radar screens screwed like nails into the mask of his face

bore in on the basket, gaze focused, a thing of beauty, no shadow, or trace,
nor hint of fear, in this, his showplace, his ultimate place to shine,
rising up in time michael jordan hangs like an icon, suspended in space,

after he has moved from baseline to baseline, sideline to sideline, his coal-face
shining, wagging his tongue, he dribbles through chaos, snaking serpentine,
his eyes two radar screens screwed like nails into the mask of his face,

he bolts a flash up the court, takes off, floats in for two more in this race
for glory, it is his time, what he was put on earth for, he can see the headline,
rising up in time, michael jordan hangs like an icon, suspended in space,

inside his imagination, he feels the moment he will embrace, knows his place
is written here, inside this quickening pace of nerves, he will define,
his eyes two radar screens screwed like nails into the mask of his face,

inside this moment he will rule on his own terms, quick as a cat he interfaces
time, victory & glory, he crosses over his dribble he is king of this shrine,
rising up in time, michael jordan hangs like an icon, suspended in space,
his eyes two radar screens screwed like nails into the mask of his face

II.

GRAY DAY IN JANUARY IN LA JOLLA

for Porter Sylvanus Troupe

the day absent of sun, troubles in over plush hill tops
threatening rain, cool hours mist towards noon
wearing gray shawls of vapor, patches of blue peek through
ragged spaces punched in clouds, look like anxious eyes of scandinavians
worrying through their skins when they see snow storms coming,
in a place cold & white as anything imaginable, eye look

past green foliage touched with hints of autumn shivering
like a homeless white man in a harlem doorway in february,
look past white ice storms freezing the nation, all the way to the capital,
on martin luther king day, standing there on heated stone, bill
clinton takes his second oath of office, as rumors swirl around him
posing as vultures devouring an abandoned blood kill,

he lays out a vision for the future as good old boys dumped
like pilsbury dough into their rumpled suits fight back yawns, eyes
boring into the back of clinton's head like cold barrels of shotguns,
the cheers of the massive crowd punctuated by gun salutes,
tries beating back the cold of this day sweeping in from the artic,
flags popping trembling wings crackover the capitol,

as jessye norman takes us where we have to go, singing:
america, america, God shed his grace on thee, & crown thy good
with brotherhood, from sea to shining sea
but we remember the reality of ennis cosby's senseless death, on this day
out here in the west, where everything seems so cozy & warm, where
time wears the laid back attitude of a surfer crouched on a board,

riding an incoming wave, eye see climbing up invisible ladder rungs,
deep in his imagination, the growing power of my son
porter's angular body, all arms & legs now, eyes peering out innocent
but knowing, laid back but cold, his mind calculating the distance

his thirteen-year-old body must conquer before he understands
the meaning of roads he has just walked over pigeon-toed,

clouds breaking across tops of hillsides, light shimmying in golden
blue, the sky widening into this moment bright as anywhere
clear & warm, the voice of jessye norman touching the blues breaks through
radio, her voice evoking history washes through this poem,
implanting hints of lady day's warning of "strange fruit,"
as the threat of another storm gathers itself—as love

& hatred everywhere—north of here, above san francisco,
porter & eye see shadows of clouds lengthening here in la jolla
see them spreading down hillsides like dark amoebas, mirth,
ragged as edges of daylight slipping toward darkness,
the air cool with mist now, the hour decked out in gray shawls,
cloud vapors now puffing into shapes of dolphins, whales

sharks cruising a sky cold as these waters off the coastline

MOTHER

for Dorothy Smith Marshall

when eye was growing up she used to sit in the bathroom, each & every
morning, smoking kool cigarettes, drinking hot coffee, reading newspapers,
a hard toilet seat caressing her derrière, reading glasses in place,
serious as cancer, the way her eyes devoured everything,
finished newspapers stacked up high as her waistline when she stood
proud, erect, defiant, all of five feet two inches tall in high heel shoes, petite
she was a pistol when she was young, eyes blazing, boring in
like bullets when her temper squeezed the trigger of her ire,
hard, her rage angry scars she raised on me & my brother's backs & legs,
dealt out with ironing cords that hissed through the air like whips, coiled snakes
about to strike, it was her mother's influence (she was scared to death of her
mother—mama to me & my brother timmy—) who believed in retribution,
payback, fear, to the bitter end we watched mama slap mother around hard,
once or twice, for some perceived transgression or indiscretion,
but we loved them both deeper than fear itself,
loved mother, mama too, because we knew we were a lot to handle—
my brother & me—born to do mischief in a neighborhood full of young thieves,
malcontents, murderers-to-be, you name it, they thrived & flourished there—
the good & straight thieves we rejected out of hand as past tense, negro, square
as blocks we played with once until we wrapped hands around straight razors—
so she cracked the whip hard, raised welts on our backs & hardening butts,
legs & arms, kept fear alive in us, to keep us in line & alive

she always ha books around the house, introduced me to poetry & novels
wanted to be a schoolteacher, raising me & my brother got in the way of that
& as she grew older she left a string of glassy-eyed suitors
in her wake, my father being the first who didn't make it all the way
home, where her sweet perfume trailed through the air like flowers
blooming fresh in springtime, gardenias of lady day, sometimes
jasmine, or roses, it depended on her mood, but there was always something
about her that kept them coming back for more, time & again,
whatever she had bewitched them with, her charm, maybe,

that could be dazzling as the smile flashing above her sensuous walk
that beckoned, her step so light she seemed to float through air, meriny-yellow
in skin tone, plum, cushiony lips, splashed bright red & full, smooth,
she called herself a party girl—though she was always much more than this,
though she was this too—with a great sense of style, dressed to kill cock-
robin, could press pedal to the metal out on the dance floor,
she caused heads to swivel on necks like spinning tops
whenever she passed, her fragrance tantalizing nostrils,
trailing behind her like a sweet-smelling, invisible plume

she's in her eighties now, still sits on the toilet each & every morning,
repeating the same ritual, only now she doesn't smoke anymore,
everybody's gone to the other side on her side of the family—mama,
her brothers garfield & allen, aunts & uncles, cousins, her daddy, mine too—
men her age still sniff behind her glassy eyed, whenever she honors them
when she looks their way, still a fashion plate, the best of her time, her smile
remains dazzling, her skill to squeeze copper from a penny, squirrel away
money—a survivor of the depression, she is tenacious—for rainy days,
she's softer now, tells me she loves me every time we speak
over the telephone, tells me, with regret, she could have done better by me
but that's hogwash, because she did the best she could with what she had,
that was more than enough to get us through all the madness,
she is still a pistol at 81, has all of her real teeth, too, has outlived all of her
suitors, except this last one, biff, who she says is slowing down at 79,
still walks with a bounce in her stride, seems to still float across
& through the air, her eyes blazing bore in on you still like bullets
whenever she squeezes the trigger of her temper, ire
& eye love her more than eye could ever imagine,
love her far deeper than fear itself

JEREZ DE LA FRONTERA
for Peter

1.

in the deep black hours of jerez, after midnight, margaret is a mummy
wrapped in a white sheet where she sleeps, in the dead of night, she lies
in the center of our bed, stiff as demeanors of some european aristocrats, peter,
your house quiet as church mice sniffing gold leaf pages of a book of sacrament,
a cool breeze licking in over white walls & slanted roofs from the east filters
heat, announces morning light is not far off, wedded, as it is, to daybreak, soon
the white bridal gown of first light will spread out its hem, lift its white lace
veil, while a lengthening train of clues breaks the dark into spreading
blues, which are current everywhere, common as lyrics of muddy waters,
john lee hooker, lightnin' hopkins, somewhere deep inside
a snoring voice of lament breaks through the last vestiges of quiet hours,
at the center of a slippery moment full of dreaming, a motor bike zips through,
leaning around corners, it escalates the language of its speed as it shoots, veers,
clues itself into somewhere it is due, gearing down towards silence as it blows
past white walls & roofs collaged in bold relief against a spangled black sky,
they look like still lifes from my second floor window over the garden,
while margaret's sweet fragrance rises like seduction from where she sleeps,
her body a stand-in for a mummy wrapped in white linen, her face sweet,
is turned toward the window as if to kiss first light when it comes

2.

now a sliver of moon smiles through our room above the tiny chimneys,
they seem to wear small hats cocked ace-duce, like the icon of tio pepe sherry,
peter has told us of the burning hot wind of dust & fire called la vente,
which brings grief from the east, when the weather vane's arrow head points
in the direction of seville, granada's alhambra, lorca's moorish part of andalusia,
its craggy mountain peaks sharp as alligator teeth, their skin the color of chalk
brown mixed with ochre, greens, reds, white villages & towns—
& one the shape of one of miro's floating birds—sweep across this heat-
stricken landscape of late august, up & down rolling, warbled landscapes,
rendered mysterious by el greco's surreal, strangely beautiful canvases,
they seem to be rising up from some moonscape, somber dream,

but today the weather vane arrows north, towards madrid & morning
breaks through smells of coffee, footsteps that crack hard as castanets, or skulls
being popped open when smashed against old cobblestone streets, spilled brandy
that stained tiled squares checkerboarding the walkway of the plaza plateros
last night, is being washed clean, right before daylight breaks apart my dreams,
eye hear in the center of my imagination the roar of a bullring, erupting
cheers in the arena roll up & down, a cadence of emotive conundrum,
& in the middle of it all eye feel the matador slaying the bull,
in the center of the arena, see its blood flowing bright as the matador's red suit,
emblazoned with golden epaulets, hear in my mind's ear clapping castanets,
cracking sounds of flamenco dancers shoes slapping the floor staccato,
in a rhythm reminding me of popping sounds of conga drums, miles' lamenting
trumpet on *Sketches of Spain*, now that the sun is high in the blue eye follow
the curve of his mournful lament, fully awake now, walk down
to your walled in courtyard, peter, bright with green, yellow chumbera cactus
buds, bright birds of paradise shoot out blooming tongues that burst into heads,
geraniums fragrant as the sparkling water fountain is lyrical, tantalize
the senses, you want to sit here forever amongst these red & yellow lobster
claws, scarlet red begonias laddering, emblazoning these old walls,
want to sit & write poems of hope & serenity, but today, back in the states,
president clinton is being deposed in front of a grand jury, people are screaming
his head be axed off, thrown into a bucket like fish, or snakes

but you wring out words of joy, peter, they roll off your tongue lyrical
as a happy mantra, relieved that the weather vane's arrowhead still points north,
the breeze tongue cool as springs of water high in mountains of italy,
you are relieved the day is not scorching hot with la vente,
though we hear words circling the american congress like declarations of war,
on that day we went down to the blessed beach between cadiz & rota,
where the waves washing in rough & warm were beautiful, the sun setting low,
in the west, just before evening wrapped itself around us like the arms
of a favorite relative, my spirit reaching out across the straits of gibralter felt
the tip of africa, so close, so far away, the promontory of cadiz pointing
like a finger full of white buildings toward the dark continent,
when the light grew dark as the sun dropped like a ripe orange into the sea,
where ships crawled into port like giant bugs, sea gulls glided over & through

the sweet, cool air, like toy planes banking over waves thick as molasses,
the air here thick with andalusian spanish, syllables cracking rapid fire,
machine-gun staccato, the laughter sudden as terrorists explosions,
spontaneous as great music is always, everywhere it is played

3.

night has come again to this place of caballos, noble horses & brave fighting
bulls with curved horns trying to kill a matador with a red cape,
toro, toro, toro, bravo, toro, the cheers rise as the bloody black bull charges,
toro, toro, toro, a man & a red cape & a horse, the spectacle beyond what
eye feel is beauty, though eye see there in movement the sheer power,
choreography of war, the grace of man & beast during a moment
at the edge of death, locked into a mode of survival, is as far as my heart can go
in the service of destruction for beauty, but who am eye to say what is or isn't glory,
the lance poised in the air like a scorpion's tail before the strike is art for so many,
murder to others, in this land of the inquisition & franco's execution of lorca,
what is there to know but your own heartbeat pulsing love, peter,
the blood of friendship pure as your smile, these bodegas of wine you have shared
peter, full of the finest sherry, meals scarfed down & laughter shattering moments
like gunfire, these are the things you remember, castanets & flamenco dancers,
the chimneys cocked ace-duce like icons of tio pepe in the cool evenings,
your gracious, spontaneous welcome, my friend, your friendship that brought us here,
for me to see margaret's body wrapped like a mummy in lacy white linen,
asleep in the center of our bed, the shades open, in the dead of fragrant nights,
her face sweet, always turned toward the open window, as if to kiss
the first morning light when it comes, is a blessing & a gift,
eye tell you now, peter, it is a blessing & a rare, poetic gift

III.

THE POINT LOMA SERIES OF HAIKUS & TANKAS

for Mathieu Gregoire

I.

beauty all places
here, look inside yourself now,
look deeper, it's there

II.

gray day underground
in tunnel, bright, warm sun
outside in the blue,
inside your own deep working
time, thoughts of making sweet love

III.

think of making love
to work that you do here,
think of it as song,
music whispering, a breeze,
a tongue of someone you love

IV.

think of a sweet place,
now that you are here, in all
this darkness, light where
you are standing with yourself,
wherever you have to go

V.

smile whenever you
think of the sweet love blooming
inside your hard head,
think of it as a flower
you will hand to someone soon

VI.

down here in darkness
think of roses when you look
at these concrete walls

VII.

your mind a window
to look inside yourself, see
a rich garden there,
bright with flowers, whose faces
pop the air like sweet music

VIII.

deep rumblings in air,
is sound of sea waves smashing
skulls of wet black rocks

IX.

somewhere on a hill
burning candle flames—tall pines
shoot up, reach skyward,
their V, for victory signs—
lick hot tongues, scorch the air

YOUR LOVER'S EYES SPEAK

your lover's eyes speak
to you so softly in this
place of wind, sea, bright blue sky,
sunlight after the gray lifts,
stuns your face into smiling

IV.

BELLS

after Gustaf Sobin

eye am hearing bells in the music of poetry, bells
inside laughter tinkling like silver, bells rinsed in colors, shapes
& forms washing wave after sonorous wave, bells washed through
wind chimes, swept through morning's first breaking light, rolling
bells shivering in damp cool speech hip language seduces
& imitates, bells coursing through syllables spilling from lips,
bells tinkling through raindrops, pooling on rooftops,
spreading like rosebuds, airborne on wind tongues,
drooling down storm drains, riding water through whirlpools,
drop by dropping drop, bells spooling electric
through hearts in sacred himalayan mountains of tibetan buddhists,
bells swirling through pooling deep eyes of lovers, trilling inside bright voices
raised by small children, bells seducing through winds that play games
with our minds, with the way we hear time slipping through our ears,
& there are bells heard in kisses when sucking lips meet, vibrating
electric bells, strolling bells, breeze-blown bells that tongue
through fragrant afternoons of spring/time,
bells in silver dewdrops shimmying down bright green leaves
that land & float like rafts skimming surfaces of glass-blue rivers,
bells that dive through sparkling waterfalls like voices or solos
rinsed with clear welling sounds that tickle our senses
like crystal runs of bill evans laying down clues, bells sluicing through,
in flight, the way a thief steals through the night's deep music, like a sleuth,
the way blues tiptoe over piano keys dropping bell notes here
& there, as chords shimmy-shangling through the thick night air rinsed
in shimmering, electric beauty, bells that render us spellbound,
as when the heart seduces sound by locking pure
rhythm that is light, conjuring, bells that speak in voices dazzling,
church bells that ring inside seductive sweet strides of dancing women,
as when bells roll through their hips swaying lyrical, incredible magic, & eye heard
bells in the heat of summer language making sweet flowers rise,
heard bells in the voice of pavarotti's "nessun dorma,"

heard bells clanging & rolling through the square fronting westminster abbey
heard bells in the sound of african dew mornings rising, trumpet blaring,
saw bells in the silver ice of hale-bopp's streaking comet tail,
heard bells ringing throughout plazas of freedom everywhere—
but not from the cracked fluke bell squatting mute in Philadelphia—
heard bells inside all beauty heard or seen anywhere,
bells, bells, splendid sweet bells,
heard bells in the seduction of great poetry singing,
heard bells ringing through luminous language of sweet birds
riffing, bells, bells, splendid sweet bells,
swelling inside the air's sweet music

V.

CHORUSES

for Allen Ginsberg, 1926-1997, and Lucy Goldman

I.

within the muted flight of daybreak, inside its leaked trembling light
of birth, after the cracked shell of night's dome has spit open,
cut loose a flurry of pitched voices grown from different, linguistic sperm,
we hear a cacophony of opposing rhythms integrated inside the body of a song,
carried as if upon the widespread feathered wings of a bird across the sky
of imagination, as in circling, beating mantra the heart knows
as breath becoming choruses, becoming soundtracks
lifted off a poet's chanting tongue, syllables become moments
within moments, are transformed into song
beautiful as any morning glory colors when the sun slants down,
cuts through whatever is there with its golden blades, become beams
bright & sharp as voices heard anytime hands meet drumheads of skin
tightly pulled, the rhythms vibrating there in skimming waves
washing in or out at you as if they were imitating foaming sounds rolling in from
the sea, curling tips of its waves into shape of grigri lips that can be cataclysmic
as foam sudsing off lips of madmen moaning, or roaring,
or doing whatever it is madmen do, in katmandu, in the center
of nepal, or on the streets of new york city, where voices fire up pitches
fast as old satchel paige threw a baseball down the heart of the plate
or snaked it across, inside or outside corners, disguised as an aspirin,
like sound nicks edges of language, chips off syllables & meaning
until the voice cracks words electric as static,
perhaps resembles the sound lightning bolts make when ripping
off small pieces of dark sky & space
when thunder cracks its jagged whip in the night high gloom

there, where wolves sing love songs to the moon, where looky-loos crane
necks on freeways trying to spot hale-bopp comet's streaking silver ice tail,
who listen to songs of beck over the radio hightailing it lickedy-split through
the dark out west, burning rubber signatures into asphalt, as cars
wheel in & out of traffic, screech brakes, shape a kind of music, a new language

only the initiate know & imitate as it twists itself around again & again,
doubles-back in the way rhythm turn in & back on itself
like a concrete pretzel claiming its own place as it curls into space,
lifts off in the shape of interwoven, interlocking freeway ribbons carrying cars
& speech above heads on conveyer belts as motors screaming high speed
octane, zooming around curves like crazed vagabonds
hitting moments of sweet need, as music fills the air with magical incantations
wrapped in voices that track down sound, then double back blue as terror
recycles itself through years when good old boys guzzled beers
on back roads of america in a slew of cars that sped down roads twisted as limbs
of people suffering from rheumatoid arthritis, gun racks over their faces,
grinning like cheshire cats who just ate a slew of canary birds,
yellow feathers scattered all over that sordid history
& everywhere blood on whiskers of hyenas, blood frozen in ice-
cold stares of serial killers, blood in drawing rooms of politicians practicing
blood sports, bullshitting us in washington, blood on the cheese face of a leering
moon after eclipse hung down over rancho santa fe, blood on grimacing faces
bursting from bloated black bodies in rwanda, blood exploding from that
incinerated house in waco, texas, blood shooting from the eyes of a child before
he pulled the trigger in paducah, kentucky, blood in speeches of ministers
pontificating from pulpits, bloodall up in the curdling screams sliced clean
through by razors, blood smeared all over the blues
choruses of screams heard chilling after explosions in jerusalem,
in the choruses of hand grenades tattooing the nights of bulgaria, colombia,
in the choruses of machine gun bursts stitching the evenings of mexico city,
los angeles, that snuffed out the life of notorious b.i.g., tupac in las vegas,
choruses of fire meeting choruses of bullets, choruses of hand grenades
greeting the imploding language of love, blood on the syllables of choruses
spewing blood on musical notes that sing of these times everywhere

& blood on money pulled from ocean bottoms by deep sea divers,
blood up in the voices of poets impregnating stanzas with music,
blood on the tongues cut off because they sang beautiful images of love,
blood where the landmines littered the earth with eyeballs,
skulls & severed hands that point accusatory fingers stiff as bones in the mud,

& choruses & blood & choruses & blood & choruses & blood,
behold, time-clocks ticking inside blood irrigating flesh,
inside the moment when the poet knows language as a wellspring,
inside the moment when truth is understood as a two-headed sword,
duplicitous as the notion there is true beauty in flesh, lyrical with movement,
final as death, time marches on, leaves flesh imprinted with maps of spiderweb
sites, that spread across the body's internet, as songs pealing across
this embezzled air tantalize us with history of our continued failure

II.

when we sing we hear & know the music best, hear it with hearts
imitating breath, the rhythm of drum beats in cadences
true poets hear, the heartbeat of their breath in time signatures spread,
scored like music across fleet pages scrolling the mind, dreams composed within
language, when words become musical notes or chords language is retraced back
where it first burst from song as anchored root,
grew into a melody (a sweet flower smelled in springtime,
summer, when birds clear their throats of seeds, open piccolo beaks
& run tremolos beautiful, at dizzy gillespie speed)

& there is joy in the sweet singing of melodies,
beauty in the voice marveling at the sweet, blessed curves of a lover's
ripe body, in the way a woman's mind is shaped, her thighs, breasts, her lips,
caressing in the way a dress might caress the sensuousness of her body,
pure joy in the rapture of her kiss, blood boiling over there with sweet heat,
glory in her song, glory in the choruses of blood singing
beneath her flesh, choruses of heartbeats drumming faster & faster still,
glory in the mind running over from a space rooted in love,
where a poet creates from inside a moment of stillness, silence,
when metaphor is ejaculated from mystery into language,
sluices from the brain as words scaffolded onto the page like archipelagos
strung out in a sea of air like notes blown complete from a bell of a trumpet,
becomes poetry when form connects structure with magic, when breath
carries poetry with the indelible smell of damp rooms after lovemaking,
rumpled sheets stained with semen, history, the claustrophobic odor of cigarettes

when jamming their crooked burnt-out butts into overflowing ashtrays,
into rooms drenched with stale smell of whiskey & garbage,
& all this forms a question mark, a gesture—
a hand curved in space & bent at the wrist—a fragrance of mystery evoking
the color of pastel drenched in the lilting speech of the caribbean hinting of soft
seas, the air there filled, fragrant with garlic, peanut oil, saffron,
orange-gold sunsets laced with magenta, pink streaked magical coral
reefs, purple threaded like veins through blue, the feel of it is a chorus,
is a song lifted from the blood of the sky by a poet who sings
another prayer at sunset, practices ancient science of cabala,
cabala lore, cabala, cabala lore, cabala

III.
& eye heard you died today, allen ginsberg, heard it over the radio—
like eye heard about miles' passing over the idiot tube—that you went home
surrounded by friends & peace, heard you wrote till you slipped into a coma
after you wrote a last poem called "fame and death,"
you left great poems, allen, poems that fused blues & jewish chants, rock 'n roll
& jazz riffs, you left behind as gifts to remind us of a life lived fast to the fullest,
in "absolute defiance," you were a bridge between the sacred,
the transcendental, the underground demon & the buddhist-shaman-priest,
you were the guru speaking of wars when skulls were used to cradle silver coins
flashing under the light of human skin stretched tight into lampshades
used to filter heat from glaring lightbulbs—& the silver flashing there
like gliterring smiles, evil as death—o great bard breathing in & out,
spoken blues chants coursing through your lines gone home to rest,
gone home to rest besides your mother & father in spirit & shiva,
it was a great love you gave us, allen, a great love that makes me remember
you now with and affection & awe, o great son of whitman , blake, & williams,
your love of mystery, gemara, your love of flesh & magic, blood of poetry
coursing through choruses of your river-veins, love
coursing through memory of chicken soup, roasted eggs, love,
the smell of challah bread evoking candles burning on the sabbath,
on the lower east side where you walked hip-di-dip, a little strut & bounce
in the dip of your stride, you walked amongst jews wearing yarmulkes—

& though you moved here a little odd down there on passover,
buddhist that you were, you still moved,
many of them will still sit seven days of shiva for you,
many will lift their voices in solemn kaddish prayers—

so eye baptize you here with rhythms of the black church gospel,
with rhythms pulled from some of your favorite voices—
ray charles, bessie smith, ma rainey, charlie parker & john coltrane—
have washed your memory down with holy cadences—cool & hot
as water—rinsed in blues & jazz riffs, chanted from voices
& baptized in holy rivers of cabala, cabala lore

cabala, cabala lore, cabala, cabala lore

& blood & choruses, blood & choruses,
baptized in rivers of blood & choruses

& cabala, cabala lore, cabala, cabala lore

coursing through poetry that burst from your river-veins,
coursing through poetry that burst from your river-veins,

shalom, o great mystic bard, shalom

WORDS THAT BUILD BRIDGES TOWARD A NEW TONGUE

you begin with a sound wrapped around a syllable, or syllables
a word (or words) like razzmatazz or ratamacue, then you listen to
a red-boned black man playing a horn like a clue,
like a train or john coltrane or bird, then you play around with sounds
your ears done heard, lift them off a rebound, spellbound inside a roux,
because of a cue your memory remembered & knew
                                now you add a few nouns & vowels,
words singing like birds, flying through a spring wind thunder clapping,
                with roiling, rolling consonants, their feathers echoing colors now
black or white or blue, as a ranky dank pressing flesh beneath them
was immune to trailing blues stretched out behind him
voices that flew rhythmic as queued soundtracks through the night's
sweet longing, choo-chewing like wailing engines hurtling down isolated
                        tracks, way out in the dead of night's hushed music,
                around the voodoo, bewitching hour of bats, who liked words
bruising from a crew of mad hatter good old boys were circling inside
a hushed cave, where a strange blend of language was fashioning itself now
from cries & screams, the whooshing of beating wings
drumming pell-mell clues through
            the dark cinematography of a dream bordering on nightmare
as it wraps itself inside around you now as would a cocoon,

you find yourself there inside the cave of your head
& you are whatever it is you think you are there, brand new,
you are what you believe in as truth, right then, right there,
when you hear sheets of sound rushing out of the bell of a saxophone,
it is a stomp down cornucopia of magic spiraling out of a dream,
from a golden axe, shaped like an elephant's trunk, the shape of need here
is a question bewitching us with breath, power, mystery, stealth,
is what new language is shaping itself into now inside the neon air
hip-hopping & rapping in voice rhymes of young people,
before us right now is what the mind's ear reminds the tongue of here
chasing the sound of a freight train moving at full speed, is a syntax,

the jackety-jack of wheels rolling through the slick flow of tracks bedazzling gears,
the song of it all beguiling us with amazement, the rackety-rack of steel spinning
over & down rails, underground or overground, tracks,
                              the sound we hear is real when we know it
coming from the terrifying mystery of a hip shaman's horn,
we see the music form in the shape of the hot tongue of a bic flame lighter
tonguing out gushed heat
                    flames as sounds, as words inside the scorched flow of lava,
inside a tongue that is red, white & blue laced with dues paid in Philadelphia,
                    in hamlet, north carolina, where a language was fractured there,
congealed, until it hopscotched itself to its on own back beat
conundrum, before it pealed across the air clear as a bell ringing cold
on Sundays, unleashed a rage in rhythm & tempo, heated voices in sermons,
became a fire there in flight, was volcanic with syllables aglow, the night
flaming with embers washing through the breeze like a tribe of fireflies
swarming the night sky, a voice pure & guttural
                    a primal scream looping clues of a prophecy here, blue,
or sweetly singing as a slew of birds
                    tracking across a fondue sky laced with magenta,
their music heard in ringing silver bells as the wind tongue trills melodic
as it breezes lilting language through chiming leaves trembling

like lovers in heat/time, when the air is all aglow & splendiferous
with greens, yellows, & golds,
                    bright reds of bouganvilleas
jacarandas fragrant as voices of doves cooing, sweet pink of flaring
rhododendrons that burst into shapes of trumpet bells evoking
miles playing muted live in memory, clean as a whistle,
is where a poet stretches rubber sentences into bridges of music now,
language reinventing itself daily out of lost & found words,
constructing what it is to speak as a true American here,
today, right now, words moving through poems as magicians through parades
clowns dressed up as verbs, adverbs, adjective surrounding nouns with bright
verve, reminds the senses of sweet odor of frangipani perfume,
rhymes and rhythms intoxicating the senses,

this moment sluicing across the air in a rainbow of races
seductive with music, images moving as quickly as faces in an MTV video,
across screens blazing fast as beats moved through bebop, urban slick
as hip-hop brothas, chilling wicked in blooming fubu color schemes
rad in baggy jeans, their hand jive flicking & stabbing the air, constantly blur-
                    ring images—blink & they're gone like pop goes the weasel—
their rhythms nicking edges off slick time in stop-gap measures,
voices locking & leaking into currency, flip & zip,
on the box locking in the back beat,
can-you-dig-it, inside blaring boxes clocking back beats stitching threads
through the culture of hip-hop, attitudes holding everything together there,
as when a guitar player picks blaze out of funk noise,
his cadence up inside & outside time,
as in this poem swinging its voice downwind to cross fragile bridges
strung together with cadences & words, structures underneath
form the bass-groove swaying back & forth over deep chasms,
between mountains of language , where a child hears vocabulary in a swing,
in the backyard of a favorite uncle waxing real with his sho-nuff-to-god
hope-to-die-ace-boon-coon-throw-downs,
                    the ones that always got his back each & every
time he smacks scary, wherever he goes, their attitudes high-fivin' their eyes
& everything silent here except the wind's screaming terror,
words trying to cross over to the other side, to where the nephew swings,
right here, right now, words flowing through seamless
as eye (w)rap of my tongue around of johnny ace or nat king cole
stitching together a profusion of sweet cadences frank
sinatra & elvis stole, words that breathe inside a living language full of colors,
as choirs of birds singing atop hot telephone wires carry aretha's gospel
a symphonic elocution of elegant voices
                    a cecil taylor bedazzlement of lyrical, discordant chords,
swinging double-blade axes cutting down trees as they slice through all this
blue air, the bird man still singing now over steel tracks
snaking through & in between landscapes, where tupac & biggie now sleep
beside coal train(s) blowing through the night's voodoo air, sweet
the feeling here now, still blue as you were, charlie parker,

& truly American as slow trains choo-chooing twelve bar blues
through your old stomping ground of kansas city's twelfth & vine,
where you first showed your razzle-dazzle,
                        your feathers spreading their beauty through wind-chimes,
aching with your soliloquizing voice, always on edge,
triple-timing the fire that flowed through your genius ire on time,
until a chicken bone stuck itself inside your throat & damned up your music
(like that legendary finger stuck in that dike did to tupac, did to biggie, too)
pure smack snaking venom through your veins,
in a deadly slow dance with death you stumbled & scratched,
poisoned your brain until your head nodded off for real, then the bells tolled,
but boy did you jam, jam, boy did you jam until you left, no sweat, boy did you
jam, jambo, jambalaya, gumbo, boy did you jam jam, boy did you jam
& play that horn for real before the pain jammed vomit in your throat,
left those hot cadences cold as methuselah,
fire bird of stricken-heat, chicken-gumbo boy of sound language, boy,
did you jam, jam, boy did you jam, boy did you jam, jam, boy did you jam
riffs run through scales & chords, inverting electric

everything you heard you turned inside out, structures,
blew past every note—& through them, too—
rooted them in your own blue expression of turn everything inside out,
you jambo, gumbo, chicken-liver boy, running up & down jambalaya scales,
pastiche, a coal train before Coltrane blew down the hushed voodoo night,
a coal train burning across flat plains of kansas city, flight & barbecue
sauce up in the flavor of your drenched hot giddiup, scorching as red pepper
chili sauce, yo boy of bebop phrasing in *groovin' high*, you blew:

bebop, bebop, beedoo beeboli, doodle-li, bebop, bebop
beedoo beeboli, doodle-li, bebop, bebop,
beedoo beeboli
                bop baw baw baw bo de baaaaaaaa daaaaaaa . . . .

& you ran it all the way to new york city, minton's & birdland
chicken eating boy turned hip man skedaddling choo-choooing chords

so fast the air could hardly digest them, not to mention some human
ears, playing *salt peanuts, salt peanuts*
you & diz beautiful beyond words tradin' fours in duet,
fours in traffic, boppin' & rappin' before tupac & biggie were even born
bird, you uptown in harlem, creating language that reinvented itself again
& again before rap seduced rhythms down to scratching old records & words,
skating over samples of james brown & george clinton, toasting & roasting
the language like you & diz did in a *dizzy atmosphere*, jammin'

beedle-loo-beedle-loo-beedle-loo-bop,
beedle-loo-beedle-loo-beedle-loo-bop,
beedle-loo, beedle-loo-beedle-loo-bop
beedle-loo, beedle-loo
beedle-loo-beedle-loo-beedle-loo-bop
beedle-loo-beedle-loo-beedle-loo-bop
beedle-loo-beedle-loo-beedle-loo-bop
beedle-loo, beedle-loo

words & sounds building bridges toward a new tongue,
& it all started back in africa, mixed with europe over here, everything else,
that found itself here, too, in this gumbo stew, jambalaya,
this salad bowl filled with all kinds of flavors,
this pastiche, collage of language reinventing itself everyday,
every moment giving itself props, wherever words are
spoken, patch themselves together with sound, form a sentence,
that becomes a musical line, perhaps lifted from armstrong, bird, or miles
a phrase snatched & grafted into language of tupac & biggie, buzzing
in the attitudes of Alanis morrisette or jamiroquai scatting
phrases metamorphosed into dance when he reaches back
to grab hold of a language to swing & sing

today, in this moment in time, when everything is evolving
right now, from cue tips of tongues, a new language
is waiting for you to discover, listener, for you to give it some props,
to speak it, wrap your tongue around it, roll it off your assembly line of new

expressions too, so give it up for the new, right here, right now, so speak it,
don't diss it, give the new some props right now
freak it out with your own
dash of flavor,

                            say what's up in the air as sound, now
know it's rooted & shaped in the vortex of truth-change,
constant with language & words, sounds & attitude now,
say what's birthing in the womb of air, now
say what's birthing in the womb of air, now:

bustin on the scene clockin benji beastie boys actin like fiends:
down with the fave, funky jam, the noise up in the legit
jack up, someone screaming to kill the ill funky noise living large,
with an ace keepin it real, poppin the rip, doin the nasty to the bump
breakdown in the bricks, where the homies roll bones
to clock dollars, chillin hard through the calendar, gangstas flexin
profiles, while they kick it on the real decked in doo-doo pants
saggin slow like low riders over their doggy-grips
as they watch aces ball with the pill takin it hard to the rack,
skyin down the box, risin up like god to deal, or flash for the count,
pumpin treys from downtown, nothin but nets

words that build bridges toward a new tongue

beedle-loo-grab-a-groove-drop-some-slick-talk,
jazz-a-phrase-pop-a-blues-new-as-hip-hop,
cruisin-through-rappin-clues-sprung-from-bebop
me—&—you, groovin through
me—&—you, groovin through

me—&—you, singin new

from
TRANSCIRCU-LARITIES
New and Selected Poems

9/11 EMERGENCY CALLS COMING INTO MANHATTAN

I.

a crystal clear morning greeted you, dazzlingly blue
as a sweet water lagoon on some caribbean island
is blue, blue as the beautiful eyes of some
swedish woman is blue, as the deep true licks on the guitar
voice of robert johnson is blue, the alto riffings of charlie yard-
bird parker is blue, blue as a blue dress,
lady day's voice wore, searching for meaning on "strange fruit,"
blue as miles davis on "blue in green" is blue, coltrane on "alabama,"
blue as the sky death flew & turned into a flying missile,
a flying coffin, a heartless bomb glinting silver after sun rays
struck it, glanced off as it flew low in the blue sky just above roof tops
& chimneys, flying true as an arrow aimed true
at the heart of new york city, this first glinting missile coming
straight in from the north is blue, as it struck the world trade center
north tower, high up, is blue, blue as a fireball igniting tonguing
flames turning to smoke billowing upward, outward, blue as screams
wailing & piercing through the darkness, flames eating through steel,
flashing teeth of heat chewing, blue as horror of people
stunned for the first time into panic, into real fear after leaving loved ones
at home & somehow & somewhere behind them the terrible slow
feeling begins creeping through the bones, seizes the heart
with the terrible possibility that this could be it,
but it couldn't be, because some of you have just arrived
& it's morning & it's dazzlingly clear & blue, a brighter blue even
than the policemen in uniform downstairs who just greet you
blue & beautiful & warm as caribbean waters are crystal blue
this time of year, when you look out into blue space
you see the second coffin of death arriving out of the south,
it strikes the heart of the twin spirit of the skyline, you watch it erupt,
become a twin fireball, then you know, all who have seen it now know
what terror is, really feels like, is the dread you are thinking of now,
what is running like madness through your heart & brain,

horror is what you feel suddenly now in all of this,
your life flashing before you now as if it were a movie,
as some seeing it live & on TV thought it was a movie—but not you,
so you move with the others toward the windows high up in the blue—
some move like sleepwalkers, others screaming hysterically loud—
move toward the clear windows you loved so totally to look out of
as the flames, smoke, heat & terror increase—
tell me it is a movie, you thought, *a hollywood thriller*
& arnold, or bruce will come rescue us all soon, very soon—
& you thought you could see your god from up here,
inside, behind all this clear glass, where you took in such expanses,
such power you felt, so high up, each & every day coming here,
to witness all this sweeping glory was a miracle, now this sudden fear,
this swelling madness burning a black hole through the miracle that is
now a place an overwhelming fear, crawling like bile to grip
your spirit in your stomach, as the billowing smoke blooms
& flames keep licking toward you as you move with co-workers,
move toward the blown out windows, what were you thinking
as you climbed out on that ledge, a fierce wind up here licking,
whipping around you like an avenging spirit, taking your breath
away as you looked down, then stepped out into nothingness,
tumbled head over heels, your clothes flapping & tearing
wildly around you, the wind screaming, like you, for a moment,
then it was over before it was over, though you knew what
you saw before the end as truth, what were you thinking
out there, when you saw the whole building imploding down,
coming toward you like the hairy brown-gray legs of a tarantula
spider, crawling down the sides of your beloved second home,
so ominous now as it pancaked down, floor-by-floor at you,
toward chief ganci, father judd giving final rites & so many others
& when you hit rock bottom it all fell hard on top of you roaring,
choking acid smoke billowing as from a phylogenic cloud
after a volcanic eruption incinerated the day,
then everything went black, black as the skins of delta blues
singers from mississippi, whose voices imploded before they rose,

rose back up like tonguing flames & smoke billowing black there,
before they wrapped their black voices blue-black around song
& turned pitch-black nights, tar-baby nights into blue days,
down in the scorched earth grounds of unknown lynched bones,
those black voices full of blue tones of raise-up redemption . . .
but here, at ground zero, when the hush fell down,
the voices went silent as ghost-people emerged
& things would never, ever be the same again,
things would never, ever be the same . . .

2.

9/11 emergency calls coming right at you
9/11, emergency calls screaming

what were they thinking as they steered flying bombs,
flew them straight into their targets,
what were they thinking, "why did they hate us so?"
freaked out voices mutter

9/11 emergency call coming right at you

did we look into their eyes, how deep back inside themselves
they were, burrowed back in their skulls, cold as pinpoints,
because they had left all feelings behind
inside experiences they had gone through full of chanting prayers
five times a day, that brought them to this moment of redemption,
high up in the crystalline blue, confused people all around them,
going through fear, rage, quiet acceptance
of what was about to occur,
until they saw the towering symbols of capitalism before them—
those seemingly impregnable double edifices of everything
wall street stood for; power, arrogance, hubris & money—
standing before them now, so very clear, so hard-on phallic,
looming & glittering like millions of razors when sunrays hit them,
glancing off those 43,000 windows, they were coming closer to now

they were so very clear, looming, coming closer until
everyone who didn't know suddenly knew,
as the flying bombs held on course straight as a crow flies,
or a screaming arrow from the bow of an expert,
everyone knew now as they flew into the looming hard-ons,
erect with the blood of gold, silver & green backs & hubris,
they knew as their panic shattered into countless shards of fear,
as those 43,000 windows that were razors glinting
when sunrays hit them suddenly blew out now
like the pinpoint eyes of those who flew the bombs
blew out, at the moment of impact, prayers chanting in their heads,
then we suddenly knew, right before the world suddenly knew,

heard 9/11 emergency calls coming straight through
9/11, 911
                                    emergency calls
coming straight at you

3.
it was a castration, pure & simple, a cutting off of phallic symbols
of greed, money & hubris, they came down blooming clouds,
blowback coming to wall street, turning it into a war zone,
a war zone of weeping, screaming, unreal horror,
clouds black as those delta blues singers, color gloomed now
this once blue day, gone now, like the gold coin we knew this morning
as the sun was gone now, like those once gleaming phallic edifices,
everything down here was shrouded in mourning dustcoats,
as if in a movie, stunned ghost people stumbled through streets
ankle deep in soot & paper, wrecked fire wagons, police cars
& bodies—what was left of them—& street lights glittering through
the unreal light like flashing hyena teeth,
blink down on paper clips, chairs, telephones, pieces of bone,
shoes, blood & guts, shocked eyeballs looking up mute from the soot,
glinting earrings next to hats, an arm, office supplies, pieces of paper
fluttering through the stinging air like bat wings,

gone now the innocence, gone the hubris of impregnability,
gone now the arrogance, the jaunty haughtiness in the step,
in its place this new blueness, a blueness of spirit, of whatever
the future holds, a blueness of not knowing what you thought
you knew, who the person standing next to you was, is, is he an arab,
is he—or she—a terrorist, what does an arab look like anyway
without a head wrap, or veil? a jew, an italian, an american indian,
who, what? who? what? who? what? who? do they look like
mirrors of ourselves? ghost people hiding in corners?
white people full of anger? who hate everythingabouttoday,
like timothy mcveigh whoblewupthenotionwhitepeoplecouldn'tbe
terroists&noonepointedfingersat them, even after
the uni-bombertheodorekocinskiblewup those people
with those booby-trap letter-bombs, so who is a stranger,
who can know you now, since you don't know who you are yourself,
you don't even know what you're thinking even now as you speak,
because it changes from day to day, from whatever is said on TV,
talking heads on talk radio shows, all the flag waving now,
all this saber-rattling jingoism, boiling talk of war,
it is a blueness of revenge burning
red-hot through the language of the day—
though this, too, in time will calm down, fade away—
when the cameras drag slowly across the bombed out scenes
shown daily now—though this, too, will fade in time—on TV screens,
it reminds you of surreal disaster movies made in hollyweird,
swarming with high-beamed lights, thousands of made-up
extras, who shuffle through their shots with bone-weary faces,
like ghost people, as shadows of soldiers with machine guns
drift through the horror that is palpable now—
though this, too, will wind up & fade away—imprints
in soot the form of a footprint, a hand clawing as if for clean air,
an upturned face frozen into a wooden mask at ground zero,
though it looks like a movie this is real
terror & panic, frazzled voices, real, the stumbling strides of ghosts
the plumes of gray-black-brown smoke belching, flaring upwards

to blanket this eerie, sacred burial ground of pulverized dust/rubble,
soot-coats worn by heroic firemen & rescue people,
all races of weary volunteers from everywhere,
this spot marked forever by a jagged six-story tombstone—
                          which, too, in time will be taken away—

all that is left of two once gleaming 110 story towers,
two phallic symbols seared into memory & onto postcards

& 9/11 & an emergency call sweeping through manhattan,
engulfing the pentagon, exploding in pennsylvania,
spreading out to ensnare most of the globe
9/11, emergency calls wailing through all of this . . .

& what is terrorism but a faceless, invisible presence
suddenly here, there, completely in your midst,
then gone, then back again,
like a sudden death on a highway in the form of someone
drunk & out of control, in a runaway car hurtling right at you,
perhaps, a mind-set blowing your world apart on a bright, clear day
in september, or anytime, like now,
in this eerie time in the world

where there are two gaping holes
in the snaggle-tooth skyline of downtown manhattan,
two gaping, empty holes that ask questions,
are silently screaming for forgiveness & redemption,
two gaping holes that beg the questions

will we ever be able to fake innocence again,
howdy doody cornball smiles, daffy duck head-in-the-ground,
black-birds-sitting-on-a-wire-in-a-row-follow-the-leader,
wherever the bushies words say go, "let's roll,"
in this land of redwhite&blueapplepieflagwavingbombers?

doesn't all this saluting remind anyone of the slippery slope
germans found themselves on heil hitlering genocide in the day?

will citizens become suspect for not waving the flag,

will things will ever be about peace & sanity & love & respect
& different opinions listened to anywhere in america, now,
anywhere in the western, christian world?

9/11 emergency calls coming straight through to you,

9/11 wake-up calls, wake-up calls, wake-up calls

ringing up in the air, coming straight to you,

sluicing through the soiled air voices of the blues

coming straight at you, straight at you . . .

RECONFIGURATIONS

there are moments when we are what we think we are,
bright suns burning deep with love, white moons glowing,
lighting up the sweltering darkness, beauty,
the center of our imagination
but in revisiting old music, rhythms are sometimes heard
in a fresh light, a language you thought you knew
now sounds radically different
in the way a musical phrase suddenly turns,
makes your body move in a way you had hadn't known possible,
before, shows you, once again, surprise is always lurking
within a moment of deep creation,

so you follow this new way of hearing,
a kind of reinvention in your ears, so to speak,
it reminds you of a time you once knew, heard, without notice,
a flaring cadence butaning a fragrant night sky
inside a voice, a piece of music rooted in an expression suddenly
there, transforming itself, is both familiar & unfamiliar, but there
anyway, new your faculties, retooled
fresh inside the center of your imagination,
where you had refitted your faulties, retooled them,
without knowing—the way you took things in—
perhaps, you had fallen in love,
or dropped out of love, who can say—
but it had happened anyway, was some kind of miracle
the way you had reconfigured things
inside your spirit—red things turned into blue,
metaphors pinwheeled into stars, became
a kind of fireworks of language holding brilliant
words, chords, shining faces spangling the darkness,

where you lived, caterpillars became butterflies,

babies killers, geometry architecture,
night day, noise music, sounds ordered & shaped into forms,
poetry sprang alive transformed by new images inside language,
the way the voice digs itself out of a dark hole & breathes
again in light, fresh air, is a miracle, eye tell you now,
again & again, that reconfiguration is a miracle

& a miracle is always a blessing

PULSE & BREATHE

for Charlie "Yardbird" Parker

eye remember bone under skin as gristle of wings
beneath bird's feathered flights, solos, up in the tone,
music inside syllables echoing light, up in the steep night
transparent as an ethereal shimmering,
as a shower of colors laced through the sight, is a necklace
of white pearls strung around a black woman's neck,
from where we stand with plumes of flares in our hands
we see her at the edge of a looming vortex
as a fanfare of trumpets blooms from somewhere,
she starts to dance a fandango with herself
& everyone standing there, looking, is amazed

WHAT THE POETIC LINE HOLDS

the line can be taut as a straight clothesline
strung across a patch of field full of sun
flowers, a whip in the hand of a lion-tamer,
cracking out commands, a geometric groove between
two points, straight as an arrow flies true to the target,
like a flat jump shot leaving the hands of Michael
Jordan, with the game on the line, a ruled line,
upon which sets a string of words perched
like a flock of black birds gossiping high
up on a telephone wire, their dark shapes silhouettes
against a day sky, their black shapes holding true
forms a series of black hole seductions for our speech
to flow through there, is like what improvisation does whenever
it changes up whatever is said inside & through a line like jazz
riffs, is perhaps what "Bird" passed on to Miles in an instant
of rare beauty, is what his sense of liberation was at that time
& so on & so forth, ad infinitum, on the other hand
the line can be as loose as a goose frolicking in clear water,
shaking a tail feather baby, whatever the mind holds
true as its artistic inclination, is what the poetic line stretches
our deep limits out into, is a moment we can dive through,
find the other side & that is what possibly shapes the line,
whatever the imagination is able to manage,
hold onto, the music there following a snaking flow
of words, that act like notes embedded inside
a composition, is what the poetic line holds, clues,
perhaps a fragment, a sliver of bright sound,
glinting, as a gold tooth hit by a glancing ray of sun
can evoke a solo & so on & so forth, ad infinitum

ONE SUMMER VIEW; IN PORT TOWNSEND, WASHINGTON

for Sam Hamill

soft blue wind caresses ease in off the sound,
the waters cool surface shimmers
blue diamond-rare, miles up in the air a trumpet slips
glittering hard licks true & fast, slick as a moment
eclipsed in a wink
                  & quick as a hair-pin turn
you're looking out across the diamond-blue shimmering to see
a low, long land mass rising & swimming out to sea,
where the blue becomes a darker, deeper blue,

where the land's end is the brown-green
sandy snout of whidbey island, seemingly swimming—
a whale's head jutting—out to sea, then back over here again, where
green leaves brimming from branches & bushes are hands
waving *good bye, good bye,*
like farewells of weeping lovers,

now you see trees standing guard, high on black bluffs
overlooking the waters, foaming death as it exhausts itself
washing on shore, as the trees above wave their branch-arms
everwhichaway, like those of a music conductor,
whenever the wind blows hard, the music
a serenade of flutes imitating the tongues of breezes,
this is what you see looking out the window of alexander's castle,
overlooking the straits of juan de fuca,
at the tip-end of port townsend, washington

everything serene here, blue, green & brown, sun-
light dappling around edges, hard black masses—
the shape of shadows—spreading, over which one piercing bird call
tingles, pricks the senses
as it wheels, slices its double-winged comma shape right through

the blue singing, like a solo of miles davis cutting right through,
clean to the heart, true as a surgeon's scalpel,

these moments are a shopping list of natural wonders,
beauty, all the things we ever imagined leaping off of postcards
we receive from faraway locations,
most times always somewhere over *there,*
     on the flip side of imagination

& then bam! it's right there, dead center in a blind/spot,
clued into a glance, at the edge of where your eyes are looking,
just now, where your vision fell just short

& the moment completely escaped you

FAST LANE

for Victor Hernandez Cruz

fast lane, the ball is up in the lights
& you are breathing hard, there
& wherever the flight of the sphere takes your eyes
in its arc, you find yourself there, chasing
the music of the curve, up in the air, slick as an eagle,
or a red-tailed hawk, when it turns & dives,
its wing-tip become a blade,
sharp as its beak breaking the flesh of prey

& from here you are there, too,
inside the blood-letting, the death of the prey
horrible, but pulsating as an image
inside your imagination
& you are riding a wave of creation inside your mind,
a current of light & air that takes you to a fertile place
inside that imagination, deep down within, perhaps,
an imaginary circle, where you now consider
the path of the ball as it flies arching
through the blue, it is a cut-out object,
an image, black as a period on a white page,
then you fast-break your mental juices forward,
your improvising twists & turns inside
the possibility that you can do whatever
this thing you thought you could do,

& it, like you are running backward,
way up inside the music
you are listening to, now, inside your head,
you move the tempo forward, because it is your own
creation, way forward, past the dot up in the blue,
that is black now as any moment you considered
murder as an answer, then shrugged it off,

as one would a coat swarming with fleas & flies,
than you bevel yourself into a groove,
but very much still on time,
inside this moment you are creating for yourself
now, you are present there, but here, too,
on this page, looking out at yourself,
but that can get very boring,

so you press pedal to the metal & shoot
your mind out ahead, running fast
as the image of that black bird with spinning legs
in the old road runner cartoons,
or like a space shot trying to connect earthlings with the moon
you try catching up with your dreams, fusing them together
here, with everything you are thinking, now,
but you are still, by a beat, behind time,

though inside time, too, & the language, like seasons
is always changing, is always out ahead of you
& you are what the music hears inside your DNA rhythms;

language created everyday by you, by someone else
& played out here, or anywhere else, for that matter,
in an improvised way, too, you are

the possibility of what you are listening to, now,
the music up in the rhythms—soukas, salsa, maracas—

words of a poem pulsating jazz notes toward the light

SHADES OF BLUE FOR A BLUE BRIDGE

For Mildred Howard, Joe Rudolph & Yori Wada

1.
three shades of blue
evoke minnie's can do,
soo chow's, yori wada

2.
jimbo's bop city,
john lee's boom boom room,
history riffing blue matzoh balls,
fried chicken, soba

3.
the jigoku club inside
j town, bold rebels jamming
cross from black town, udon,
grits, barbecue

4.
cherry blossoms blooming
in lady day's hair, greens & fat back,
sashimi staining kimonos

5.
you walking filmore,
crossing geary with duke,
street cars running over ghost-tracks,
pigfeet in vinegar

6.
indigo-blue & white,
red satin, sticky fingers handling
chop sticks, hot cornbread,
sweet potato pie

7.

memories brought back
in a blue mirror, gefilte fish,
kimochi, lox & bagels

8.

filmore auditorium
jamming beneath miles of blue,
bird, monk, nihomachi,
a fake dividing line

9.

mixing it all up
this cultural jambalaya stew,
kabuki, white linen,
silk, coltrane

10.

music the glue singing
new images of multi-you
rapping in the sweet blue air

TRANSCIRCULARITIES

across, beyond, moving toward the soon other coast,
transcending a change of appearance, as when
transfigurating a moment that is circular,
as the O of a dead man's mouth is a circle
sometimes after his last deep breath has been sucked in,
becomes the shape of a spinning snake chasing, or swallowing
its own tail, can be a sign, an omen, perhaps, of what has been
forgotten, erased from the circular thought-waves
history provides, the highway of metaphors:
bombs & bullets & flag-waving guiding the way into madness
drunk on power, the hypocrisy of slaughter bombastic
with language rooted in opposing religious fervors, greed,
the sad war dead made over into blood-dripping saints,
converted to propaganda-iconography,

now we find ourselves once again here, as yesterday,
our speech a copy of a copy of a copy,
our histories located in roots, clues underground, bleached
bones, skulls without vanity marking the spots where
ancestral voices once swelled & grew colorful as bright flowers,
were there, rhythmic, beautiful, full of surprises, bold with new
twists inside language grown fresh in an instant,
then suddenly gone, erased in a blink,
as history quickly removes those who lose wars of iconography,
even as music of their speech echo choices they made
when they stood visible, unbroken, inside their own loved skins,
their heartbeats thumping drumbeats in time with their spirits,
their voices musical instruments, they sang & shaped
a language they danced to then, even now you still hear
echoes of its rhythms on our own tongues here

now the faces of those ghosts are invisible as death
coming in the dark, after midnight when most eyes shut down,

close themselves off to light, live only inside shifting dreams,
it is a roundabout way that we have brought ourselves here,
shrouded in this moment of looping shadows,
whispering in this graveyard of rundown tombstones,
whispering to the memory of what could have been, like autumn,
brown leaves scattered across asphalt, or dirt, or stone,
after the chill of coming winter's tongue sentenced them here
to the fate of dried corpses rotting on a battlefield,

the eyes of owls, their whooping language of mystery
our only companions here, as time tick-tocks down,
our eyes rotate upward toward where we think heaven is,
as if looking for a sign, hoping for a savior

from
THE ARCHITECTURE OF LANGUAGE

I.

HAIKU SCENES

faces of leaves fall
red as kisses stamped on cheeks,
pile up brown on streets,

as pine needles wave
outside my window, dance slow
scherzos on the wind,

the landscape green here,
dazzling, bird-calling colors,
fragrant la jolla,

lavender ice plants
explode on hillsides in spring,
glistening with green,

my thoughts reach out blue,
look like the ocean when viewed
high up in the sky,

also blue when viewed
from down here, whispering trees
remind of sea waves

lapping rocks, spent brown
leaves crumbling in winter's cold,
skeins of words flying,

geese in summer skies,
kites, their strings unraveling,
planes up in the blue

II.

VERSACE

eye watch my cat, versace, roll over on her back,
four paws boxing the air, she is striking there,
soft white, brown striped & spotted fur,
with the coat of a small leopard, she is beautiful flipping
& flopping, her tail up & down, stretching
her long, lean body outside my window, in the sun,
blue eyes opening & closing as she naps
                              in a world of her own, at first glance
she seems so innocent when she yawns, revealing
those long white nail-like fangs hinting at the possible
terror she is when she awakens,

suddenly she is alert, her ears twitching & turning around
like crazed antennas, tensing she leaps quick as a cobra striking,
uncoiling in midair, strikes some hapless victim
she was clocking while she appeared to be dozing
& it's all over in a blink except for the futile, spasmodic twitching,
the horrible death struggle, then she eats the thing whole,
licks her paw, scratches behind her ear, then
stretches out again & goes back to dozing,

but don't get me wrong, she's a beautiful, loving friend
inside the house, always giving of her love freely,
but outside, in the air—even inside if it's a shadow that moves—
watch out, especially if you're a tasty bird, rat, or lizard,

watch out, you'll pay the ultimate price for not paying attention,
sleeping on the job, it will be all over quicker than the blink
of an eye glazing over, or closing, in death

III.

THE HOURS FLY QUICK

the hours fly quick on wings of clipped winds
like nonsense blown from mouths of hot air—
people—including my own—form syllables, suds,
words shot through pursed lips like greased sleaze
& bloom inside all these rooms dominated by television
babble sluicing idiot images invented in modern test tubes—
clones—blinking, slathering all over controlled airwaves
of an up-for-sale world, blinking a paucity of spirit,
so dance you leering ventriloquists, marionettes,
you greedy counterfeits, dance, dance, dance

THREE SEVENS: 21 LINES HOPING FOR CHANGE

an opaque sky streaks tears down from clouds
on the other side of murmuring
a language understood by flies
after decommposition has been broken becomes
clear syllables rolling again from a bird's vibrating tongue
& music is heard by those who recognize its beauty
when sound penetrates love to beating hearts

listen to the antiphonal flow coursing up
from rivers of ancestors a breathing history lives there
to know the secret mysteries voiced with codes
you must first feel the poet's lashing words
you have buried deep inside sleep their resonance
under pitch-black clouds of acrid amnesia
you have forgotten even the sound of your name

ghoulish apparitions of flames dance under shadows now
spreading umbrellas of smoke billowing wings over hunger
advance through the world like pestilential plagues
nuclear as evil intentions of men with unchecked power
unleased under guise of unholy gospels
& lethal when pulpits are aligned with bullets
& guns put in the hands of praying congregations

EYE AM FOREVER LOOKING FOR SHADOWS

eye am always looking for shadows dropping hints
where they lost their old bodies, is a matter open
to question, a conjecture full of mystery,

eye am watching for bird wings eye imagine
are eyebrows over two moons in a blind man's face,

now my ti-punch is speaking to me
full of rum, limes, sugar & gingembre, in a language
full of zouk, clear blue-green caribbean water,

it reminds me of the translucence of my cat's eyes,

now the moments are filled with hesitations,
the sounds exploding in music so quickly
they remind me of skiers blowing down mountain slopes
slick with hard ice & snow,

but who are we fooling during these frivolous moments
slick with silly infomercials flooding
the language we speak, created in test tubes,

what is the drilling sound we hear inside our heads,
the loud jackhammer of woodpeckers tapping out
thoughts with hard sharp beaks like machine-gun fire
ricocheting off walls & exploding skulls,

it's time now to pay attention to where this creaking
ship is taking us, leaking, taking on water as it goes,
it's time to get nervous about not being nervous,

because if you're not jumpy you aren't paying attention
about being worried, aren't giving consideration

to being edgy as a crash & burn junky absent cocaine,

you're not paying attention while entire worlds burn

IV.

MEMORY, AS A CIRCLE: FOR THE LOVE EYE
LOST IN HURRICANE AUDREY

because it is beyond midnight somewhere,
between total darkness & daybreak,
light, pure & simple
is an echo of someone hidden far back in memory,
an echo pulsating like a heart beat here, it has intensity,
like a drummer keeping time alive,
it follows the rhythms of an artist breathing
music through a face jumping from a canvas, extends itself
way up into a future you can't even see now but know
is there, perhaps a moon sliding slowly across
the geography of black skin that is sky, is like a notion
a pearl once evoked in the mind when it first saw it coming,
that it was a globe lit up like the round, gleaming eye of a panther,
or the idea of a black hole imploding with light,
was your smile, love, come here again, back from memory seducing,
a light pulsating through imitates your face, where you once were,
where all these years a hole shaped like a cut-out of you
flattened itself out daily against my longing

& eye see a fire burning way out there in the pitch
black desert of midnight,
perhaps it is a camp fire encircled by lonely spirits back when
eye knew you as a deep sea diving lover, always underwater,
entombed inside your own breath bubbling circles,
your silent voice now a chain-link of bubbles climbing forever upward,
toward the surface, light pure & simple,
an echo of itself, when the light was fading fast
the way out far up above your memory, light still beyond a doorway,
perhaps through which a lost fish swam once looking for the way
back to that baited hook it refused to bite on,
back when the promise of light above this language was clear,

reflective, was shimmering like great music, or poetry,
before night came back washing everything away in darkness,
before they dredged up your once shining face from that lake,
fish eaten, bloated beyond even faith,

our hope a memory now eye have held onto all this time,
beyond even what language is to great music,

beyond even what metaphor is to this poem

DIVA

again for Dorothy Smith Marshall

my mother walks with certainty, ballerina-style
she glides by up on the balls of her feet, tippy-toe,
her back straight as a plank of wood,
there is an air of haughtiness in her manner,
the way she looks at you is a command
about to happen, no doubt in what she says,
in her own mind she's already convinced herself
it's right, she's eighty-seven, a tiny woman,
when she's all made up, decked out in her finest clothes,
her arms, fingers, ears & neck dripping jewelry
she's regal in her bearing, but can blow warm & cold,
radiant when you catch her just right, in a good mood,
she will bless you with a beautiful smile
wide as daybreak, her laughter spraying light
mist all over you as when waterfalls hit rocks & liquid
bottom after dropping over a cliff, makes you think of music
entering your space with notes shimmy-shangling, but please
don't catch her wrong, say something, rubbing sandpaper
rough up against her tempermental grain,
could be anything, large or small, everything changes,
her temper hisses, then explodes like a lit firecracker,
better pull back quick when her face clouds over
her mood turns black as a day about to drop a tornado
you better pull back quick before she flips her switch—
her once-warm eyes suddenly turn into twin smoldering
nuggets about to spit singeing fire all over you—
better turn your back & go the other way, *tout de suite*
before her verbal anger hits you like a category five
hurricane & you wonder how it all came to this
from this small, dainty , high-class looking
proper woman with the ballerina style,
who just a heart-beat moment ago was flashing you

a soft, bright smile wide as daybreak, her laughter
spraying light sparkling bliss all over you,
made you think it was music entering your space
made you think it was light in this place

LUCILLE

for Lucille Clifton

if you were a guitar, lucille,
b.b. king would play beautiful blues
songs all over your ample spirit,

but you're a poet, sister,
so you play your own wondrous riffs
through notes of your honed words,

they dig down deep, sewn within
your music, boned, you keep them inside
your brief luminous sentences of echoes,

sounding like sonorous utterings
flight seeking light inside a flute's breath,
bird wings lifting on the wind's

rustling flight, your elliptic absences
pregnant with caesuras arrest us with their sorrow—
winged loves gone too fast from you now

always test the elixir of your rooted
deep faith, everywhere in your poetry
the conviction of living spirits, beauty

shining through the bravery of your life is
a bright, flashing beacon pulsating harmony
in all this darkness, your embrace

warm as the sun during summer,
it is your faith that holds me fast to you
now, inside your sweet nourishing well of love

eye know there is a "river between us"
we can always cross over, we can,
cross over it again & again & again,

can always cross over it with faith,
can always cross over it with love,
again & again & again,

like you do, lucille, like you do

THE SHOT

for Tiger Woods, at the 2005 Masters

we watched him loft a chip shot from the rough
on the 16th, the ball dropped from the sky
like an aspirin in the middle of the green,
then we saw it move right like pure magic,

like a basketball player pivoting
before making a deft move to the hole,

this spinning little white ball made a beeline
in the direction of the cup,
crawling over the green it had twenty-twenty vision,

everyone watched, held their breaths,
when it got to the lip of the cup it lingered,
trembled at the edge like it was afraid of heights,
before dropping like a ball of sugar
into a cup of black coffee,

then the crowd erupted as he kneeled,

then stood, ramming his balled fist into the sky,
celebrating having being blessed by a miracle
cameras caught him in his signature logo

& everyone knew then the rest was pure glory

FOR RICHARD PRYOR: 1940-2005

you danced on wing tips of raunchy humor, richard,
danced on edges of words flying high up in the blue(s),
you were the flight of so many birds soaring
toward freedom of expression, an idea clued you
in your in-the-pocket profane language, words mirroring
the jazzy tongue-lashing put-downs we blacks heard all
our screaming lives laughed out in barbershops, churches,
in beauty parlors, on street corners where gun-slinging local
black wordsmiths slapped down cruel, embarrassing all-comers
with their oral boasting toasts, so funny they leaned into caustic
hard verbal shootouts everyday, sardonically hip they thrived
on cutting down to size all pretenders to their thrones
though none were even close to the genius you were in stand-up,
richard, you were the cat's meow, *the man* who had the gift
the quickest razor-tongue flashing under any & every sun
& everybody knew not to raise up & bother with your "dirty" words
words slicing clean to the bone in head-on comedic cutting sessions
& eye loved you when eye first heard you dishing it out on TV,
on records, you made everyone's hair stand up straight
with your machete-wielding stories rooted in peoria
eye knew you were the real deal throwing down *our* words
on stage, our african-american prometheus, fragile as you were
you had steel in your backbone, steel in your everyday
commitment to truth, flawed as you were too with drugs
so high you set yourself on fire, lived to tell about it
lived to laugh at the stupidity of yourself in self-deprecating
screaming routines, filled with truth, sadness, & hilarity
you are always with me, richard, & eye will judge
other comedians, how their words stand up next to yours

V.

CONNECTIONS

for Robert Antoni

I.

on a drop-dead clear day you took me down the waterway,
riding the miami river in your small motor boat, robert,
the skyline of miami back-dropping or journey,

                                       like on *miami vice,*
suddenly I was looking for a flock of pink flamingos skimming
low over biscayne's waves to burst into view, take over
the scene, alongside don johnson & michael phillip thomas
streaking by, squeezed into a wave-skipping cigarette boat,
front-end up, chasing drug-dealing "bad guys,"
but the scene was so tranquil here as boats slid through oily,
dark, smelly, flotsam-filled waters on this november day,
so different from the sparkling blue, pastel images
surfeiting *miami vice* on celluloid,
with staccato with gunfire blending with colors,
complete with rhythmic soundtracks& stunningly beautiful people
fused with all matter of races, dressed in linen,
wondrous bodies of women bursting from skimpy bikinis,

            none of this was present this day, though the sky was
lovely as any eye have ever witnessed,
the mood—except for our laughter—was pensive
as we passed the venetian islands & san marco island
(where you used to live before barcelona, spain, robert, new york
city), silent now, except for the sound of wet fish slapping
& flopping around metal pails after fishermen hauled them in
over concrete railings of the venetian causeway,
running low past islands of the same name,

                                  spanning biscayne bay,

connecting miami beach to miami

& beyond here, out to the east the atlantic stretches,

its foaming waves to touch the caribbean,
                              latin america, africa & europe,
all these places blended inside you here, robert, where
your genes fuse genomes of all the modern world, your DNA
pumped through veins & arteries bright red
as your two-year old son gabriel's vexed face, screaming now,
at the top of his lungs, his innocent displeasure real,
contorts his beautiful face with roped veins
bulging from his temple & neck, his voice catching,
                              coughing, until you give him a drink,

then his transformation to calm is swift,
remarkable even, in the way his eyes laugh
with glee, now, as rubber car wheels squeal above us
over the causeway like scherzos, our laughter breaking,
skedaddling, shimmying through the air like skeins of yarn
sky-diving from our mouths in musical notes

& we, too, robert, are like children, here in this world,
our blood fused within the nexus of history,
flowing within interconnecting musical tongues,
moving us—like this soiled river we are riding over now
is moving us—toward some secret rendezvous
we will discover later on when we get there

2.

what is the real meaning of any journey, mental surfing
through connections of our minds made real when we see
at the end a possibility for redemption,
brought to life by what our eyes pick up along the way, we keep
information vital as blood plumped through the veins, is sacred
as heartbeats drumming through language as life-force,
glue, a synergy, perhaps, of oppositional music,
caught within the ebb & flow of sounds that each hears,
inside the moment, is close enough, as well, to rhythm, waterloo,

is beautiful enough to go there with ears & eyes wide open, too,
as to stand buffeted by a hurricane wind & crow,
"no wind exists anywhere like this but here," but how
would they know, having been nowhere else but here?

3.
nomenclatures of miasmas are sweeping the world,
oxygenating, they become looming specters of prophecy,
synergistic connections to the past,

if we pay attention to what connects us all, robert,
we might more easily move towards a real state of beauty

move into a more blessed state of grace

IN SAINTE-ANNE, GUADELOUPE

for Jacque-Marie Basses and Derek Walcott

we awake to days in august bright with emerald
foliage shimmering around us,

      as if we were living in a lost paradise
somewhere, abundant with wild hummingbirds darting
through extravagant leaves, as orange flamboyance peek,
red hibiscus flowers dance high among the leaves,
as shining palm fronds wave like warrior sword blades
lance through lush, whispering air heavy with heat,
sticky, even in the shade,

      as the ocean's murmuring bric-a-brac
is a low, constant reminder in the distance,
foaming to shore wave after wave terracing in,
one after the other, evokes memories of white pages
being licked open by wind tonguing a book
left in the salt wash (it reminds me of history,
its far-flung journeys piling up here as sand wedge now
between my toes, next to the webbed imprints of birds,
the zigzagging trail of lizards wriggling through
the hieroglyphic ambrosia of amphibious ambivalence,
soaked in amber), just before the whispering goes

still, then, just as quickly, a fresh new breeze startles
with its coolness, licks a soothing tongue
wet across my sweating forehead,
blesses open my eyelids, weighed down now,
with a gathering languor so heavy eye find myself drifting,
as in a dream, toward sleep,
nodding a herky-jerky head dance, imitating a junkie's,
so pronounced at times my noggin reminds of a cork

bobbing above a fisherman's line & hook,
                    after a hungry fish has bitten
& the struggle for survival is on,

eye linger here for a moment, think of the breadfruit
leaves waving in benediction after the wind's blustering
command, rustling groves of mangoes & strawberries
just off the black snake of a road twisting into bouliqui
from sainte-anne, in central guadeloupe

& there, in bouliqui, the hibiscus are pink
buds imitating pursed lips waiting for a kiss,
while above birds lance close heavy air, plunge through amber
filigreed light between the lattice-drop of leaves
as the sun passes behind & over the treetops,
starting its daily descent toward a frigid pacific
a sudden wet breeze startlesmy dreams with its here-
then-gone sweet tongue of my wife's sool breathing,

then, back in sainte-anne, wrrnchd out of my dreams
eye watch dragonflies swim the air
sweating toward twilight, while white butterflies wobble
& float like tiny sacred ghosts between the scarlet, yellow
flamboyance, the emerald leaves holding the hibiscus's
red lips, deep within our own paradise here,
                    at auberge le grande large,

among the lengthening shadows, palm fronds waving
like servants above a giant frog, who seems to be leading
a deafening choir of other toads in a symphonic offering,

eye listen in awe as nature's orchestra boggles my senses
once more with its beautiful perfect pitch & rhythm

A WOMAN IN THE WATER

eye see a woman in the caribbean sea—
water off the beach of sainte-anne,
she is walking with curlers in her nappy hair,
a pink net, a straw hat on top like a crown,
she is black, walking through the sea,
the sun is high in the vaulting blue,
she is humming a beautiful tune,
the sea is clear light green to its sandy bottom,
as some cats' eyes are green, some striking women,
the water is warm as a freshly drawn bath,
the woman's tune is so beautiful
eye want to know the meaning
under the words married to the rhythm
there, inside the song, a feeling of joy
eye hear in her deep voice walking
through the sea there, wearing a red dress,
the water is warm & clear & light green
as a cat's eye, those of a striking woman,
all the way down to their sandy bottom

A KITE ABOVE THE BEACH

coconut leaves shiver, wave, dance, green-golden, stream
like manes of flaxen hair behind galloping racehorses,
high above auberge le grande large, in sainte-anne,
pulsating voices of croaking frogs, buzzing crickets swell below
the gathering darkness, yeasts like bread, just before night falls,
raises a winking, full moon—a one-eyed cat's view—
a cyclops looking at the world, just before lights click on,
headlamps of cars pop bright into view, before twin lanterns
guiding two watchmen on their rounds, a lone, fragile kite trailing
a snaking train of trembling ribbons, flutters skyward, a speckle
above the beach, a hint of uncertainty there, like a young bird
searching for its mother before climbing upward toward curiosity,
riding a lifting *alizé* might climb further than perhaps
its mother taught it to fly, now its ascent hints a fretful hesitation
just being up there, higher than it's ever gone before, suddenly
a gut-wrenching fear of the unknown seems to consume it,
like a beginning swimmer being pulled farther & farther out to sea,
right before a freezing panic sets in, grips him, like now, like this
young bird, this fragile, drifting kite fluttering ever upward
before darkness swallows them with its daunting black magic,
here full of sounds, sea waves washing in hissing & foaming,
voices of people, frogs, & crickets fusing their orchestral miracle
& a full moon up there, in the night sky, staring like a cyclops—
a one-eyed black cat looking down on all this teeming planet

THE MOON IS A LEMON WEDGE

the moon is a lemon wedge over guadeloupe
in the night sky, its likeness swims bold
inside a cold, tall glass of rum & coke
standing on a table, on a white veranda wrapped
around an airy home somewhere around high noon,
on a bright, clear day, somewhere in sainte-anne,
as flamboyance bloom orange, high up,
or low-down in shimmering, lush green leaves,
beneath the sun's wicked eye, in a blue sky paraded by clouds
soft as cotton candy riding over forms of swimmers in emerald
warm caribbean waters, but you are not there
except in your poetic imagination, but here, under this
starlit sky, right now, in all this blooming darkness,
driving the back roads of grande terre, on a clear night
& looming the moon is a lemon wedge suspended
above you, a still life in an artist's paint-splattered room,
a beacon wedge lodged inside a lover's dreaming bloom,
a milky-blind eye of ray charles, or stevie wonder

SOMETIMES IN MONTEBELLO

rain storms come swooping in wearing veils of dancing
mist, come whooshing in over guadeloupe with a switching,
swishing motion of women's skirts when they swing
their wondrous hips, as probing tongues of scandalous winds,
who, if truth be told, are nothing more than peeping gigolos
prancing around, lifting dresses of women with the sweet,
whispering sounds of their breezy tongues, they are lyrical,
these winds, fleet, sometimes, soft as scented talcum
caressing skin with soothing touches, these rains
murmuring secret lullabies rustling through leaves,
bending tips of grass with fingers curling softly around
them as if they were follicles of a lover's hair,

eye watch veils of rain wash over the green body
of a lizard as it darts through luminous grass quick as fear
when it drops down on you & you run lickety-split
into the unknown, suddenly eye become the lizard
running for cover when lightning strikes,
zigzags across a sky gone black as miles davis's skin,
his smile a sliver of moon in the distance where clouds break,
the sea murmuring secrets beneath them now
are foaming waves of histories fish know but will not tell us
until their flopping bodies or still deaths, appear floating before us
bloated, reveal the poison inside their spirits
they could not tell us of when alive, now
they are washed over by cascades of foaming music,
polluted waves sweeping the greed of men, filled with blues
they always forget, just ask george bush, dick cheney,
ask them if they know ajoupa blues coursing through
sad raging eyes of people in iraq, haiti,

ask these men if they know anything other than greed, power,
ask them if they have ever taken time to understand

the beauty of rains sweeping in wearing veils of dancing mist,
fanning out, whooshing across the imagination, the magic
singing in the swishing sounds of a woman's skirt,
those marvelous hips switching back & forth,

just ask dick cheney, george bush, men like these
if they know the deep secrets of a deep, human love,

ask them if they understand the history of blues & rain

THE OLD BLACK MAN WALKING

the old black man walking montebello road,
swinging a rusted machete seems angry
as he chops off heads of flowers,

                             perhaps he's thinking

this flora represents heads of french government officials
he sees oppressing him, black bourgeoisie stand-ins
on the island for the long, machiavellian

                             arm of france,

perhaps he is just a simmering image of anger
now, at everything surrounding him he can't control
in this new world of computers, globalization,

where he doesn't fit it; who knows what triggers
the whys & where-fores, the fire igniting a fuse

EYE AM THINKING OF MOMENTS

eye am thinking of moments when my thoughts run
free as twisting wild vines growing under the sun,
soft rain gathering new puddles around roots,
dew drops of crystal on flower petals, mist swelling
in the air, the sound of language percolating everywhere
music, the hum of creation improvising rhythms,
mysterious as soukougnans shedding human skin,
throwing off light, magic comes when you least expect it,
is a *lewoz* of drums, pippiree birds serenading, colibri eating
bananas, *gwo kas* speaking in seven-rhythms, time, bonda-butts
responding to deep ancestral memories, a dirge
becomes a kite, is a beautiful sight up there flying
free until a strong wind comes, breaks it apart,

like syllables of poems gone wrong, surfers on waves,
the mind miscalculates the power of rhythm,
the deep notion all things have, memories of their own magic,
to change directions, as when volcanoes explode, floods
take back space where fingers of its rivers once ran,
where water first came from, is as mysterious
as why tornadoes, hurricanes swirl across time, space, creating
conditions for their own destructive artistry, heard in the syllables
their winds bring, is a certain clarity inside their own savage beauty,
an indelible music in the ferocious howling gusts of rhythms
screaming frightening secrets throughout their lifetimes,
everywhere either of them passes dreams of men flung
stunned into the air, where they fly like beats of drums,

what do we know of ancient secrets, magic, pippiree birds
singing in the sweet, gathering sounds of evening,
bwa-kabritt crickets, large as small boulders screeching loud
as some scary, imagined zombies flying through the night
to bring us ancient cries predicting rain, sounding mating calls,

they land high up in leafy branches of trees, rooftops,
surrounded by darkness, what do we know, those of us blah-blah,
in violent, industrial cities, living on the run, zooming around
like bats out of hell, or crawling around our steel-encased homes
gridlocked on freeways like shoppers on a sale day at the mall,
or underground in subways smelling of pee, oil, & metal
what do we know of *mofwazés*, soukougnans shedding skin,
throwing off light, pippiree birds singing sweet love
songs of *gwo-ka* drums gathering *lewoz* rhythms,

magic can come when you least expect it, from anywhere,
mysterious as the sources of hurricanes, tornadoes, language
in the air percolates everywhere, music, like mist, suddenly there,
swelling here, blooming fresh as new flowers after soft rain drums
bonda-butts in to the air responding to ancestral memories

climbing from the earth, through the body, like duende
climbing from the earth, through the body, like duende

WE HAVE COME HERE AGAIN

for Margaret & for our friends Maryse, Richard, Luc & Micheline

we have come here again to hear the talking drum of our galvanize
rooftop beaten with hands & feet of falling raindrops
speak to us here, inside rhythms, to listen to choirs of leaves
whispering secrets outside our wide-open windows & doors,
speaking a language bringing the world outside inside to live with us,
is close to paradise on this earth filled with terror,
as a swirling wind sluicing through all openings probes each
& every corner of our little house here, searching like snakeheads,
feverish tongues of heat-stricken lovers circling inside each other's
mouths, right before their twin orgasms explode, together,
right before a gray day turns green in montebello
& hummingbirds preen in whirs of spinning wings, hesitate,
stop in midflight, like tiny helicopters in front of ylang-ylang flowers,
drink the sweet fuel-nectar with nozzle-beaks,
then dart away clean into massive clusters of green leaves,
shadows serving as hiding places ripple under deep cover,

below, eye wait for the sun to break through with laughter,
wait for blue to crack open clouds like a can opener,
to lighten up the sea's lingering gray frown on the water's surface,
wait for the aqua-green palette of waves to be burnished clean & glow
with the sun's clearing focus, so eyes of all of us swimming here
can see through saltwater from top to bottom,
sand shifting gently beneath our feet, from bottom up,
the water soothing my toes, clear as a church bell ringing slow
in sainte-anne's square is lucid on sundays, the air fresh with lemon
smells, mangoes, pregnant with people speaking salt-&-pepper
creole, their breaths laced with scents of ti punch—rum mixed
with sugar, lime, or gingembre—counterpunch each other,
their boxing styles depending on what class or color strata
they're in, a different rhythmic code embedded
inside the tongue's DNA, is a microscopic chip
recognizing, or rejecting tonal shifts, nuances,

so margaret & eye wait here, outside of it all, familiar strangers
as we are inside our own country, friendly ghosts
passing through these moments with people refusing to fuse with us,
or themselves, for that matter, the *other* inside everyone here, too,
always in front of us, as here, or there, it doesn't matter,
though here the moments are still beautiful, calm,
we are inside a wondrous flora, brilliant with lavish colors,
as is this beautiful mix of jambalaya races stirred together,
though beauty is in the eyes of the beholder, here,
as elsewhere, we move through rhythms knowing the key
to tongues swapping spit is love, the passion of language, music,
reaching out to convert ears to listen to sweet, strange
rhythms deep down inside, is familiar as great art is, is a dance
step coming through the night's tongue carrying secrets, love,

is familiar as heartbeats, familiar as drumbeats of rain-
rhythms on rooftops, choirs of leaves whispering ancient secrets
outside windows & doors, clouds riding swift wind currents high
above, threatening or softening throughout the day, like history
when it moves at the churning speed of a gathering hurricane,
or caresses the moment with a licking lover's tongue,
carries a sweet soft beauty some never understand

VI.

WHAT IS IT POETRY SEEKS

what does poetry seek beyond
turning a phrase, or two,
cutting a figure of speech with a word
sharp as a shaver's wish
to rid the face of hair,
                    slicing through the tangle of texts
as a razor blade would lopping off

an ear, a way of hearing,

what is the path pruning takes
in revision when it cuts back unconscious
flows inside language
the way lava flows edit themselves, perhaps
in a manner a tree trimmer goes about
eliminating dead leaves,

on the other hand winds

become a kind of reordering
inside fury of a storm, is a form,
perhaps, like the way a poet rewrites a poem,
a painter re-imagines a canvas,
a musician re-invents a solo,
a politician changing what they meant
right before our disbelieving eyes,

is a constant re-invention

is all of us who daily reshape meaning,
is language always in search of itself,
new ways to express the moment,
                    to create freedom

in an instant, like a bird or a trane moving through
sound in real space, in real time]like miles,
like picasso or al loving
with an eye, a brush, or a splotch of color
re-creating a moment through an image,

a feeling in an instant is a changing of the guard,

eye tell you, metaphor is a way of hearing, seeing
things, being in the moment, in real time,

right here, right now

SWITCHIN' IN THE KITCHEN

after an art show of the same name by Mildred Howard

rhythms be switchin' in kitchens when cooks work magic
through pots, out on dance floors hips gyrate
like poets constructing lines sometimes switch & drop
from proper to colloquial, new days are forever changing color,
weather, voices switch back & forth in the sky,
down here breezes caress bodies, sashay through thoroughfares
inside language, doing whatever flip-flops it has to

to survive, inside music everything matters, a poet steps off
the count syncopating syllables, meters, the voice-music falls
over the edge of a cliff of chromatic scales, shades splash bright clues
as water skedaddling new diamond-drops imitates flushed birds
spraying syllables through showering waterfalls, mist,
skeining language skews, stretches, slips & slides through
space, sounds crack ensconced rapture somewhere here, listen
to these hairsplitting ruptures politicians spew every day
in sad convergences of bad, flat notes,

as time signatures skip-to-my-loo through lace
grace notes bloom in poetic lines, loom posthaste, push
& zing the voices through sound, shimmy-shingle,
juxtapose in place the poet's high-energy gymnastics, highjacked
words switch up in double-backs, pivots, crossovers,
as sky walkers wing word-plays deep beyond boundary lines,
where NBA gunners drop treys, pop cords, create balladic
touché, body-magic up inside rhyme schemes rhapsodic,
their body music reflects light as sprits lance curling through
prismatic flight, oh, tell me about it air jordan, kobe bryant, lebron
james, up there in lights imitating bird, bebop, well
you needn't, because great solos are tracer-bullet flights, sun ra
& coltrane breathing solos as they zoom riding high-priest monk riffs
into any rooms they played, brought high-jinks-magic for poets

to play, eye put a little bloom on this poetic language-tip, riff
diglossic, scatology, piss-zoom in on a neo-logic trip, rapology
dripping words of obfuscation, filo-plumes, orgasmic dolos,
zip through traces of fizz on the rebound of a champagne bliss,
eye telescope hubble inside flues, constantly scope bubbles, link
strings of pearls inside champagne glasses, sans clues,
my attitude fed by gas rises to the top, floats over blown grass,
grows like sassafras, my voice a reverberating echo
inside a memory dome, eye communicate with my mother,
break through the fog of old-age disconnect, eye ask you now, brotha,
where's your boom box, are your false teeth lost in a jar somewhere,
is your ego drowning inside an old piss pot, funky as this sick war
invented by chicken-hawk neo-con bush-wags, rumsfeld

& is this an early morning alarm clock going off for you,
sans hard-on, a wake-up call, a tall drink of confusion,
are you a two-watt on a dimmer-switch belching gas, ignorant as snuff,
a moron looking for conundrum, inside a bait & switch pimp niche,

but don't panic just yet, run out to investigate chromatography,
lapis lazuli, do you think you might need a tad bit of viagra
to get your love-thang juiced out on the dance floor,

as you're listening to an echo-chamber of words, what
was that reverb eye heard glancing off those winged syllables that flew by,
like birds inside a sentence laced with miles & miles of blue history,
stitched with trumpet blasts, obbligatos, obdurate
against past abracadabras, running like doodly squats,
who only drop dimes on the rhythmic line,
while some only drop treys from behind set screens,

which one are you, mr. flip-flop, slow on the crossover,
"switchin' in the kitchen" is what eye mean to do here,

this poem's trying to do a dance on this page with words,

metaphor & reverb, switchin back & forth through rhythm & time
signatures, improvising through space, switchin' up on a dime,
my lines trace words looking for birds winging through dirges
blue as lady day's words on "strange fruit,"

sluicing through language this poem's tracer-bullet tip
tries to put hip bloom on the rapolic verbal trip,
pigology, filo-plumes, fusing words to create a new syntax
with no nonsense from politically correct verbs to slice & dice,
as eye string out a proper poetic sentence, turn them into solos, hello,
my voice shooting through syntax quick as a string of escaping
bunny rabbits looking for a way out of a house of glass,
rising to the top like a linkage of pearl-drop bubbles,

eye jazz sassafras, telescope hubble-constantly

inside the galaxy, eye raise a champagne glass,
offer up razzmatazz, rhythms carving out

meaning inside language, images that might last

VII.

THE ARCHITECTURE OF LANGUAGE

For Allan Kornblum, Carolyn Holbrook, Lois Vosson,
Christopher Janney & Al Loving

I.

the wind swirling through the blueprint of speech,
bare bones of utterances found wrapped there
inside sound, a language, history
    stitching itself together, where bodies wrap themselves up
inside measures, reinvent syllables,
sprout wings, where voices lifted up by spirits
        hurl themselves
            into singing, echoes,

as a man with a drooping handle-bar moustache slaps down
a hard black domino bone-white with stars
embedded in the night of its color,
its shape & form square
      stares up from its hard skin of black ivory,

as another man lights a fire under he said-she said innuendo,
his constant bantering setting up rules of the game,
the way it will play itself out
when the playing field is slanted toward the speaker,
his words controlling the flow

inside the subliminal seduction of sentences,
where language can become anything, mixing words,
mata hari shots of heroin manipulating the brain
during a first sweet moment of celebration,
just when you thought you had pulled everything back together
again, in that first moment of half-light just when you thought
the words you heard singing could possibly become
the very wind you always needed to lift your spirit
up into flight, to hear a music that was always there,

always possible, but somewhere hidden outside
your comprehension, its chords encoded
in mystery but there all the while chasing invention,
magic, now & forever, a breathtaking moment hovering
over shimmering blue water rippling with waves, intensity
& heat, a line of words sizzling with ingredients of jumbalaya,
foo-foo, cooked like a clifford brown solo, was replete,
ingress was possible there through which words could flow
to point a fractured finger of an archipelago out to sea,
to show where the great poetic muse of wind might build
a scaffolding from rhythms, stacked up from word-plays, puns,
jokes, caesuras, enjambments, fused in a burst of language,
flight, in the first cracked moment of daylight,
when the moon has slipped back undercover
& the sun begins to blow out its houngan's breath
of fire tempered by distance, calibrated by a man high up
inside the blue skies of his imagination,
inside the heat of creation, deep in song, a man who could be
you, could be me, could be a woman emitting a high sharp cry
shrill inside a call of divination, worship

beneath these words a street of boiling tar way down deep
stretches out now as a track for this poem
sizzling like a ribbon of asphalt at high noon in phoenix,
burns flesh like lava flows in hawaii

in the dog-day's heat, microwave oven of august,

where fat earthworms fry crisp to black wing tips on pavement
where they pause, looking like detached stingers
of scorpions, replicas of fish-hooking commas arresting words
inside clauses, shaping the ultimate breath of our sentences,
speech oscillates here like winking membranes,
quick as tongues flicking liquid fire down scorched throats,
lye of incendiary words flaming hot as wind-driven forest fires

in california, burning leaves dropping from branches
like faces in nazi ovens, melt from memory,
like days burned from calendars,
as the pages of our lives are numbered here
where we stand up or fall down, ears wagging heads
full of blues inside the sound musicians spawn
inside test tubes today, where our speech becomes
                          hissing snake tongues
outside our heads, words flicking fast as popping sparks
from the snapped off-end of an electrical wire tip,
after a storm dropped its coiled tail into a pool of charged water
& is (yes) like a snake's body (well) shaping itself into an O
or a cowboy's rope looping itself (yes) into another O
                          like the shape of a dead man's mouth
after sucking down or blowing out his last breath
(well, yes) is like a black hole there

in space (another O)

could be an apparition of fakery
could be an apparition of skullduggery
could be an apparition of organic metaphysics
                          political theater
could be an apparition of hiccupping drudgery
could be an demigod of miasmas, holocausts
could be a holy shaman leading to song
& is its own particular kind of passageway to language
filling up the blooming opening of that place
with its own music, its own kind of mysterious magic, a space,
a language filled with ambiguities of silence,
sound buried deep there like light during midnight hours,

a paradox silence, as in death there is always
the living breath lurking somewhere in a song

2.

sometimes new language is a storm dropping songs
suddenly from some secret place high up
inside a swirling system of weather—
itself an ever-changing code of utterances—
it communicates the alchemy of nature when it appears
assembled by God's mad architects of sound
it explodes new rhythms out into the open in a whirling,
cacophony of calamitous syllables
full of mysterious soundscapes, lightning bolts shattering
the moment, unzipping dark clouds clothing the sky,
rips it into veined fissures of an old woman's legs,
reveals an elephant trunk of spinning winds howling
in the half-light as it drops down, it evokes in me
moaning voices of ancestors thrown overboard
during the middle passage,

it is a scaffolding of tongues we hear crisscrossed
with different rhythms & cadences, meters,
forms from which newly found structures of poetry are created,
we hear birthed & sprung into the air there fresh music
mimicking today's speech, mirroring thirsty syncopation, sound
cross-thatched with distinctive cultural DNA seduces voice
through poetic architectonics of lingua franca,
architraves of crossbeam sentences lay themselves
floor by floor, build new structures of language that speak
to us, intersecting at crossroads everywhere

3.

kind of blue in green miles music sings to us
inside the ether flow, sounds as alphabets blow mean
solos high above cumuli, a language of silent dreams
flows through darkness with speed & longing, embraces
light spreading across a pregnant sky, through cracked lips
of morning, a voice heard imitating a flute

where clouds bloom their heads like pop-up ghosts,
yeast through long segues between black & blue intervals,
down below, blowflies torch another pregnant pause,
deepen the space between ahmad jamal & clueless doodoos,
between "lady day" & test-tube imitators
the memory chip of voice richness is lost somewhere in between
the two, replaced by marketing frenzy
because of cleavage & greed, eye ask what greatness is lost here,
what should we remember when speaking of imitation
in the name of song, comparing it to the real thing,
                                        what made american music great
was not physical beauty enhanced by breasts bouncing through air,
not platinum/gold teeth flashing, doo-rags,
but pure voice/genius making music in blues, jazz, country
& western, rock 'n' roll, gospel, rhythm 'n' blues, bluegrass,
rap, classical, all beautiful when deep richness is there,

tradition is innovated deep in the grain, beyond image,
beyond the cloning sameness of musak,

is a language communicating with people everywhere
intersecting at crossroads throughout the world,

4.
at 116th street & 7th avenue in harlem,
english mixes with french & wolof, pops
like senegalese talking drums, impregnates bootylicious air
with rap-rhythmic speech scatting out on the streets
where new voices mack the juba-rattle of flying hands down,
slap tightly strung skins, mix jambalaya riffs into flow
caca flow inside rhapsodic rapology,
clock new inventions scratched across grooved tongues
spinning & springing from vinyl,

bodies break-dancing across airwaves like syllables

track trends coast to coast, cross international boundaries, rap
new-wave crack language-beats, seduce hearts & cultures
as architectonic magic fuses clues inside colloquial rhythms,
harp everyday popular speech, everywhere bringing the news
as everything is changing in this very moment,
everything is changing everywhere poetry grows
word by word, sound by sound, form by form, cadence by cadence,
mack by mack, wordplays sluicing under the syllables
stitching evolving language into innovative soundtracks,
found in the very air we breathe every day

everywhere, everything is changing

5.

each new day begins with the sun rising after night
swooped down with a black cape full of stars
& moonlight shining like diamonds left in the afterglow,
but it all passes, is cyclic, things change again & again
like poetry, it's normal the way the world reorders itself
time & again the highs become lows, systems
destroy themselves, it is the nature of things,

when night becomes day moments are viewed, flashed
in & through a different light

                                    architectural structures are altered,
their language full of shifting metaphors in the slinking
half-light, new rhythms replace old ones,
music is syncopated with improvisational modes, moto-flows
push aside goose-stepping syllabic metronomes
stomping through time & space on white pages, in speech
when spoken in entombed air it echoes,
sometimes fractures inside the ear,

surprise happens every day, different colors mix
inside speech, a jambalaya-paella fused speech complete
with fruits of the sea, clacking chickens, stomach sounds

full of rice & bean palava feijoada gumbo speak,
it is the natural way to create new cuisine, poetry, music,

mooing cows, woo-wooing owls, lyrical birds, the winds
natural syllables rolling from fluted mouths in spring, summer,
whispered softly as a lyrical caressing breath seductive
as a lover's sweet undulating tongue,

they enter the world, become a new way of hearing/speaking,
everything changes, the way we hear
sounds we never heard, never paid attention to,
everything changes, the way we hear,
see & know things from different angles,

                                    everything changes,

                        like new architecture rising into the blue

as glass & steel fingers pointing up to where
religion swears God is—is the Spirit really there?—
                                everything changes,

it is normal to be afraid of the unknown,

normal as cracked mirrors throwing back changes our faces see
every day we look into them as we grow older
                                everything changes,

day changes to night the sun replaces the moon
it is normal the way our world turns every day
on its axis like a roulette wheel spinning
our lives, our fates locked in the luck of the draw,
the spoke-gears driving the wheels of a speeding car
losing control on a black highway slick with ice,
the throw of the dice at a gambling table
is what this poem seeks to express through voice

6.

the pure voice is heard best in solitude, silence, like when
eye watch a small crab enter a dark hole
in damp mud in deshaies, guadeloupe, at taino village
cottages looking over the beach & waves of a blue-green
caribbean sea, later in the distance *gwo ka*
drummers crack night's stillness with rhythmic genius, machete
chops of their flying-hands slap tightly drawn skins, track sounds
seldom heard in america, their voices
mixing with brilliant orchestral scores of crickets
improvising with voices of tiny frogs, wind-tongue speaks
wet with salt off the caribbean as bats dive low through trees,
the droning threat of a humming dengue mosquito
can be heard, poised to strike, suck blood from me
equal to its own weight, but eye smash the threat
before it becomes real, leaving a mangled
blood-spot trembling on my skin,

when day breaks again the miracle of deshaies rises,
black humming birds stop on a dime in flight
drink nectar from a flower, their beating wings a blur,
transcendent choirs of birds serenade in this place
wondrous as ladera resort between the pitons

        in st. lucia to the south,

as the sun sets in the west, darkness swoops down again
an ancient shaman unfurling a black cape of mystery
full of diamonds we call moon & stars, bats dive
here again slicing through shadowed latticework of leaves
like fighter jets, they give off weird shrill cries,
it is a kind of poetry, a different music
my ears adjust to listening for its rhythms,
alert for any surprises bat voices might bring

7.

with their music rhythms structure, idioms slip through air
into fragments of speech in flight throughout the world,
light up the night inside refracted air,
organize themselves from improvisation into sentences,
sluice through our ears like laser beams, musical
chords & notes chewed off spitting syllables
shot like bullets from young mouths to explode inside our ears,
shape breath through songs of griots, the lives of people
whose voices build block by block from call & response
antiphonal neologic constructs,
like sunday morning preacher's throwing down hoodoo
                  architectonic-juju, DNA inventions boogalooing,
shaping the gospel, those churchified hallelujahs, mixing
boogie-woogie doodoo sounds cruising through street cadences,
rolling off soothsayer's blistered tongues,
as light glances off their platinum/gold teeth—razor blades?—
like sun rays bouncing off insect-looking mirrored windows squared
in sleek skyscrapers stabbing through polluted air like stilettos
throughout mestizo cities of the post-modern globe,

everywhere this architectonic-juju creates new metaphors
inside musical sounds blending fresh articulations, mix
moto-cell phones ringing in bathrooms, showers,
hang from their own hooks
                            voices entering the digital age,
sashay through a maze of computers,
download into iPods hip-hopping the globe,

this poem articulate a language seldom heard
in the mummified academies filled with tweedy gatekeepers,
tight-mouthed rejection stretched across their wire-thin lips,
                      unable to hear wondrous music
swelling through the air, unable to dance in celebration,
their bones refusing all movement,

unable to recognize any language other than their own
metallic goose-stepping military rigor, their flat-footed sentences
straight as lines on EKG screens

no mellifluous magic, no syncopation, no surprise,
there, no improvisation,
but close-minded poetry mirroring ethnophobia,
decrepit with deep fear

& claustrophobia replacing light

8.
this poem calls for a poetry of openness in america, now,
where voices skedaddle through time & space,
signatures riffing, creating on the margins,
screeching like cats at a cutting session, out on a fence,
like bird & monk up at minton's in harlem,
playing music like they owned it, like mahalia jackson,
leontyne price, willie nelson, johnny cash, chuck berry, aretha
franklin, the beatles, los lobos, u2, & bono,

like voices of whitman, paz, neruda, márquez, hughes,
walcott, baraka, brooks, ellison, shange, rich, césaire, or cruz
(riffing on the language we hear in our hearts & ears
is a new way of hearing & listening)

the american voice is not white or black, european or asian,
middle eastern or african, but mestizo, fused with jambalaya
palava feijoada gumbo, it speaks a musical language
bewitching our ears with what grows from a collective linguistic
flow, is a fusion of new syllabic magic rolling off the tongue
in a mélange of rhythmic sounds,
like la cucaracha is more syncopated than roach or bug,
(means the same thing, but is a dancing word
full of power)—can you say, la cucaracha!
can you hear power in language flow as beautiful, spiritual,

the pulse of being in the moment instead of the past,
on time instead of behind time,
feeling the breath of wind in your face can last
as it happens, like music tracking heartbeats pumping
in your own chest right now is a flow

9.
great language is a shower of words inside a blizzard
of tongues full of rhythms & syllables, is a flow,
is snowstorms of meaning coming & going everywhere our ears
turn, hear rainstorms, tornadoes, lightning bolts unzipping clouds
towering around the calm, savage eye of hurricanes, is a flow
coming & going, bringing new systems of music,
new ways of listening connected to hearing,
structures carrying a host of evolving languages, roiling tongues
inside cross-fertilized speech of immigrants & new poetry,
is a flow also located in the evil eye of katrina, rita
swirling in from the gulf of mexico carrying thunder & death,
foaming with cataclysmic omens, terrors beyond any understanding,
categories beyond any knowing what horror will bring

through cracks of daylight destruction unfolding, rancid bodies
bloated, floating in toxic water, is a language, is a flow
                                  we hear but do not know how to recognize

thirty-foot storm surges speaking in tongues more violent
than any language we think we hear or know,

is a flow disjunctive beyond any application of money,
is perhaps a cosmic spiritual payback
for bug-eyed children who mirror the language of hunger,
murder, no sympathy, or empathy for blues people festering
in a place full of heat, water, mosquitoes, poisonous snakes,
high prices for gasoline for cars thirsty for petro, is a flow
of anarchy spreading like a plague in this place, is a form of language
ignited by category-five winds & angry seawater foaming salt

& screaming in the voodoo language of the sea goddess, erzulie,
houngans blowing calamities ashore through their mouths
of long bamboo horns, is perhaps a payback
for all the terrors released in this flow

when coffins, mummified corpses, leering skeletal bones
unearthed by katrina's savage flooding tongue
are scattered like dead leaves & broken branches all over
louisiana's devastated countryside, it tracks the fall posthaste
of america's once promise of greatness,
lost here in this macabre jumble of unknown spirits
evicted from their graves with no names, identity,
no race-ticket or skin color has privilege in this space
of spirits displaced, scattered from former resting places
of chipped tombstones—also scattered—
their skulls reminding us of broken teeth of ex-fighters, junkies,
these corpses grinning teeth set in jaws of cracked bone,

is a powerful language screaming for redemption,
if we look deeply into this moment it reveals our true selves
in these spaces we live in corrupted by greed,
skin color, class, religion, power at all cost,
                                    is a definite language
suffocating in claustrophobia, ethnophobia, no connection
to the real world, to the flow (caca) flow of humane language,
poetry inside the most profound beauty of utterance
sings still inside the deepest grain of that flowering word,

sound by sound, word by word, speech evolves into beautiful
architecture, creates a scaffolding of cross-fertilized utterances
crossbeamed inside poetic sentences fused with music,
where metaphors spring from deepest sources of community,

these are the seeds that will link, bond us together

10.

after tongues of fierce winds howl full of calamitous journeys,
ship-wrecked adventures swept astray by circular history,
where are we going feeble question marks of human embryos
bloating after the wind's anger has died down, turned soft & gentle
as a sweet tongue of breeze caressing the passion of naked lovers,
where are we going led by troglodytes in dark suits selling wolf
tickets, tiny metal american flags festooning their lapels,
violent little chicken-hawk men in seats of power,

where are we going re-running all this bric-a-brac fear of hitler's,
germany, murmuring a language full of evil secrets, murder,
mysterious as the ocean's salty sandpaper tongue of screeching
felines carrying sounds evoking warnings,
where are we going on this stormy sea full of huge treacherous rocks,
100-foot waves looming toss our premonitions like match sticks,
thunderclaps of vowels flooding the peaceful conversations
we try to evoke within a spiritual connection,
where are we going carrying this toxic speech full of static
buzzing like hornets or flies through this pestilential
space where we live out our lives full of fear,
trepidation, & hateful loathing,
where are we going on this stormy sea,
heading into a space full of huge sharp rocks,
behind time instead of on time,

where are we going, going, going

11.

thunderclaps of vowels, raging rivers flooding
conversations, carrying languages, coming & going,
as the wind blows a mango out of a tree it speaks, too,
the moment it hits the ground, in the future there will be
new sounds when buzzing flies start feasting on
the mango's sweet nectar as its flesh rots away,

sinks into a swarm of feverish maggots,
is a kind of language whispering close to silence,

speaking inside this moment, it marks an instant
inside time, like musicians or poets riding the rhythms of wind,
the ocean's improvisational breath of misty saltwater, now
catapulting a fish into the sky, locks us into the moment,

as does the bootylicious murmur of a woman's taut flesh
rubbing bodaciously up against silk, evokes sin-
ful dreams in men & women eye know—a politically incorrect
thought eye know, though true in the track of reality flow—
is seductive as kisses tonguing inside passion sweetly,
sucking sounds flowering inside locked mouths
as she pulls you deep into the volcano of her song,
bodies moving instinctively now, poetically, mysteriously,
bodies come alive in the moment—on time, not behind—

as when poetry is poured into language, great sounds of music
scaffolding up buildings, architraves of syllables
hanging off edges of pursed lips, like dripping notes there,
can be heard building into an improvised cadenza as it flourishes
when sound is thrust into the sky as a inventive idea,
is like a wondrous sleek building—an eagle soaring above it—

architecture can create memorable language up there
pointing fingers up toward where religion swears God is,

where we know the spirit of great poetry sings & lives

from

ERRANÇITIES

(COFFEE HOUSE PRESS, 2012)

I.

AN ART OF LOST FAITH

for Robert Farris Thompson, Maya Deren, & Ishmael Reed

1. BEGINNINGS: A PLACE OF SILENCE

in a place beyond our knowing silence reigns, darkness
perhaps some light, echoes, in this vast space,
perhaps it is a netherworld, an etherworld of maybe,
if spirits amongst us know what *It* is they have never spoken,
perhaps shadows have, over/underground in some invisible space,
surrounded by air, water, where spirits of creation exist,
swimming or zooming outside our comprehension,
a place where only imagination through prayer can take us,
to a road, perhaps a passageway stretching long & far,
deep into the past, perhaps, a doorway leading to nowhere,
nobody knows, only silence knows the language echoes speak
& in this vast place beyond our knowing, are bones, teeth, hair,
ribcages, skulls, toes, fingers here, are maggots here, too,
do they speak some kind of music in this beyond world,
do they understand silence, the twilight world of myth, the memory
of water, earth, sky, wind, the memory of fire, earthquakes, thunder,
the memory of storms, lightning, ice, the memory of creation,
birth, death, the memory of everything here & gone, everywhere
a mystery, is what we know is certain, an idea of something
without shape or form, pulsating with what we know is power,
It is a metaphysical presence, a blessing with what we know
is the ability to heal & destroy this space we live in
only by *Its* invitation, sanction, only by *Its* blessing,
this place we've been born into with so much amnesia

2. LOOKING THROUGH THE MIST TOWARD AFRICA

in the beginning was a sound, a crack of light, fissure in the dark
dome of the sky, earth, from which a resonance of air echoed,
perhaps something like a note, a sudden sound,
or wind moving toward expression, a beginning, a seed of language,
perhaps a hum, a grunt moving toward something clearer, perhaps

a voice, which became visible later, as a stroke of whatever was needed
at the time, some kind of music beating like a heart
in time with a first act of gesture, imitating a shaking
in the ground, something close to a rhythm,
a grain of language, something like a word, perhaps a growl, something
the ears of earth, air & sky might hear & know what was coming was
a kind of improvisation, a phenomenal act of creation,
perhaps shadows in a garden, under what we know now are iroko trees,
moving the way humans would, fusing memories, music
in a beautiful rhythm, undulating, coming together,
moving apart, in an act of expression we know as joy,
perhaps love, a feeling of ecstasy, an act of vital conception,
invention, making, in fact, an act of copulation
in the holy Yoruba city of *Ile-Ife,* where Olorun, god of all things Yoruba,
(*the* vital force, neither male or female, the ultimate embodiment of *ashe,*
spiritual command, the power-to-make-things-happen)
slithered down from the sky in the form of a royal python snake,
bringing with it *Eshu, Ogun, Yemoja, Oshun, Oshoosi,*
Obaluaiye, Shango, Obatala, Oko, Egungun, bringing
the power to give life, take life away, *ashé, ashé, ashé,*
as an earthworm, white snail, woodpecker, gaboon viper,
ashé represented by iron staffs, long-beaked birds, iron sculptures
of serpents in the form of kings, chiefs, wise old women
coming in the form of birds, sacred beads on the crowns of kings
hanging from their masks, covering their faces during moments of prophecy,
ritualized during times of possession, *ashé*
in these forces watching us through spiritual eyes,
with the power to give life, take life away, *ashé*
on an old ceramic bowl, *It* is the thunder of Shango,
a meandering patterns of pythons, gaboon vipers twisting through sand,
lightning zigzagging through space, unzipping the black bowl of the sky
above an iroko tree, its trunk tied with white cloth as an offering,
semen at its base, drops of blood sprinkled around too,
is a gift to the gods, as a person dressed in red is *ashé*

then everything was lost in sandstorms of confusion, tribal rivalries,
blood spilling reduced to ashes civilizations of prophecy,
divinations began to lose images of faith after Europeans arrived
with greed in their eyes, storming off ships with guns spitting fire,
carried away priests, their faith, across the middle-passage, to the New World,
though these chained holy men still whispered under their breath the holy word
ashé, ashé, ashé, the rhythms of talking drums held tight in memory
on wide seas, in the sky lightning flashed, kaboom, gunfire, *ashé*
then silence

3. THE NEW WORLD

many priests died during the middle-passage, shot, whipped dead,
their bodies thrown to sharks in the roiling salt water,
when survivors arrived in the New World *ashé* was a memory
under their breaths, the tempo of talking drums transformed to something new
though it kept old roots beating close to the rhythm of hearts. Gods changed, too,
transformed through language African prayer fused with Native American Indian,
Frenchh & Spanish ones, too, *ashé* grew new animating forces,
loas, houngans—priests—stirred the pot, rediscovered powers over the soul
spirit, self, bloomed as new voodoo avatars anchored in old ways though
transformed here into new ways of bringing spirits down,
in this New World all manner of tribes, races, metamorphosed into creole
culture—languages, faiths, music—old drum rhythms innovated new accents,
added them to ancient measures, fused into newfangled tempos,
married fresh New World time-signatures—Congo rhythms became Petro beats,
music/dance of Rara, compas, Rada songs from Dahomey—
visual arts were expressed through shimmering voodoo flags holding mirrors
reflecting souls in lakes of glass—whispering poetic rituals of *ashé*
married Catholic, indigenous Native American Indian religious mantras,
the dead began serving the living, ritual became reclamation of the soul,
everything was transformed as night sounds cooed, undulating
sweetness found in mangoes, papayas, red flesh of watermelons
unlocked primal mysteries as hurricanes howled & swirled,
vèvès invoked *loas,* retainers f the vital force, mireacle fireflies
of spiritual command, the power-to-make-things-happen,

bestow life & take life away through possession,
black seeds of language loomed in the fresh silence

4. SOLO

eye have come to this text to sing the gospel of Neo-Hoodoo
the rediscoery of self in this new, cruel whirl
of dilettantes seeking greed through senseless wars, who machine
gun down any spirot who can dance words across empty white pages
who refuse to recognize any culture save their own as a vital force
in the world, who speak with forked tongues,
who think they know everything when their hisitory is so short
& bloody, charlatans who raze the world with bombs, spitting bullets,
whose religion is greed, who cannot hear wisdom or music,
whose time is finally short, whose storehouse of stolen ideas is empty,
whose ragtag culture of hobos went up in flames like so much in the West,

many of us are here now, have been transformed through memory of *ashé*,
its drum rhythms synonymous with our own beating hearts,
we know the lost faith—now recovered—as our own vital force, its syncopations
reborn in *Voodoo/Santeria/Candomble/Neo-Hoodoo* in the New World,
we got High John the Conqueror in lines of our poetry, got mojo hands
guiding brushstrokes of our paintings, Papa Ogun in our sculpture,
Yoruba/Petro rhythms infusing blues, spirituals, ragtime, gospel, jazz,
merengue, salsa, rhythm 'n blues, rhumba, tango, zouk,
soul, rock 'n roll & rap, we move our feet & bodies to dance
entranced with recovered rhythms of a lost faith, infused here
in art of a New World expression probing deep,
it connects us to an ancestral faith we embrace here as our own
magic, mystery, power, grace, expressed through our hearts
as an ever-evolving, powerful Neo-Hoodoo expression, voiced through priests
like james brown, sly stone, miles davis, jimi hendrix, charlie parker,
thelonious monk & marie laveau, voiced through every man, woman
viewing themselves as sacred innovators, improvisers of the spiritual body dance,
the art of lost faith is not lost when reinterpreted, is everything
griots & shamans know to be real on earth, surrounded by air,

phenomenological, Voodoo transformed to Neo-Hoodoo here,
transplanted in the New World space with magic, faith of the Old World,
American fusion is iconography rooted in the new/old transmogrification,
a logo for America, perhaps, a pathway to a future of the new, Neo-
Hoodoo, perhaps found through the words, *ashé, ashé, ashé,*
is perhaps a fresh, innovative life-force gathering in the air

LAS CRUCES, NEW MEXICO REVISITED*

for Keith Wilson, Donna Epps Ramsey, Andrew Wall, Charles Thomas,
& Thomas Hocksema

I.

you have come to this space of light & pure beauty
from the love-song tongues of ancestors ringing
you have risen from an earth soaked in human blood
animal blood bird blood fish blood slicking polluted water
singing the gospel you have bloomed like a desert flower
under the cross of crucifixion your pain deep as poetry
river deep pure as love flowing back to jordan
blood-holy from africa you have come reborn to us
with the spirit of healing, you cleanse us now
baptize us in clear water of your sun-warm words
& you have carried the holy flame of god through stone rain
kept it burning like a candle in the church of your heart
& you have kept the faith with your holy gods with jesus
with malcolm with martin luther king in everyman
& you have come wearing the mantle of adam
your own sermon on the mount in your own throat
O gentle native man luminous with tenderness,
your commitment, your faith in love is so very holy beautiful
as the spirit of ancestors tonguing through your blood
their pain veining river-deep through your gospel of holy feathers
your sacred text of healing deep singing in your sacred mountains
your sermons bringing us here to this clear sweetness of place
to this space this moment where you are light & beauty
your words drum-scripts we listen to, see in your dance steps
carried in hearts throughout the world where you live

---

* When I was putting together my work for *Skulls along the River* (I. Reed Books, 1984), I discovered that I had lost the first part of this poem. But I liked what I had at the time and decided to include it in the book. When Coffee House Press published *Transcircularities: New and Selected Poems* in 2002, I did a little re-writing and included the revised version. Finally, on September 21, 2009, I found the original text of *Las Cruces, New Mexico*, with the original "part one," added it to the rest of the text, and then revisited and revised the entire poem to make it into a single new piece, published here at last.

2.

eye have come here to these sacred great mesas, high up above
las cruces to sit meditate on these mesas flat as vegas gambling tables
rock-hard as red dust swirls into miniature tornadoes
dancing down roads red with silence silent as the faces of solitary
indians here where white men quick-tricked
their way to power with hidden agendas
of bullets & schemes of false treaties
& black men alone here in this stark high place of mesquite
bushes white sand mountains colors snapped in incredible
beauty eyes walking down vivid sunsets livid purple scars slashing
volcanic rock tomahawking language scalping this ruptured space
of forgotten teepees so eye listen to a coyote wind
howling & yapping across the cactused dry high vistas
kicking up skirts of red dirt at the rear end of quiet houses
squatting like dark frogs & crows etched silhouettes high on live
wires popping speech caw-cawing in the sand-blasted wind
stroked trees caw-cawing all over the mesilla valley

& here along the rio grande river dry parched tongue bed snaking
mud cracked & dammed north in the throat of albuquerque
mescalara zuni apache & navaho live here
scratch out their fire-water breath peyote
secret eyes roaming up & down these gaming-table mesas
their memories dragging chains through these red breathing streets
while geronimo's raging ghost haunts their lives with what
they did not do stretching this death strewn history back
to promises & hope a hole in the sky a red omen moon
where death ran through like water whirl pooling down a sink
& this shaman moon blown here a red target of light at the end
of a tunnel of blackness where a train speeds through now
towing breakneck flights of light, where daybreak sits wrapped
like a blanket around a quiet ancient navaho wrapped in american colors
who sits meditating these scorched white sands flat distant high mesas
shaped like royal "basotho hats" chili peppers churls
pecan groves roadrunner chaparral birds salt cedars sprouting

parasitic along bone-white ditches bordering riverbeds thirsting for water
meditates these wide flat black lava rocks holding strange imprints
of fossilized speech that died before it knew what hit it
as did those silent clay-faced ancestors of this solitary navaho sitting here
wrapped in breaking colors bursting sunlight meditating the lay
of this enchanting blues land changing its face every mile or so

& in their faces indians carry the sadness of ancestors
who wished they had listened to those long gone
flaming words—battlecries!—of geronimo whose screaming ghost
prowls these bloody muddy streets baked dry now by the flaming eye
torching the sky wished they had listened instead of chaining
his message in these coyote howling winds kicking up skirts of dirt
whose language yaps like toothless old men & women
at the rear end of quiet houses whose lights dance slack
at midnight grow black & silent as death's worn-out breath
beneath these pipe-organ mountains bishop's peaked caps
holding incredible silence here in the mesilla valley,
where the rio grande river runs dry
its thirsty spirit dammed north in the throat of albuquerque
at the crossroads of fusion & silence, in the red gush swirls

whispering litanies sawblading through ribcages, dust memories—
snaking winds tonguing over the mesilla valley brings back
long-gone words of geronimo haunting las cruces, new mexico,
long-gone wind whispering geronimo geronimo geronimo

WHERE HAVE THEY ALL GONE

for Ojenke, Eric Priestley, & K. Curtis Lyle

where have they all gone to, those exuberant edgy misfits,
those glorious madcap poets of precise inexactitude,
those lunatic purveyors of transcendental flights through space,
verbal high jinks sky walkers of jazzified hyperbolic scatology,
rhapsodic sleepwalkers selling screaming jay hawkins wolf tickets,
echoing skull & bone dances of dahomey voodoo smack downs,
emanating from beyond watery graves of middle passage,
from the genocide of millions

all the spiritual six-fingered witch doctors brewing up revenge
secreted deep in hidden holes of linguistic thoroughfares,
those sacred red-robed wilt chamberlain maasai spiritual hunters,
who chase hunters of lions running free around ngorongoro, tanzania,

eye say, where have all the stork-legged soothsayer space cadets
traveled to, disciples of sun ra's bamboozling cloudbursts of words,
those smoke signal purveyors of mojo language hypnotized
through music,

those schizophrenic soothsayers practicing loop-de-loop tom-toms,
rhythmic scavengers of esoteric metaphors stitched throughout
knuckleheaded sentences, illuminated by yardbird parker
excursions through solos exploring outer limits of scatological space,
thelonious monk comping along as acoustical solar sidekick,
riffin' off only he knows what "mysterioso" piano licks,

where have they all gone to, those insane rollerblade skaters
decked out in silver asbestos suits & caps, wraparound shades,
zooming, weaving through manhattan traffic like lone ranger silver
bullets, those slingshot word magicians, loup-garou wordsmiths
shooting out rhythms hidden deep in thickets of reared-back cobra
tongues, who flick out hypnotic spells, undulating spellbinding

tempos at seductive dances, where beautiful full breasts
bob up & down like ripe melons, seducing like honey,
lips dripping with sweet lusting desire, licking, sucking kisses,
tongues probing mouths when passion sweeps down overwhelming
the senses, as when in cunnilingus her body trembles, explodes,

where has pamela donegan gone to with her deep-loving-holy
gripping-sweet-seductive-suction-cup that caused men to howl anytime
they came with her, like mad wolves celebrating the moon,
where has leumas sirrah (samuel harris spelled backwards)
disappeared to, who sat upon rooftops all over watts sniffing glue,
talking shit to the sun & writing incomprehensible beautiful poetry,
what about stilt-legged, tall & skinny, midnight-blue emory evans,
from north carolina, who walked around watts wearing a long,
navy-blue wool overcoat in 95 degree weather,
wore high-top, black tennis shoes & wrote love poems to ants
& broken-winged birds & everything that moved or didn't move,
where have clyde mays & cleveland sims gone to
with their criminal schemes & quixotic over-the-top poems,

as our lives unfold, switch, turn with cycles of sun & moon,
seconds turn into minutes into hours into days into years,
people, scenes, events, time becomes history erased from memory
if not recorded, written down (even then some fall through
cracks or holes in narratives, fall victim to amnesia, or even worse—
alzheimer's, where memory falls down into a black hole, is erased—

so where have all those exuberant, edgy misfits gone,
those glorious madcap poets of precise inexactitude, lunatic
purveyors of transcendental flights through space, verbal high jinks
sky walkers of jazzified hyperbolic scatology, grace,
rhapsodic sleepwalkers selling screaming jay hawkins wolf tickets,
echoing skull & bone dances of dahomey voodoo smack downs,
emanating from beyond watery graves of middle passage, space,

where have all the spiritual six-fingered witch doctors gone
whose spirits could not be locked up in a jar, or even poetry,
have they all gone to chasing erranceties, errançities,
the sun, moon & stars inside their heads even underground?

II.

AFTER SEEING AN IMAGE IN ASHLAND, OREGON

a full moon stares like a one-eyed panther's surprised
good eye, bright over ashland, oregon,

                                    hangs in space
a gleaming silver dollar
                  stamped into the skin of midnight
                                    & is a hole
punched clear through to the other side of dreaming,
where light is pulsating energy,
wide open as surprise, a flashlight beaming
one ray brighter than faith, is a reflection of what
we see hanging there,
        complete in this moment,

                        the twin good eye opposite a blind one,

veiled in darkness black as othello's human though
demon dream, struggling to cut loose all that anchoring baggage
connected to skin-tone, all these weighted syllables

words serve as glue to bond narratives
stitched with flawed images, metaphors filling history,
as its narrative stumbles forward stereo loud
as those false coon-shows typically slurping
devouring good-old sweet watermelons, red-lipped

& scratching on white, manicured, suburban lawns

ON A SUNDAY

eye remember seeing the oblong fruit—mango,
papaya—in a photo of a lynched black man's

head fixed above the exclamation point of his tad-
pole body swaying easily in a gentle

breeze, it is summer in my memory, warm,
not yet sweltering in southern steel country

alabama, outside birmingham, where
john coltrane blew hauntingly of four little black girls

blown to smithereens on a Sunday, in church,
eye also remember hearing chuck berry playing guitar

on a sunday, in the back seat of his white cadillac car—
driven by his red-haired black wife, cruising st. louis

blues streets, singing, "roll over beethoven,
tell tchaikovsky the news, there's a new kind

of music called rhythm 'n blues," on that sunday
the sky was blue as it was in my memory—

where all things are elusively fixed
because nothing is ever permanent save change—

cobalt blue, sapphire blue, cerulean blue
when eye saw the lynched black man's head in the photograph

oblique above the exclamation point of his tadpole body,
it was a sapphire blue sunday in the deep freeze

of january, when barack obama
took the oath of office, became the forty-fourth

president of this divided nation in crisis,
the voices of reason thrown out the window

like bath-water & soap in a small infant's tub,
the bawling baby hitting the ground, breath atomized

as the vaporizing suds, mistedd into the air in a fog
like an elegy, a sunday's listening to punditry talking—

points hit the fan on TV screens, their elegies
leering all over the planet, richly paid for drivel

their infested dialogue, their blather like plagues,
prattling disinformation, sluiced through airwaves,

zapping clueless people inside side their atomized brains,
glued as they are, to these talking heads flashing

expensive dental-ware as they natter their shopworn
rhetoric into cameras, connecting us to them

through plasma TV tubes, on glory bird sundays
& the blues as a way of life everywhere, even on sundays

when all things are elusively fixed, even words of sermons,
because nothng is ever permanent save change,

the sky sometimes blue as a sapphire woman
wearing red, her hips moving from side to side, beckoning

with her sensuous, sashaying hips, come-to-me-poppa-strut,
seducing where the gospel of sweetness is elusively fixed

inside a church, a juke joint, the music hot as her allure,
hittin' it, layin' the mojo down, conjurin' up wicked

spirits, as poets raising the roof from its foundation up
into cerulean-blue, sapphire-blue, cobalt-blue air,

preachers running the gospel down on Sundays with their
sermons everywhere, people living inside their memories,

where all things are elusively fixed, but here
noting is ever permanent save change after change

nothing is ever permanent save change

MIX-Y-UPPY MEMORY

eye got on the uptown c train traveling north to harlem,
the day was beautiful up-top over ground, down here
on the subway eye pass a funky black man swaddled in rags
sitting in the car where eye choose to rest my tropical spirit
filled with dreams of mangoes, papayas, the sweet space
my wife's delectable essence holds in my feelings, eye am
at ease moving in this mix-y-uppy place, chaotic beauty

present all around me every day in new york city, quixotic
truths, moral dilemmas arriving as gordian knots, conundrums
deep inside meandering twists & turns map octopus traps filled
with tentacles inside our lives carrying paradoxical images, metaphors
weaving through labyrinthine spider-webs, crisscrossing intelligence
within moments of dreaming, sweetness, evoke poetry,
as here & now inside the prison cell of this speeding subway car,

when eye see the funky black man swaddled in rags moving slowly
in my direction, now he sits in front of me, leering brown caveman teeth,
he is very, very funky, his smell of decaying flesh wakes me up quickly
from dreaming of poetry surrounded by mangoes, papayas,
the sweetness emanating from thinking of my wife's delectable essence,
my mindset re-focuses now on this mad-max apparition hovering
in front of me, mirroring the chaotic random beauty suddenly

anywhere you might be in new york city, errançities mix-y-up-ping
in space with restless, wandering impulses—like my mind deriving information
from everywhere, from within itself—eye focus in on this man facing me now
blooming with rot as he drops his pants, exposes his shriveled private parts,
suddenly eye lose control of my hard-won discipline, blow a gasket,
leap up like a panther, confront him, he flinches, pulls up his pants, begs off,
trembling, obsequious now, his eyes pleading drop from mine,

eye tell him to get off the train at the next stop, he gets up shuffling,
dragging the shadow of a decayed spirit behind him he moves toward the door,

leaving me a blooming odor of a fly-blanketed garbage dump, eye yo-yo back
to the moment before his shock almost froze my liquid creativity, questioned
my fluidity in this chaotic alternate state of the big apple, eye do not know why,
or understand what brought his shadow to slouch an apparition across from me
a moment ago, though eye do know the mysterious truth of language failed

him—as it has for so many—did not grant him space to move with freedom
into an embracing home amongst the breathing who truly co-exist here, dream
of the possibility of this place as a space to reside in inside the chaotic beauty
that is new york city's errançities, where restless love is everywhere present,
found in innovative music created within evolving forms of communication
we recognize as speech, stirred up by mix-y-uppy sounds of poetry, cooked
as linguistic cuisines, simmered down inside pots of our poetic tongues

& dished out as creole, jambalaya, metisisse, mélange, as in a marriage
of divergence, as when a meeting of eyeballs glancing off each other fail to hold
meaning as gesture, though offer intuitive hints of bonding with what we do
not know—have never reached out to know—in this clashing culture of values,
when words embedded inside the same tongues hold love, fraternity, liberty,
brotherhood, but are not recognized as equivalent for this kaput man
who drug the shadow of his ruined spirit after him when he left the train

A HARD QUICK RAINSTORM IN MANHATTAN

a hard quick rain creates rivulets in streets of new york city—
manhattan, harlem, to be exact—glazes patinas on wet
slick surfaces suggesting bits of glass embedded in black thorough—
fares when streetlights throw their beams down to flicker like diamonds
on the backs of raging water currents as a fierce march wind whips through
trees snapping off branches, leaves, shattering umbrellas,
leaves them twisted & broken all over harlem streets
like bodies smashed by speeding cars or trucks,
winds whistling fiercely through shallow gullies running along sidewalks,
turns them into a succession of arpeggios—violent rivers now—sweeping
lie a broom all debris away—a shoe, a half-eaten sandwich
found by a beggar (who looks like he could be anyone's hard-luck brother)
& snatched from his hand by greedy, snaking airstream,
eye see his look of shock as a mangled pack of torn cigarette butts
is ripped from his hand, see his tears as his cardboard shack,
his blankets cartwheel, hightail it like caped apparitions
down these stunned, flooding streets suddenly whipped hard by winds,
now water spins into whirlpools & the beggar has lost everything
after the storm came calling, save his shoes—quarter-sized holes
punched through the worn soles—the grimy, disintegrating
scarecrow clothes on his back, a stocking cap covering
his clotted hair, where voracious lice bed down every night,

still, the rain is mercifully warm, spiritual even, it is spring,
a time when God can be blustery, full of kindness,
in the very same moment (but don't tell the beggar this,
he thinks God long forsook him in this time of pure vengeance,
left him out here alone to face this wind-fierce,
gizzard-hearted storm) when all seems to have been lost,

but after all these drumrolls of improvised thunderclaps,
rattle-rattle of rain-sticks on snare drums of metal garbage cans,
prancing dance of accents pinging through streets

flashing down from thunderheads blooming
& booming overhead, bold zigzagging lightning bolts
unzipping these towering black trousers of clouds, unzipping
the night with electrical élan, after all this rigmarole,
all this breathtaking pellets of rain driven like bullets or nails,
fired into the beggar's face—your face, too, if you're out here—
shot from an invisible gun, you hear the sounds of whiplashing
voices speaking in several tongues, dialects settling down,
become an adagio, a gentle *alizé*, as the wind transforms itself,
becomes a whispering, lilting breeze as the raging
rivers in gullies turn calm, morph into quiet streams,

when light comes in the morning everything will have gone back
became normal, things will be viewed clearly again
in the brightness of a fresh new day, after the storm has passed
you might think of it as a cleansing dream,
you might just see your image frozen there, framed
inside a clean store window, snapped like a self-portrait from long ago
you dreamed of, recognize it now inside this clean glass—mirror?—
& it's like seeing a twin you never knew you had, for the first time
in this moment everything might become clear again
as you pass this window, after such a fiend-of-a-storm,
everything might look new, beautifully fresh, again,
even smell sweet after such a storm has come & left
you here, within the refreshing light of this reborn day

SOUNDS OF NEW YORK CITY

FROM HARLEM, 116TH & 7TH AVENUE

for Miles Davis

sounds quixotically mix human languages—wolof, french,
patois, african-american-english, spanglish sprinkled
with pure spanish—inside music—salsa, rap, senegalese mbalax-
the rackaderack of jackhammers rattling streets, cracking asphalt,
shaking minds with noise inside skulls wrapped with skin,
black tar where cars zoom over, shoot down chutes of boulevards,
hang abrupt changes of direction—left or right, what does it matter—
then disappear like insistent car horns in times square
through whatever chaos confronts them—the reality of buildings,
very tall structures with orifices swallowing stuff if windows are open,
allows all the quixotic mixes the big apple lives with every moment—dirt,
debris, pieces of conversations sailing in through open windows like pages
of ripped-up newspapers, voices salty with accents, the squeal of rubber wheels—
to enter, commingle with the city's vociferous languages residing here in the air,
slipping & sliding, punctuated by buzzing flies, mosquitoes, yapping wings
of dog tongues, cats yowling, lightning slicing though air over central park,
where birds skree-skree & yerp-yerp, caw-caw over green grass
in summer, the welcoming whoosh of winds serenading through tree leaves,
like eye imagine charlie yardbird parker soloed long-ago in minton's
in his love affair with the way music looped-de-looped during april,
when rains come shimmy-shingling down wet pavements whipping soaked
newspapers swim down chutes of streets around broadway, close to times square,
we move inside ourselves when we enter the subway as it screams back uptown,
the rhythm of train wheels riding the tracks, laying down the syncopation
underlying the rhythm sluicing through this poem, double-backs,
trumpets, bass clarinets & saxophones riding over the clicking licks of steel wheels,
reminds me of lenny white, jack dejohnette pulsating on *bitches brew*, gumbo
screeching sounds, when miles ran the voodoo down, the prince of darkness
stabbing his trumpet breath into a jimi hendrix guitar solo, like a bluesman
a cat mewing in the dark at a full moon *on the corner,* like muddy waters,

howling wolf—through all this chaos of sound all around us in this place,
so beautifully vital, so creatively imagined in this city of magic
& mystery full of gargantuan appetites & tastes, art congregating
in spaces we pass through every moment, everyday, uptown, wherever
we move through this mesmerizing place all others try measuring up to,
this galvanizing metropolis many imitate—its beehive overdrive,
its quixotic mix of skree-skree, caw-caw, music, languages—
whatever the human cost the energy here is always at a boiling point
& those who live here recognize the blowback of this scintillating chaos,
music slipping through cracks to surround you like nirvana & you
love it, deal with it—if you plan to stay here—just keep "getting' up
on the one," everyday, miles used to say—just keep "getting' up
on the one," on the one, just keep "getting' up on the one"

2002 MANHATTAN SNAPSHOT: THE WAR ON TERROR

two overweight white policemen set up
a roadblock, at 95th and Amsterdam
in new york city, on a cold, windy, november
morning, cars backed up for blocks blared horns
stuck in their anger, my cabby told me
it was money spent on the war on terrorism, eye thought
did they really think osama bin laden or saddam hussein
would be caught dead or alive in a car
in manhattan, maybe they thought they'd catch
some other kind of criminal riding in a van,
as if they would come this way since everybody
& their mama knew on this side of town
the roadblock was there—our cabby blind—
sided because he was from downtown—
& especially since the men in blue,
their bellies bulging like necks of croaking frogs
strained buttons of their coats, as they walked up
slowly to check the cars or vans,
but any terrorists worth their weight in fear,
paying any attention would have been long gone,
so what is this farcical drama all about? eye asked,
my cabby said it was higher-ups in government
just letting us know the transfer of tax dollars
they took from us was working to keep wool
pulled way down over our eyes, to keep us blind

A FEW QUESTIONS POSED

every sunday morning for many years now white people
from all around the globe have flocked in droves
to the first corinthian baptist church, across from where eye live
on 116th street & adam clayton powell jr. boulevard, in harlem
where they stand in long snaking lines sweating bullets in hot
humid, summer sundays, dressed in un-hip clothing—a few even show
up in shorts—shivering in ice-cube winters, dressed like eskimos—
camera-strapped tourists carrying maps of the neighborhood

they flock up here to hear & see black people decked to the nines,
listen to glory-bird eating preachers deliver holy scriptures,
choirs belting out bring-the-house-down-rhythmic-glory-be-to-god
rocking gospels, sung in voices so alive you can hear & see angels
strutting the black experience of joy & suffering with wings—
flapping head-nodding blues—though you can't hear real blues up in here
in first corinthian, that would get in the way of the lawd's holy gospel
the black & white-washed christian message of a blood-drenched legacy
so foreign, it must be made acceptable to these white listeners
with their beaming earnest unquestioning leave-it-to-beaver apple-pie faces,
who keep coming up here full of unreachable complexes,
mysterious maladies, impulses, perhaps thinking their convoluted conundrums
will somehow be fixed, healed absorbing these holy ghost miracles
sung by aretha franklin clones , like many thought when they voted
for barack husseim obama to be president he would fix everything bush
fucked up, simply because he was a brilliant black man—though none of this
glory has ever seemed to have helped even the most regular
black devotee-clones listening here at first Corinthian—even though
many old-timers have been drinking this same holy ghost kool-
aid for decades now, fanning away their heartbreak every sunday

which begs the question why do these white people really come
up to harlem to listen to something so far outside their own tradition,
what would happen if the tables were turned

& blacks flocked in droves into their neighborhoods on sundays,
would they suffer us, give us directions as we have them
with the same grace, would they welcome droves of christian
others flocking to churches in their neighborhoods,
as native-americans welcomed them way back in the day
when they first arrived on these shores from whatever country they fled from,
would they remember all these years they came up to harlem
by subway, taxis, on foot, in cars in large rented buses
taking up all our parking spaces every sunday morning

would they remember the sermons, the gospel music
they *said* changed their hearts, their spirits would they/can they change
their DNA of privilege, of never ever embracing the *other*

FOGGY MORNING IN PORT TOWNSEND

heavy fog blooms in the straits of juan de fuca
like tear gas did in boot camp back in fort
leonard wood, missouri, when we practiced fighting wars
& O how the years have run away quick as cats darting through
the dark, to enter this boggy morning of almost silver
rinsed shadows, of trees standing still as silhouette cutouts
outside my windows, on my next to last daybreak here
in port townsend, in another fort
called worden, so still, so quiet here, where
eye am listening to the music of mozart bloom
from speakers of my lap top computer's cd player

& O where has all the time run to, wolfgang amadeus,
from your time to here, when we can write & play music simultaneously
without missing a beat though a technological wizard like this laptop,
what would you think of this invention, old maestro,
you who died so young, like so many musical geniuses,
at thirty-four, crazy as charlie yardbird parker, who went bloated
& drunk to the other side, full of "smack" around the same age as you,
amadeus, have you met him there yet, O great maestro,
have you talked together about how all great music is the same,
have you introduced yourself to miles davis, duke ellington, louis
armstrong, john coltrane, all of whom loved your music,

have you seen them clean in their white bone suits,
polished clean as yours, mozart?

O where have all the years run quick as cats darting through the dark,

to find your music rising here, on a foggy morning rinsed silver?
did you know we would be listening still to your music,
that it would be as familiar as this billowing fog, now lifting,
would be as familiar as memories of tear gas & war on boggy mornings,

trees still standing as silhouette cutouts, shadows of ghost trees
greening up, as the fog lifts to reveal wonders of a new day,

did you know, great maestro, we would still be listening,
as the future will be listening to duke, bird, miles, louis & coltrane,

did you know, old great maestro, did you know?

that after the fog lifts the day will shine golden green here,
three deer will have already come down out of the woods,
come up to my window, with their luminous eyes wide open,
their wet, soft noses pressed against my window

listening to your music right now, frozen, seemingly in wonder

did you know, old great maestro, did you know?

THE ALLUSION OF SEDUCTION

even when you sat in the glowing embers
during that day as any other, the sun
sinking quickly as the breath of a dying man,
who felt the light dimming in his sunken eyes, lingered,
just for a moment, you remembered the soft touch
of a woman's sweet lips you loved
like a cool breeze on your flesh & you lingered
after she left, her perfume hanging in the air there
like seduction, you remembered her incredible tongue
licking so softly, so feathery-light across your keening body,
it was so electric then, is so electric now in your memory,
as this moment is electric when you feel
the beauty of language growing inside a poem,
inside the incredible music of its reference

on the other hand it is a different moment now
under this black sky filled with stars silent as people
walking around down here imitating zombies,
where you sit, sifting through the wreckage of memory
you hear voices swelling from somewhere deep within
hidden crevices of an invisible stillness, perhaps inside
history, now a plunging hush when once there was a clamoring,
a nervous cacophony filled with agitation, was marching
people around the globe speaking in one voice,
waving banners, thrusting fists—of all colors—
into the glowing air like pistons, then the light suddenly dropped
over the edge of the world during a sunset you remember, when
the police surged forward wearing gas masks,
looking like darth vaders swinging steel batons,
cracking human skulls as if they were piñatas

& hidden behind their sparta shields made people dance
when they shot them with voluble water hoses

in the glowing light dropping over the edge of the world
at sunset, in this moment here, this eerie silence,
the presence comes rushing at you with garrulous urgency,
drowning out all nostalgia

& you think of guantanamo, guatanamo, O the shame,
of guantanamo, abu ghraib, the silence,
the creeping national silence of voices ignoring the known,
the cold-blooded depravity of it all, the insulation of ignorance, the silence
we freeze into so we won't recognize the horror
in front of us now, the silent drones hovering,
slaughtering over afghanistan, pakistan, it's all so familiar now
as apple pie, the graphic scenes of a tarantino movie,
the impoverishment of spirit we find located
inside ourselves, we have no language that speaks of it

& yet you remember still the sweetness of her lips
brushing over your flesh like feathers of a bird's wing,
her incredible licking tongue lathering
your body with its honey, its seduction of your keening memory
made so electric by her touch, her wondrous perfume
hanging in the air like beautiful language inside a poem
& you linger over the remembrance of all of this,
feel hope is still there, as long as there is love

PRAISE SONG FOR SEKOU

for Sekou Sundiata, August 22, 1948–July 18, 2007

it stormed thunder & lightning the day you passed, sekou,
a sky carrying deep sadness hung down over new york city—
it reminded me of drooping bags under mourners' eyes
after hours of deep, sleepless despair & weeping,
huge eggplant tears dropped from gloomy clouds for you, sekou
drenched the daytime boppers, flooded the hot, screaming thoroughfares
right before a steam pipe exploded on 41ˢᵗ street near lexington avenue,
blowing a boiling gray cloud of debris through a gaping, sweltering hole
&swallowing whole a screaming black man alive,
roasting him inside his truck
after burning his clothes off his cooked body,
sending him pleading for help & mercy from horrified, cringing onlookers,
who turned their backs, except for one white man,
who wrapped him in his expensive suit jacket, took him to the hospital,
saved his life on the day you went raging to the other side, sekou,
you threw thunderbolts of lightning into this sky as you went, so angry you were,
we watched them unzip the mood of the day
the place where you were born, lived & died,
watched them zigzag through an onyx sky deep black
as the shining coal of your skin, my luminous friend

& you had so very much to live for, so much still to do—
but look at what you *did* do, my brotha, all that beautiful, living
stuff you laid on us full of all those memorable voices on vinyl—
hoodoo priest of sacred magic, singing into this place
a great dance you were, my friend, a black blues fusing rhapsodic
doobop & jazz, so cool inside your prince of light persona
you turned poetry into your own new bop, attitude you had in spades
a dip in your stride, a knowing look blooming like mystery
inside your been-there-done-that, ever-alert sparkling brown eyes

you were a walking, breathing barometer of hip, out of miles's tribe
always at ease inside your sin, your glorious musical language sly & knowing,

a little wink here, a subtle, humorous put-down there, so wise you were, so fly
always magical, running easy, gliding through who said what to who
& did who do what they said they would do, did they believe in magic, mystery
when who said they believed in voodoo, then flew, but you knew why
they flew, did what they always do when they are turned around
by directives & go the other way, sekou, you knew why they did it

knew why they went in the wrong direction to get to where
they *said* they wanted to go, knew why *they* went in the wrong direction
because of their deep conviction they thought they knew the *true* way,
never mind the fact they had never been there before,
but you knew, sekou so you just flashed a knowing smile when they got lost,
called you back in time again for the *right* directions, you just gave up easy
laughter, shook your head, 'cause you knew, sekou, you knew
they didn't like dancing with some meanings under certain words,
like following orders, 'cause you knew they knew the history of the blues,
which meant following some commands might leave a black man in deep,
deep doodoo, confused, because of the history of being black in America
but you loved them anyway, because you knew
some of these people, who sometimes wore suits two sizes too small,
with high-water pants showing tops of white socks everywhere they went,
buttons straining, seeming about to pop off—though they never did—
from the front of their suit coats, 'cause they thought it looked hip, avant-garde
like ornette coleman, who wore bright red clothes when told to wear all black
who took strolls in the park when asked to watch someone's house
& left the front door wide open, then scratched their heads, looked puzzled
when they got back, found all the stuff in the house had just upped & left,
who read twenty-page poems at readings of fifty long-winded poets
when told they had no more than one minute to do their thing

you knew why they always did it like this, sekou, you knew

so we celebrate you in all your who-went-your-own-way voodoo,
talkin' about who copped the sweet bop of all the hipness inside the language,
who hung out with mystery needing to put magic inside music,
so musicians could take their imagination over the top

so, solo, sekou, hello, we gonna miss you brotha, your sweet
daybreak-wide smile, though we know you still doin' the holy bop
where your deep magical spirit took you, sekou

wherever your deep, hip music flew, we will always hear
your music, your solo, sekou, always saying, hello

solo, solo with your sweet musical, poetic tongue,
with your deep, humming mysterious voice, that was song

TAPS FOR FREDDIE

for Miles Davis, Freddie Webster, and Randy Weston, who told me the story

when freddie webster died after shooting poison called "white girl"
through his body/veins, that burned like fire back in chi-town,
in 1947, he thought he was mainlining top-of-the-shelf heroin
but it was strychnine,

                                  maybe battery acid—
bad shit, meant instead for his good friend, saxophonist sonny stitt,
who was beating everybody & their mamas out they money
he came in contact with
to satisfy his own big-time junkie habit,
freddie was a junkie too, though he wasn't marked for death
like sonny was—though sonny didn't know he was either
when he passed on the "white death" to freddie, as a gift,

freddie's death hit everyone in jazz like a lightning bolt, especially
miles davis, who was as close to freddie as a brother,
so when he heard freddie had died he freaked out, became
inconsolable like so many other players in the jazz, music orbit,

now, sixty-one years later, down in gosier, guadeloupe, at the creole beach hotel,
may 26, 2008, on what would have been miles's eighty-second birthday—
he's dead, now, too, since september 28th, 1991—
sitting out on the veranda, looking at the sea—the great jazz pianist
randy weston tells me the story of how he, max roach,
& the "prince of darkness"—miles davis—went out to coney island beach
to celebrate, remember the short life of their friend, freddie webster,
& miles (a junkie too, back then, like so many others
during those dark, bright days of music & death in the time of bebop,
during the reign of the biggest junkie of them all,
charlie "yardbird" parker, whose example many were following)
started walking to the edge of the beach, carrying his trumpet
in a brown paper bag—he had pawned his trumpet case
for money to satisfy his "white girl" habit—

randy said miles walked slowly, deep in thought, head down,
walked toward the sea, kicking up sand as he went,
then he pulled out his golden horn, pointing the trumpet bell east
toward africa, where he said freddie's spirit was now resting,

blew a mournful taps for freddie—who played a mean trumpet, too—
as the atlantic ocean foamed in waves of dying bubbles

like they bubbled from freddie's mouth the moment he died

MILES'S LAST TUNE LIVE, AUGUST 25TH, 1991

when you listen to miles davis live on "Hannibal,"
on his album, *Live Around the World,*
at the hollywood bowl, you hear a memorable solo
performed in a voice emanating from a unreconstructed leader
cracking notes, sliding through changes elusive as hot
mercury, breath slipping out of his horn as quicksilver nuance,
perhaps he knew he was going to the other side soon
not long from that smoggy summer moment

perhaps though because it was his final performance live
he knew, felt all his extraordinary gifts bleeding out
from his once indomitable, mysterious spirit as if they were
running water whirlpooling down the drain of a kitchen sink,
he seemed too know the end was near—just a little over
a month away—because his playing hinted at this
in a very spooky, haunting way, even though
he wasn't ready to go just yet, had so much more still to do
in his own calculations swirling around inside
his restless, edgy mind embracing errançities

but death don't wait for no one—not even pure genius—
it just comes when it's time to pay its final visit
like a stealthy thief, whenever

it chooses to snatch away someone's last precious gift of breath,
but miles could go away thankful, knowing he had given
so much enduring, magical artistry,
had left so much beauty to enrich all our lives
left so much great music to remember him by

A POEM OF RETURN: CIRCA 2008

1.

there is something sounding like the ringing of bells
when you arrive, its music clear in your heart,
you feel the cleansing beauty of its wondrous tone rinsing
through your weary body, carrying rivers of memories,
sweeping over the familiar landscape
until you come to the beloved place, the small house
where so many moments are cascading waterfalls,
moments shimmeringly green as guadeloupean mango trees
are green after clouds drop buckets of rain, after the sun rises
bright clearing the darkness with its brooms
of gigantic, mystical beams of light flashing radiant
& you are there once again inside your head
where everything seems serene, in its place

memories are seductive things, beckoning you back
to the young women you knew—as you grow older,
their firm, lissome bodies ripple with perfection in memory,
evoke volcanic desires—as you wake up next to
your wonderful sleeping wife holding your body firm,
her tenderness a bell ringing beautiful as any
you have ever heard, a waterfall of spirits
cascading through serenading songs of wind chimes
reminds you of a very deep space that always springs alive
in her, gripping from the very first moment you kissed her
so many moons ago, she still holds you there,
even now, in her warm, magical place of voodoo,
her deep suction pool of sweet love,
even while she is sleeping

2.

there are moments within moments
when you find yourself feeling at home,

as in a smiling face of a stranger walking a road
in st. felix, guadeloupe, on the boulevard st. michel,
in paris, where you see an old black man beautifully dressed
in white linen, a red boutonniere in his buttonhole,
starched white shirt, red tie, a gold tooth flashing like a razor
in the front of his mouth, underneath a wire moustache,
sporting snappy two-toned shoes, a bowler hat & a silver cane
counting off the beat of his hip stroll, two sleek,
beautiful women strutting besides him, arm in arm,
dressed to the nines, their four pointy breasts are invitations
like the stiletto nipples of the women in wilfredo lam's
surreal drawings and powerful paintings

the three of them seductive, remind me of brash men & women
eye saw way back in childhood, in st. louis, missouri,
in the good-old heydays of the 40s & 50s,
when the riviera & peacock alley were jumping

clubs, in high gear, with wondrously hypnotic people
high-stepping it through galvanizing, innovative music
pulsating clean to the bone of rhythms,
when everything about being hip then was about style & timing,
the promise of new days emanating—
silver breaking from everyone's eyes bright
as scales of fish glinting sparks when sunlight,
or moonlight glances off its back as it swam
close to the surface of the mississippi river,
before the stainless steel arch rose like an indian bow
bent to its limit, ready to send an invisible arrow
flying true into the heart of america's tortured soul,

eye hear crows caw-cawing now in the gray, fetid air
blanketing the river's slow crawl through muddy slime, see
pollution in the form of oil slicks snaking toward the choking
mouth at the gulf of mexico, where future katrinas are

waiting to scream ashore in the soon-coming future,
unleashing howling banshee winds & boiling water beyond
anything—even the most cynical—had ever imagined,
thirty-seven years after john f. kennedy came preaching
the fresh, visionary good news at his inaugural, evoking
dreams seemingly on the verge of really happening,
before assassinations swept the giddiness away—
john f's brains blown out in a motorcade in dallas,
on a cold november day, five years before martin was gone
like a wilted flower in memphis, two years before malcolm
was snuffed out in new york city, five years before
robert kennedy in los angeles, california,
too many others to mention here—before vultures
flopped down slowly from blue notes of storms
weeping all over schizophrenic america—
land of the troubled mocking the millions un-free

still, great american music inspired many of us with obama
to move forward, into a new moment with gusto,
we heard again the genius melodies, memorable as moonwalks
sashaying through the air in the strut of barack's language
so original it began to spread like a great vintage wine,
everywhere you could hear its intoxicating rhythms,
its matchless vigor, its miles davis élan, its coolness, thought

the nation had entered a new age, but we were wrong

IV.

MICHAEL JACKSON & THE ARC OF LOVE
AUGUST 29, 1958–JUNE 25, 2009
"He was a very fragile soul in a very cruel world"

I.

it was always about love from the moment you heard music michael
love of hypnotic rhythm sound when it embraced your heart
penetrated your spirit with a deep worshipping feeling love echoed sweetly
seductive throughout your being with a resonance devoting you to the beat
jumping out of jukeboxes, radios long-playing records singles voices
witch doctors speaking to you in tongues became your hoodoo clan
heroes pulling you into their orbits weaving glorious love
the air pulsating there with magical signature breaths

you heard all this enchantment before you were five in gary indiana
listening to your older brothers sing in a group sucked you into the magic
your sweet-singing mother katherine your cold-blooded gizzard-hearted
father joe abusing you all with bare-knuckle beatings
razor strops whipping you & your brothers into line hard
with constant rehearsals—joe pushed everyone with ambitions of glory
he could not reach as a part-time guitar player with a house full of stair-step
children he had to bring the bacon home to working as a crane
operator—though if truth be told joe thought his rigorous rehearsals/
beatings were necessary acts of sweet love training y'all to deal with
the treacherous people up ahead you boys had to face down the road
you were a musical prodigy michael—a sponge soaking up everything
you recognized innovation from jump—james brown fred astaire jackie
wilson charlie chaplin sammy davis jr. diana ross stevie wonder elvis Presley
smokey robinson frank sinatra were your mentors—you learned firsthand
the complexities of love you picked up in your own house wanting to please
with your genius you blew by your older brothers by the age of five
so into entertaining you never had a real childhood so busy you were
rehearsing you got so good so fast you became lead singer of the jackson five
rocketing everyone with you to fame (your little sister janet watching

in the corner of the family nest absorbing like you
& who later would zoom to challenge even you hooking her own
copycat power act of you to your dazzling shooting star/nova)

from the beginning there was no question your coming was a gift
a changing-of-the-guard in pop music merging the complex syncopated
beats of james brown to the holy ghost spirit of your own magical pulse
so genius it soon brought the house down with a new funk hypnotizing everyone
to dance & move you left your four siblings in the dust
because your singular musical juju required you go your own way
without your blood brothers you flew so high with off the wall thriller bad
we are the world dangerous man in the mirror memorable MTV videos
shocked everyone with your breathtaking élan extraordinary to the point
millions were amazed listening to you watching you work your high-wire act
of vocal pyrotechnics coupled with gymnastic "hip-jabbing" dance steps
grabbing your crotch you pirouetted singing billie jean a sequined white glove
slanted like a snake's head high above your head cocked your lithe body
at an angle live on tv we watched you create your iconic moonwalk
your silhouetted razor-sharp cutout image of black & white fingers saluting
your hip-slanting black fedora hat in a memorable pose we can't forget

your dominance was complete after *those* mind-blowing images
showed off your unparalleled hoodoo stamping your image into the air
on stage your conjurer presence imprinted there in our memory
mysterious as a sculptural magician—you carved out your space lived in it
practicing a kind of musical cartomancy melody still your seductive secret—
you had no need though to pronounce words correctly in songs
you had poetic license to create neologisms spontaneous magic on the spot
you improvised modalities you were a beautiful geegaw we all looked at fascinated
until the shine began to wear off your bobble when you broke your nose in 1979
then your hair caught fire in 1984 filming a pepsi commercial
flames left the top of your head burnt bald as a cue ball consigned you to wear
that weird-looking long halloween black witch's wig in public forever
after that your facial changes began—by 1986 your face was transformed
changing the beautiful geegaw we all knew & loved into something strange—
after all these tragedies your bubble finally began to burst

first you were over-loved then totally misunderstood after your flower
bloomed into something beyond comprehension for so many
who knew nothing of the deep pain you were going through every day
trying to find love—as your power turned special your image was ubiquitous
everywhere suddenly you were no longer the cute little black genius geegaw
boy you had suddenly morphed into a creepy man-child
metamorphosing before our eyes you looked so otherworldly
wearing the long black witch's wig no matter it covered your scarred head—
who knew why it was there the plastic surgery bleaching your skin from encroaching
vitiligo those images of you carrying bubbles the chimpanzee around
buying bones of the elephant man sleeping in that polio-looking oxygen chamber—
you began to seem so out of step with everyone
divorced from even those who still loved you & your music

when you outbid paul mccartney for the beatles music catalogue
everything began going wrong for "wheat" folk/critics—
they started hating you—after all you were still just a little black boy to them
they thought you were getting too big for your britches making boatloads of money—
no matter your genius worldwide celebrity your hope to love everyone—
for you what the world always needed was "love sweet love"
but few knew how to get there then or now or whenever
because love is a deep life-changing thing hard anytime maybe
impossible for many though it still is the answer if truth be told

all this malice caught you by surprise since you were an innocent—
though sharp as a razor when it came to business—who only wanted love
to please everyone with your art for everyone to love you too
the heart of your music taking wings in rhythm striking love
like lightning zigzagging your iconic beats across a menacing black sky

2.
suddenly you became a piñata in the 24/7 corporate media world
for anyone to swing at in public because of problems they thought
you had—sleepovers with macauley culkin emmanuel lewis at neverland—then
tom sneddon the santa barbara sheriff wanted to look for vitiligo on your penis
drove the bogus 1993 child molestation charges

though many knew the charges were made up by greedy parents—
then you married lisa marie presley divorced her married weird debbie rowe
had two children by her before you divorced odd debbie too spoke on that strange
martin bashir—now an msnbc anchor—documentary showing you buying that gaudy
expensive junk then you dangled your son prince from a berlin balcony
went through that bogus 2005 trial before being exonerated though
your spiritual image in the media was in total tatters after that

dealing with you became a bolus stuck in many people's throats—
it wasn't about the music we all loved but about you michael—
your strangeness dominated was fed intravenously to your critics
like the prescription drugs you were taking now as lupus came down on you
vitiligo changed the way you looked as white spots spread like a plague
over your brown body forced you to bleach yourself all white if you still wanted
to entertain in public & you did because entertaining was in your blood
was what you always needed to do to be whole—but few wanted to see
your spots on stage the cartography of your skin—when you let us view it
not covered with clothing—hands face neck slivers of arms wrists
fingers/tips palms your lips turned all red now with fresh lipstick though
the most bizarre change in your face was your newly reconstructed nose
looking as though it had been assaulted in war showing all those battle scars
no plastic surgeon could conceal—the grotesque changes—
when scrutinizing cameras zoomed in you couldn't hide the damage
no matter how much money you spent it couldn't hide the bizarre transformation
of your face with any kind of makeup—for this there was no grace,

all this bizarre renovation took a toll on you—& us—dominated the media
instead of your music your deep abiding seductive spiritual love—
this was the tragedy of your long fall from grace michael this new definition
fixed you in the media—racist as it always is for black people—
with snippets of facts false truths innuendo—though in the end your love
& your music will be your timeless gift to us all not some prying camera news-
reader/voiceover who never wanted to know the real you

but at the end you were a little boy isolated in a fifty-year-old body
deep sadness in your once beautiful round light bulb eyes
though you were ready to bask in the spotlight onstage once again
with your "this is it" london concerts to show everyone you still had it
the incredible seductive magic to amaze but death—a kind of weird suicide
when you rolled the dice for seven it came up snake-eyes—ending it all
pulled us into profound grief mourning left us pondering the question—
what would have happened had you not left way too soon

3.
death found you after midnight when you finished rehearsing your new show
from the staples center you went home happy that last night
because you had once again entered the wondrous zone of your artistic genius
you were trying to sleep when you checked yourself out with an i.v.
drip dripping the deadly anesthetic propofol—you called it your "milk"—
drip dripping death into your collapsed starving veins needle marks tracking up
& down your paper-thin white arms your skin almost translucent
when you entered "the valley of death" you had long spoken of—
you went there skin & bones bald as a bowling ball save a little peach fuzz
on top of your head under the long witch's wig (did you wear it to bed at night
michael trying to fall asleep through terrible insomnia) drugs running
like polluted rivers through your ghostly anorexic body
swallowed by tents of your clothing—in the end you were still
responsible for your own life michael the way you lived it with yes-people
surrounding around you giving you everything you wanted—not needed—
responsible for your own death if you killed yourself as eye think you did—
depressed as you were at the end though happy too with great joy
for your comeback tour surrounded by your children & music

when you took your spirit to the other side of the veil you went
free of the pain around you since childhood the savage scrutiny relentless
prying eyes of media cameras searching for anything they could find—
still you were responsible for yourself michael for your children
all those who loved you but you wanted all of it—the fame you craved

the spotlight shining on you with vengeance—did you forget the baggage
that comes with being a nova/star—& it finally trapped you
your beautiful spirit inside a spider web of your own making—
didn't you see the poisonous media spider of death coming for you—
in the end you didn't deserve the terrible hatred & envy that came your way
but you surrounded yourself with all those vampire vultures & that deadly
spider fed off you greedily until you were a shell of skin & bones

some say you had duffel bags packed with cash hidden in the mansion
when you died—there was news someone in your family bum-rushed your death
scene trying to take that money—perhaps it was only rumor like so much else
swirling around your life until it became a kind of truth—whatever it was
the spectacle surrounding your death was heartbreakingly sad
revealed just how important you were to making money for others—no matter
death—like elvis—your porcelain-white flesh soon will become memory
but your music & artistic élan will live pulsating magic & love
transformative as anything eye have ever heard or seen in my life

the announcement of your death was like a gigantic broom
sweeping everything off front pages of newspapers—
across the globe your death totally dominated airwaves
people wept danced celebrated your life played your songs once again—
your funeral was something to behold you laying there unseen
inside your flower-draped golden coffin as friends & family testified
honored your name your music your arc of human love

up over staples center—kobe bryant's mecca—the shape of a heart appeared
above in the blue sky—inside berry gordy spoke sage words about you
al sharpton gave a powerful speech a gospel choir sang poignantly
so did usher & stevie wonder pulsating images of you dancing singing electric
graced a screen in all your glory brooke shields spoke incisive words
evoked humor a deep personal friendship then your daughter paris
broke down weeping at the end of the ceremony
told everyone how much she loved you would miss you greatly
this brought everyone to tears in this moment of mourning you michael—though

we also wept for paris her loss—when the ceremony was over the final image
a single spotlight shining on a lone microphone standing center stage
was an homage to you as your poignant voice sang for us
to look at ourselves finally "& make a change"

CODA
jagged lightning rips open a black stormy sky over new york city
on a day late in july over a month since you went to "the valley of death"
the lightning tearing the mood asunder reminds me of you hip-jabbing
your signature fractured cutout silhouette dance jagged
white against black evoking whatever beauty comes to mind during an act
of creative power as lightning strikes bring with it a bold sense of fiery
resurrection of savage beauty the unbridled creative power of music
perhaps sudden lightning & thunder is a reminder of demons possessing us all—
especially you michael despite your gentle spirit—perhaps the sudden fierce
lightning eye saw today is like you—no iambic hexameter line could contain
your combustible zapping spirit no broken-up space-filled stanzas
all over the page could reflect the arc of your haunting voice aching with longing
though sometimes bright with hard steel glittering off the arch rising above
the mississippi fronting downtown st. louis during clear nights or days
when the moon or sunrays dance across the glittering surface curved
like a bow in the hands of one of our native american indian ancestors
your compact diamond-hard lightning-quick energy zeroing in during a moment
focused in rhythm inside the music dance your imaginative quicksilver grooves
within your electric spirit hovering in the sky lancing lightning music
with thunder thrilling with fierce beauty keening through
the firmament of our memory with a discharge of incredible energy

your iconic image there in skies around the globe reminds us
of your glory your creativity magic imagined with love teaching us
honing in on mystery & beauty—you will always be there Michael
as spirit a sudden bolt of lightning ripping open the sky like today
your arc of music beckoning us to always "make a change"

V.

THOUGHTS ON A SUNDAY MORNING IN GOYAVE

for my son, Porter, on his 24th birthday

it is sunday morning, 5:30 a.m. when the roosters began crowing
throughout my goyave neighborhood, their *cockadoodledoos*
reverberate up & down hills of this valley
in their age-old struggle to be the first to announce the rising of the sun
from its grave in the night sky—somewhere in the east, the morning breaks through
cotton-candy gray clouds cruising over a tranquil caribbean sea, mirrors
the sadness of the earth below, where strutting, preening roosters
remind me of puffed-up politicians crowing their bogus pretense at sagacity,
peddling machiavellian snake-oil schemes of compassionate hope
to neutered flocks of sheep making beelines for edges of cliffs—
it's an age-old maneuver/scheme to sacrifice the poor
in overcrowded populations—
now my thoughts spin north
to the american capital, bumbling dupes of the bush administration—
the gang who can't shoot straight, or keep their ducks in a row—who every day
come spinning complete falsehoods with straight faces in place

today, throughout this dark, desolate period of our lives
there are so many political hatchet men all over the globe—
the hypocritical lapdogs of england, avaricious hyenas all over africa,
oil-drunk royal pigs of saudi arabia, the slimy, fez-wearing fools
posing in kabul, afghanistan,
the bumbling idiots leading israel & palestine, lizard-eyed weasels
all over the caribbean, mexico, central & south america, paralysis all over
europe, canada, australia, the far east, russia, everywhere, these men—

women too—imitating fat croaking frogs wallowing in cesspools,
surrounded by phantasmagorias of poisonous reptiles
flicking out tongues, eyeing their next prey

what are the root causes of all these age-old disagreements,
these fruitless wars without end, this poverty of spirit, imagination
sacrificed on the bonfires of vanity, greed, power, racism, xenophobia,

these dangerous, self-righteous religious creeds, this exhausting
mindset of white-skinned privilege
as an unconditional birthright to do what they want,
when they want, to anything & everyone on earth

where has the love gone on this grieving, polluted planet

now my thoughts turn back to these roosters crowing
throughout this beautiful valley,
eye see their need to outdo each other when thrown together
in the same backyard—they argue, fight, but do not kill each other
unless trained by men—as we humans have since time immemorial

all eye know for certain is that it's sunday, march 25th,
it is beautiful here in goyave, today is the birthday
of my youngest son, porter, twenty-four years old, living out his dream
of becoming a professional basketball player, in romania,
we can only hope he succeeds, that he's well, happy,
hope we've taught him to love, live peacefully with others,
to do the best he can with what he's given, to be thankful
the sun rises each morning, thankful
for the sweet love & good cheer
he brings into our lives every day

& into the sacred lives of so many others

GOYAVE NIGHT SCENE

roll-up door lifts next to a yellow light bathing
the black & white photo of miles dewey davis
resting on the white wall of our house in goyave
as a cool sea breeze tongues in, massages my face & toes
where eye am stretched out on a black & white couch,
looking at the leonine "prince of darkness" dressed in black
lizard pants, open white shirt, a slender black scarf hangs
from his neck, he is young, handsome, beautiful even,
looks taut as a black panther slouched in repose,
his face looks pensive, lost in thought, he holds his golden
trumpet cocked in the air, as if about to play with the night
sounds of frogs, birds, & crickets syncopating into my house
as they serenade us with their pulsating musical grooves,
outside, imagined ghost-voices emanate from shadows,
tremble through bushes clinging to fences,
eye hear a bat's sharp cry cleave the night like a razor
slicing through flesh, bone, gristle, as a bloodcurdling
scream of a dog hit during rush-hour traffic reminds us
death is always near, right around the corner
& all is not paradise here, though close as anything
eye have ever imagined, close as anything beautiful
can be to the paradox of mystery, surprise, wonder

SITTING ON MY VERANDA, FACING THE CARIBBEAN SEA

for Derek

eye sit on my veranda in goyave, listen to voices serenading,
climbing out of foaming waves of the caribbean sea,
hear them suds on shore murmuring of past apocalyptic histories
clashing with truth,
small rocks & sand tickling bare toes of swimmers
lying on beaches here, perhaps provoke in them dreams of strolling
electric streets hip in amber, of lovers holding hands in paris,
new york city—wherever dreams carry them to magic

it is november here, right before transforming darkness falls
with its bejeweled black cape sweeping over the entire sky with flair,
then a flourish of cicadas & crickets come out raising sound from their legs
rubbing up against each other with passion, they join choirs of frogs
in a symphony swelling the night with orchestral compositions of wonder—
like lyrical casuarinas they fuse with voices of birds whispering
from leaves of trees bowed by wind-tongues until they sing beautifully

with melodies, as traffic music of passing cars climb into my ears
drummed from highway one, mix with spinning rubber tires, wash them
into a whooshing sound of charging engines trailing off into the distance,
where they disappear down the plunging road into the night—
are they going into a quick death of wreckage or a slow aging one?—
a certainty we all have to rendezvous with sooner or later—

eye turn from the echo chamber of my ears & look south
toward st. lucia, where my old friend derek walcott lives in a lovely house,
also facing the caribbean sea & eye hope he is still writing wondrous poems
as he approaches his eightieth birthday in january 2010—
we have known each other almost half our lives now,
since 1968 when eye met him in los angeles—eye first read of trees
called casuarinas in one of his poems & loved the beauty of the word,
the sound lilting with syllables evoking a dance
of the sea washing in

as now, when it is 3:00 a.m. here & the new rooster next door begins
his ritualistic crowing a little early—it is misty now,
whispers of rain are falling, though frogs & crickets are still making music—
soon the day will return, waking us from sleep again & we will perhaps catch
a moment of beauty when we open our windows to the light
spilling its radiance into our rooms fresh with songs of birds, perhaps
the new day will bless me with a gift of an original poem
& fecund ideas to compose many others

A VEIL OF TRANSPARENT RAIN

a veil of transparent rain advances toward shore
from the aqua green water carrying a rainbow
extending up top to bottom, swirls of mist
wrap themselves around the dazzling arching colors
as two sailboats enter the miraculous mix
the wind picks up everything, seems so deliciously magical,
mysterious as secrets, when salt water of a pulsating caribbean sea
off the coast of goyave, guadeloupe, changes color from aqua green
to a wet slate gray mirroring fast-moving clouds above,
motoring toward the northwest where the sun is setting

at this moment eye remember a few days before
a french plane fell like a stone from the sky,
dropped into the middle of the atlantic ocean, due east
from where eye now sit—they found two bloated bodies floating
on this day when this poem is coming to life, two days after president obama
delivered his historic speech in cairo, egypt
dealing with the middle east, on the same day he spoke
of d-day in france, one day after celebrating
the jewish holocaust at buchenwald,
a day after mexican children were roasted in a car
somewhere in another preventable tragedy—

out there another preventable disaster of death is lurking
to cause 9/11 fear beyond the uncaring selfish gaze of so many people
greedy beyond measure is what eye am thinking
as this veil of transparent rain advances softly
as luminous green leaves of my mango tree wave *hello hello*
they shimmy dance on tongues of winds over french-tonguing
words, probing, in the distance, caressing in goyave sweet
as murmuring showers sweep in, bringing the beginning of darkness

now the sun settles down behind blooming mountains in the west,

nightfall inches in as secrets nourishing winds push the clouds
further north, past the looming shadows clearing the sky
for the moon to climb bright into a night sky full of stars—
eminding me of pearls or diamonds plopped down
on the black suede rug in a new york jeweler's shop

it is magically mysterious & eye ask myself once again
how do these things always happen every day
in this world filled with miracles & horrors—
seemingly coming suddenly as that rainbow a few hours ago—

coming during moments we least expect, bringing surprise,
as now, when stars flash bright in a clear dark sky

HAITI HAIKU

nothing like an earth-
quake, to level the playing
field, for rich & poor

EARTHQUAKE: HAITI

for Monique Clesca, Patrick Delatour & Daddy George

it struck as always without notice or warning,
struck at 4:53 p.m., January 12, 2010,
the sun was smiling down on countless
people bustling home in rush-hour
port au prince traffic, everywhere crowded streets
pulsated humanity when the earth started shaking violently
for thirty-five seconds it shook, rumbled,
then a yellow-white cloud of dust rose up—
& if you were high up in the mountains looking down
you would have thought perhaps you were above
hurricane storm clouds roiling with fury—

thirty-five seconds the earth was an undulating rollercoaster,
thirty-five seconds devotees called upon Voodoo gods,
                              Christian gods for mercy, forgiveness,
thirty-five seconds of fear wrestled inside frazzled brains

someone on a balcony filming the scene below said,
"the world is coming to an end," just as wailing rose,
just as the sound of dirt and rock cracked apart
underneath the earth, grinding plates screamed from tension, broke,
one sliding underneath the other, creating fissures up above
as the ground split apart, riven, multiplied into snaking fingers
that couldn't strangle the many voices that rose
from everywhere, unimaginable horror spoke—

the montana hotel where eye wrote half of *Miles:*
The Autobiography with Miles Davis,
collapsed, pancaked floor by floor into a pile
of rubble, killing hundreds as it went down—then pain
exploded through countless brains, skulls, bodies, arms, limbs,
as concrete walls caved in on them

thirty-five seconds seemed like thirty-five slow-moving lifetimes,
thirty-five seconds collapsed edifices of religion, power, privilege,
thirty-five seconds sucked poor people even deeper
down into whirlpools of choking poverty

the end of the world as haitians knew it came suddenly,
entered their eyes as a revelation,
shocked, that a day so beautiful
could turn so wicked in thirty-five-second blinks of an eye,
thirty-five seconds of violent eruptions (perhaps more heinous than the rule
of savage dictators like papa doc duvalier
who slaughtered tens of thousands like joe gaetjens, the hero
soccer player, who scored the only goal for america when
they beat the english team back in 1950)

thirty-five seconds of shaking madness & death down
on this first day of suffering—before stench of rotting bodies
shocked nostrils & the imagination after a few days—
then on the second day a miracle happened
when homeless people began to sing, chant, dance & pray
under the moonlight and stars

then what eye always knew to be true popped into my mind

that the haitians are a remarkable people,
spiritual, beautiful, creative, strong, resilient—eye knew
they would bounce back from this over time—
they always have in the past, they will do so now—

though this time good news will be a long time coming

HURRICANES

for Monique Clesca, Patrick Delatour & Daddy George

first eye am dreaming of blue skies followed by slight murmurs
resembling lisps of people speaking, trembling through silence
(like lovers whispering in bedrooms or gatherings of friends)
followed by fluffs of small white clouds soft as cotton candy
(they remind me of scouts of an advancing army searching for clues
to take back, information that what is coming behind them is a menace)
still eye am inside my imagination dreaming of the golden eye
of the sun warming my day with its beauty & healing power

but out in space seeking a way to cross warm sea waves tossing
turning down below is a growing cluster of whirling cumulus clouds
gathering around a vortex of swirling air rising up as errançities
hissing with salted white spray starting to speak in tongues
as it coalesces around an engine of wind giving commands now
(the engine that sent the cloud scouts out searching for clues)
to explode upward into angry vapor obliterating its cousins
soft as cotton candy it begins to move forward gaining speed
these new vexed vapors wrap themselves around the vortex—
like whirlpools of shouting hissing political voices disagreeing
throughout congresses all over the world every waking day—
soon some have purple eyes—category fives of evil—
threats to everything around them they will hurl themselves
boiling into our consciousness after acquiring names like hugo
katrina rita dean will raise fear of catastrophic judgment days
as they advance with howling voices of apocalyptic errançities
churning every-which-way full of violent linguistic maelstroms
swirling masses of cumulus advancing over warm sea water
imitating whirlpools spinning into fives massive human militias—
destined to destroy everything they touch when they approach

LUSTING AFTER MANGOES

for Margaret

eye get up before the sun imitates a burst of fire,
igniting a huge explosion as light
sweeps all shadows into secret corners everywhere,
it must be—as miles davis once told me—
about timing,
eye must arrive precisely behind

my house in the yard, under the tree full of mangoes,
a split second before the rooster comes leading
his posse of hens, cute little voracious chickadees

right after the rats have abandoned the eating field—
which is my abundant, sprawling, tropical backyard—
where fresh mangoes fall in season, ripe beyond belief—

like tender breasts—sweeter than a luscious kiss—
succor from someone you love, you must be there on time,
as the prince of darkness told me, to gather that saccharine

taste those luscious sweet mangoes where they fell
when the sun burst through yawning hours of the dawn sky,
opening it up with its cutting rays as would a can opener

a tin of candy treats you tasted once & everything
seemed new, as when you wake up, find your lover there
breathing softly at your side, succulent as a mango

SEARCH FOR MANGOES: SECOND TAKE

for Margaret also

it's a race against time in our backyard
in goyave, trying to beat field rats,
ants & chickens to the sweet prizes—
delectable griffy mangoes falling from our two trees—

it's a race against sharp tiny teeth & beaks
penetrating the hard green skins brushed with rose,
yellow blush, once they've nestled on the ground

before the rats take healthy bites, the chickens peck
holes in the skin, the ants stream through the flesh en masse,
wherever they find openings they swarm all over
the sweet nectar flesh, gobble up all the tissue,
leave behind, over time, dried-up
leather-brown corpses

they remind me of slain soldiers on a battlefield
littered underneath umbrellas
of our twin trees,
where the rats prowl only at night,
the chickens only during moments of sunlight when it is safe—
they fear attacks from packs of always-hungry rodents—
the ants come whenever they choose
& eye only during hours when the sun is smiling

it is a race against some odds, too—who knows when
a strong wind will come, blowing through all those
overloaded tree branches, shake loose those sweet mangoes,
send them plunging toward an unwelcoming earth

so the trick for me is to arrive first at daybreak,
right after the rats have eaten their fill, abandoned the field,

before the chickens come out of their sleep to peck holes—
the ants are always there but need chicken holes
to stream through—just when the new mangoes have plopped
down on the ground, ready for *my* harvest

it's all about timing
as miles davis once said, who gets there first
enjoys the fruits of their labor,
the sweet golden nectar of a mango's ripe flesh,
succulent, luscious beyond description

LISTENING TO BLACKBIRDS

eye listen to a flock of black birds jamboreeing high up
in the large mango tree in my backyard in guadeloupe,
wonder what they are jabbering about hidden
within lengthening shadows of twilight approaching darkness
spreading its wings like these birds when they take flight

their jabbering reminds me of black people gathered on corners
underneath my window in harlem during summers running down
whatever game their jazzy, jambalaya language offers up
as food for thought—the loud insistent slap of dominoes hitting tables,
spiced with boasts of men—women, too—who have mastered
the sarcastic lingo of tongue-in-cheek put-downs mixed
with salt & pepper wisdom saucing up air around the game

eye have always loved listening to language like this improvising
solos spit from lips—or beaks when talking about black birds—dripping
syllables popping through firecracker sentences dropping neologic words,
sounds into everyday lexicon of hip oral speech—language
has always been the fuel driving duende/music of my poetry

but these black birds are a special case since eye can't enter
the meaning of their language—are they happy or mad, hungry
or sad, making fun of humans like me listening to them perplexed,
trying to decipher—translate—their intricate jabbering music
packed with jackhammer rhythms—a language so high-pitched,
so insistent it seems close to frenzy, as if they were discussing
important topics to themselves, relevant to survival of the globe,
perhaps what they are jabbering about is crucial for us, too,
though how would we humans know since few of us listen,
or even hear anything we say to each other
when it comes to important matters
like, for instance, the waging of eternal war
pollution of the planet with oil—what about the gulf of mexico, alaska—

the politics of corruption by outright bribery, runaway, rampant greed—
the list of human deafness goes on & on, dominates the sordid,
sad history throughout the blindness of the world

so why would one think anyone would pause to listen to black birds
jamboreeing high up in a mango tree in guadeloupe,
jabbering away about whatever in their jackhammer rhythms,
in a high-pitched language so insistent it seems close to frenzy

perhaps a poet like me—or you—would listen to that language
possibly holding mystery, magic, beauty, if only for clues
we may decipher from secrets these black birds might know—
the boasts of men—women, too—who are masters of the sarcastic
lingo of tongue-in-cheek put-downs, the wisdom saucing the air
surrounding the insistent slap of dominoes smacking tables—

what the language could offer up for me or you—if you are
out there—perhaps, is a thread, a possible connection, where
we might locate our spirits in a common, fertile space, where words

language might be the glue holding communities together in place

HAIKU SONG

the sound of the wind
becomes the tongue of the voice
sung through poetry

A VISION

the star speeding across a midnight sky
is a voice in the shape of a glittering comet,
a bird burning as if it were pulsating
with a need of sex, as are these words carrying
a primal scream, hot & dripping with longing

the star speeding across a midnight sky
is a voice in the shape of a glittering
bird burning as if it were a comet,
pulsating with the need to explode

VI.

SEVEN/ELEVENS*

UNTITLED 1

words are dice thrown across floors,

gambling tables, where language circumvents who

won or lost, comes down to bets

lost in chips when snake-eyes dooms your first throw, though

turn a seven, eleven

after bones stop rolling you dance as though great

music, love, entered your soul

UNTITLED 2

living in the world is mostly about chance,

the draw of straws, or cards dealt

in a game of poker, it's all about nerves,

how your eyes react in tight,

cold-blooded moments of chicken, will you fold,

cave in to raw fear, pressure,

will you become an improviser with chance,

probability living

inside this new moment offered you singing

as solo, the notion fresh

thoughts can carry art to new, profound plateaus

UNTITLED 3

---

* I grew up in the inner city of St. Louis, Missouri, and I watched older and younger people—mostly men—gambling when they played the game of dice. Some were killed because one of their adversaries perhaps thought they were cheating, though sometimes it was for winning a great deal of money, which made their opponents mad. So in my mind playing the game of dice contains within its mandate an essential element of risk and chance. *Seven/Elevens* is my attempt to create a new form based on the roll of the dice and the elements of chance and risk embedded in that game. To put it simply the form goes like this: in the "seven," the poem is seven lines, with alternating seven- and eleven-syllabic lines, beginning with a line of seven syllables. With the "elevens," the poem is eleven lines of alternating eleven- and seven-syllabic lines, beginning with an opening line of eleven syllables.

In my view of the form the series of poems opens with the seven form, with the next form being an eleven, though I don't see the form necessarily conforming to this strict configuration. For me the idea is to write poems that address risk, chance, as the throw of the dice does when someone is gambling, because in my view life and living is always about taking risk. Even if one approaches life conservatively, there is no way to predict what will confront you while passing through the daily activity of breathing and living.

walking beside a building
offers possibility of a falling
brick cracking your skull with death
coming in the blink of an eye, a dice throw
unfavorable to you
in that moment, the fickleness of chance,
odds, is an opaque, feckless risk

TOMAS

tomas came whipping in suddenly, winds howled
through wet morning darkness, wings
of cold rain, drenching voices swirling anger
from a roiling, angry sea,
tree branches kneeled down as if they were blessing
snapped sugar cane stalks, whirlwinds
tossing leaves, switchbacking currents, closed hands held
tight together as in prayer,
benedictions raised up to God to spare us
holy terror like this one
whipping hurricane winds in from Africa

UNTITLED 4

eye hear cold voices whipping
my language of poetry wet with snapping
syllables, flying off white
pages full of dreaming, whirlwinds of rhythms
trying to create a form
history can walk through as pure poetry
rooted in language of place

UNTITLED 5

poetry is form, draws from nothingness, song seeking language to create
metaphor, meaning, a vehicle through which words shape themselves into sound,
local elocutions mapping birdcalls, grunts, slippage of puns, wordplays, jokes,
the march of history's impact on tongues, words, the chance mixing of races

splices mestizo voices, tongues simmered down in pots of creole culture,
food we eat today is language won or lost

UNTITLED 6
throw the bones again to see
where the dice stop rolling through life's chief moments of chance, do they roll stopping
with snake-eyes, seven/eleven turning up inside luck, ability
raised up from cultural fusion, risk, fresh modes, language echoing the new

UNTITLED 7
poetic language rolls off tongues like dice throws, words tumble through poems risking
they might fall off cliffs of sheer rock-face meters, rhythms suddenly breaking
backs of sentences, veering in another direction, alongside chance,
risk the only way to dance with creation, expression, art, politics
in the hands of poets become high-wire acts balancing cool survival,
creative voices walk through space, joyously

UNTITLED 8
snake eyes in eyes of hustlers,
pimps, who throw their lives into moments of death, snake eyes in stares of lizards,
who slither belly-down through sawgrass, people, snake eyes fixed in eyes of men
shooting bullets with their gazes, guns firing, snake eyes empty of beauty

UNTITLED 9
on the first throw of words tumbling off tongues, risk, chance takes over, becomes birds,
spreads wings, lifts off into space, is a solo, music as air beneath wings,
breath of notes is a chance to where wind takes poems in the moment art lives, thrives,
takes off as tongue when rhythm rolls as thrown dice
huck-a-bucking across floors, carrying the sound of possibility artists creating in air
carved out by miles davis, monk, jimi hendrix

UNTITLED 10
where is the courage to sing
songs no one plays over airways, radios, television, internets,
where are great poets celebrated as news

anywhere in this country,
their poems & faces splashed all over tv
like that of sarah palin

UNTITLED II
it is late in the game when new dice are thrown again, where did the risk go
with the early throw of the bones, time always moves in the moment of now,
choices thrown across gambling tables become the present voices, the new
throw of language as dice roll toward edges, chance, risk, art lived in the margins
where great poetry creates in peril, loss the name of the modern game,
is fame, the throw of cold dice, no matter what

VII.

ERRANÇITIES

for Edouard Glissant

1.

the mind wanders as a line of poetry taking flight meanders
in the way birds spreading wings lift into space knowing
skies are full of surprises like errançities encountering restless
journeys as in the edgy solos of miles davis or jimi hendrix

listen to night-song of sea waves crashing in foaming with voices
carrying liquid histories splashing there on rock or sandy shores
after traveling across time space & distance it resembles a keening
language of music heard at the tip of a sharp blade of steel

cutting through air singing as it slices a head clean from its neck
& you watch it drop heavy as a rock landing on earth & rolling
like a bowling ball the head leaving a snaking trail of blood reminding
our brains of errançities wandering through our lives every day

as metaphors for restless movement bring sudden change
surprise in the way you hear errançities of double meaning
layered in music springing from secret memories as echoes
resounding through sea & blue space is what our ears know

& remember hearing voices speaking in tongues carrying history
blooming as iridescent colors of flowers multifarious as rainbows
arching across skies multilingual as joy or sorrow evoked inside
our own lives when poetic errançities know their own forms

2.

what is history but constant recitations of flawed people pushed
over edges of boundaries of morality pursuing wars pillage
enslavement of spirits is what most nations do posing as governing
throughout cycles of world imagination plunder means profit

everywhere religion is practiced on topography as weapons used
as tools written in typography to conquer minds to slaughter for gold
where entire civilizations become flotsam floating across memory seas
heirloom trees cut down as men loot the planet without remorse

their minds absent of empathy they remember/know only greed
these nomadic avatars of gizzard-hearted darth vaders who celebrate
"shock-doctrines" everywhere ballooning earnings-sheet bottom lines
their only creed for being on earth until death cuts them down

3.
but poetry still lives somewhere in airstreams evoking creative breath
lives in the restless sea speaking a miscegenation of musical tongues
lives within the holy miracle of birds elevating flight into dreams & song
as errançities of spirits create holy inside accumulation of daybreaks

raise everyday miraculous voices collaborating underneath star-nailed
clear black skies & the milky eye of a full moon over guadeloupe
listen to the mélange of tongues compelling in nature's lungs in new york
city tongues flung out as invitations for sharing wondrous songs

with nature is a summons to recognize improvisation as a surprising path
to divergence through the sound of scolopendra rooted somewhere here
in wonder when humans explode rhythms inside thickets of words/puns
celebrating the human spirit of imagination is what poets seek

listen for cries of birds lifting off for somewhere above the magical
pulse of sea waves swirling language immense with the winds sound
serenading us through leaves full of ripe fruit sweet as fresh water
knowing love might be deeper than greed & is itself a memory

a miracle always there might bring us closer to reconciliation inside
restless métisse commingling voices of errançities wandering within
magic the mystery of creation pulling us forward to wonder to know
human possibility is always a miraculous gift is always a conundrum

JUST THINK ABOUT IT

just think about it sometimes all you need do is open
a door, walk through it perhaps out into open space,
walk into the world, whether it's cold, or warm, then go
whatever direction your mind of errançities takes you,
go quickly, or slowly, but move resolutely through this moment
with your eyes wide open, your wandering brain, but move forward
toward something perhaps you haven't thought to do before,
whatever it is let there be beauty in it spreading light, meaning,
open yourself up to new music, people, vistas, spontaneous
improvisations of the day, rhythms carrying possibilities to unlock
secrets of this moment, perhaps will lead you to look into things,
people you never focused on before you walked through the door,
perhaps the opening will reveal yourself to yourself—revelation—
perhaps now you might feel different for the rest of your life

LOOKING INTO THE FUTURE

eye have spent much time looking into the future
elusive as it is sometimes hidden
inside a word a poetic line a sliver
fracturing a fragment breaking away from a flowing
conversation bursting from what someone just said
within a bright moment of elucidation

then perhaps eye might come upon it outside
a lyrical color-field of phrases becoming metaphor
as in a poem creating itself in an empty space
a white page or a secret place inside
the brain a painting forming on a blank canvas

after all is said & done maybe it will spring from
some woman's face luminous with spiritual beauty
carrying a deep elegant élan beyond
what can be captured in any photo is only close
to human feeling the heart knows but cannot explain
on an empty page during the rapture of composing

poetry is as elusive as the future
when all you see is perhaps a trembling outline
suggesting a shape a direction you are searching for
a presence pulsating with what you hope
is luminous with a pure beauty your heart will embrace

in side a clear moment of elucidation
you might hear it in music swelling within a voice
filled with a magical spiritual beckoning
perhaps it just passed when you were distracted
inside a moment of confusion now it's gone
forever inside a fog of dissolving mist
where time exists in a state of forming questions

inside a dimension giving shape to nods flurries
winks blinking within intervals of expectations
moments on the verge of arrival music a kiss

something you have been yearning for all your life

EYE TRAVEL BACK INTO MEMORY

eye travel back into memory searching for voices,
faces enshrouded in fog, silence-filled roads
blooming with shadows waving their limbs
as tree leaves do dancing on concrete when winds come,
sweep through them with musical tongues speaking a language so
naturally some bodies understand as they move rhythmically
out on dance floors, somewhere someone is walking
secure in their space, they might be an artist, pure
essence inside a dancer's comfort zone, pace
controlling movement of a body, the way music responds
creatively to tempo, improvisational movement, measure—

as when tree leaves when whipped by wind tongues prance,
dance, in tempo, as now my journey back into memory
is a dance, my eyes searching ruins,
wreckage piled high (as bleached bones dug up from graveyards
remind of living people who always take in, never give back,
their hands constantly open to receive whatever is given,
their hearts always closed, though they are beating)

finally eye come upon high-pitched sounds of male crickets
rubbing their legs against each other somewhere out there
in blooming fog, the rushing sound of water clear as wind chimes
tinkling up ahead, in the distance, perhaps, mystery
waits in a man dressed all in black, a flat, wide-brimmed hat, also black,
pulled low, cuts across his forehead like zorro's

he rides a black horse—eyes milky moons in a black sky—
& looks through me as eye imagine death would—
then eye focus my mind upon the wind chimes' soothing music
up ahead, in the distance—movement will always take me there—
in a heartbeat eye hear water rushing through reeds,
licking over rocks & grass, see the road winding up to enter

mountains densely canopied with trees like in belle basse terre
on the western tip of guadeloupe, near the silent
volcano of soufrière, long dormant as voodoo is here,
silent on this butterfly island (though you hear drums
beating lately now when darkness falls, during carnival season
when eye hear synchronized hearts pounding inside transplanted
haitian voodoo worshippers, their rara rhythms zigzagging snakes
through streets of pointe-à-pitre during mi-careme,
their breaths blown through conch shells, dancing
inside movement of shango, papa legba, ogun, obatala, erzulie—
loas long underground here until now—the old african
gods rising up through voices of people—young & old—
thumping in time with their hearts, moving as one, inside
comfort zones of their bodies, here on this island)

out there somewhere someone is walking toward me now
through this blooming fog, they are coming secure
inside their own flesh, within their own space, their comfort zone,
their eyes bright as beacons probe through the fog-like lasers,
whoever they are eye sense their spiritual presence,
know myself in them, looking back, moving forward into mystery,
magic, see them as mirrors of myself, even now, searching
back through this dense, blooming fog—when will it ever clear—
gloomy with wavering shadows slinking across the road forward,
they speak—the wavering shadows do—a language
like wind tongues, like singing birds, like my tongue sings sometimes
in poetry when responding to improvisation of any kind—music,
voices, the sound of car tires screeching, machine guns chattering
back & forth at one another during wartime—whenever
odd clues drop cunning bombshells into equations of speech—
words strung out into sentences written by juries, judges, reporters,
poets—revelation, surprise suddenly, as in a quirky chord
change, shocking in its placement, coming out of the blue
as when a new tempo is inserted into a composition, a performance,
comes with the need to improvise, then control has to take over

as in this split second after this blooming fog opened up,
suddenly a doorway there, eye step through into a clearing where
time stops, inside my memory, knowing somewhere out there
someone is walking toward me & eye will know them
when their spirit mirrors mine, the music of their tongue speaking to
me in a language eye know inside my comfort zone,
inside a language of our two hearts, beating as one

UNTITLED DREAMSCAPE

eye relive that moment after first laying eyes on you,
once again in my mind—in that dreamscape
long ago—in the dream you were still stunning as eye remember,
the spiritual beauty shining in your face was as radiant
as when the light first caught you in my sideways glance
then surrounded you with a blue-ray aura—
now—as then—you are deeply inscrutable,
mysterious as daybreak, or sunset—the interval between
those two called twilight, when our minds play tricks,
fool us all the time, when what we think we see
could be a mirage, an illusion,
a magician's dazzling sleight-of-hand trick
a moment infused with sweet seduction

as when you first undressed & eye saw you naked there,
your body supple as any eye could imagine,
so perfectly sensuous, your swollen, plum lips
so ravishing—as they are now, in this present rapture,
your tongue lathering my imagination down,
licking over the glistening honey of your pursed kiss,
an invitation, your mouth open, your curling tongue
beckoning my lips & tongue to suck your peeled mango breast
our pubic hair a mound of sweet dark moss,
my lascivious thoughts focusing like a laser on
the ravishing sweetness eye imagined was there,

it was was what eye remembered as eye reached
out to embrace you—when the lights came on
& the dreamscape vanished, poof, just like that,
wiping out your lovely, seductive likeness,
though the memory is still there—a longing,
a miraculous dream, mysterious
as ever, as now, your inscrutable loveliness

always beckoning, like a drug, an invitation,
so rapturous it calls out to me always, as now,
when eye am dreaming, you always beckon,
seducing me, as now, as long as eye dream

A MAN WALKS IN SLOW MOTION

for Usain Bolt in 2008

a man walks in slow motion as through a dream,
above the sky listens to blue heat waves
rolling across the miracle of its deep expanse
as pulsating clove-rhythms of music come & go,
improvising as they please, voices sashay
through syncopated beats, dreams suddenly
appear naked & clueless all over the globe,

time dressed as a sleek jamaican thunderbolt zips
quick as a blink through shot-gunned meter dashes,
cracking like a whiplash he flashes down chutes
lined with white, red lanes on a track, shoots
like a bullet through dazed sprinters bunched in
an arm-flailing group behind him dropping tears
sprinkling like bombs detonating in their blues-
drenched dreams, as they watch the thunderbolt
zap to victory in awe, dashing their hopes of glory
as he slingshots across the finish line, suddenly
he is their fear, a lightning bolt/flash zapping black
through a blue sky deepening above thoughts
when a mumbling man stumbling like a drunk
inside slobbering, flummoxed speech, where
a poetic thought was just chopped off
(reminds of surprise in the eyes of a guillotined
head after the sharp blade slices off
the neck clean) and quick as a laser beam
scalpel inside the man's brain, leaves him silent
as a rock looking mute at a coconut cracked
open rolling mysteriously by his feet

& the moment is heavy when the blue heat wave
surrounding him vacillates its rhythms of love

just when an oscillating storm cloud appears above,
exploding the sky, darkening the pulsing music,
joggers get wet from God's sweat falling from the cloud,
then everything for the man becomes confusing,
flows, though syncopations still come & go as they please
improvising upon rhythms of speech

the man hears inside his frazzled brain words grooving now,
beats flashing quietly quick as blinking strobe lights
through his thoughts, he sees the thunderbolt zap—
a whiplash across the sky in a moment
of speed—then truth enters his spirit when he moves

as through a dream, walking in slow motion
as a breeze tongues in as a song in a voice,
the sun breaks through clouds again much brighter than hope
people swirling around chaos in the world feel

walking through a dream a man hears music surrounding
his spirit, senses it syncopating end to tend
through the day, chords whiplash athwart a lucid blue sky

as rhythms come & go inside heartbeats as they please,
around the globe smiles break across people's faces

replicate daybreak cracking through night's deep longing

CONNECTIONS #2

1.

eye look out my window, see mangoes hanging sweet
on tree branches starting to block my view of the sea
as they grow larger, somewhere a man sits with a rifle
pointing it at someone's head or heart without sentiment,
without knowing who they are before shooting them,
in the same moment a bird lifts off a branch
where it just hatched an egg above the crouching man
who just pulled the trigger, now someone *else* who doesn't know
who the sniper is locks in on *his* head—X marks the spot
in the center of his forehead—with a rifle scope, pulls the trigger,
time is always changing across the globe, around the clock
seconds are constantly moving *tick-tock* about its face,
tick-tock measures time, moves the bottom line
of the balance sheet, what do we really know of shifts,
crack crack happening in mini-seconds, onomatopoeia
clocking intervals brief is what senses recognize
when music changes tempo, rhythm moves the body,
somewhere else a fault line shifts the ground underneath our feet,
deep under the earth there is movement, violence we will not know
until we see dirt opening up in front of us, concrete streets,
sidewalks splitting, buildings shaking to rubble
is a message from God connecting us all to an awesome, avenging
power, is an omen from a God we have never really known,
would not recognize if the Spirit sprung up in front of us

2.

what are the connections between people waging war,
who have never met each other in the flesh,
who drop bombs on people making love in their bedrooms,
drop bombs on children playing in their own backyards,
doom doom from somewhere high in the blues, *doom doom*
explosions because someone said *they are our enemies,*

who said what to whom, what did they do to us
we didn't do to them first before we *doomed* them
as in iraq, afghanistan, libya, panama,

why do they hate us so we said after blowbacks on 9/11

there are connections that bind us each to our actions,
everywhere images cross wires in mini-second errançities,
somewhere some/body is a walking time bomb
about to go off, explode, do whatever it takes
to destroy, at the same time a climbing wisteria blossoms
a purple drooping flower around santa fe,
at the foot of the sangre de christos (blood of the Christ)
mountains, spathiphyllum, blue hydrangeas bloom
in the sonora desert, a brightly beaded gila monster looms,
slowly hunts for small animals, with a keen sense of smell
digs for bird eggs beneath evaporational graves

where earth metamorphoses into fine grains of sand

3.
throughout the world there are people who know secrets,
balancing competing agendas they use words of yin & yang,
in the world all people are equally human,
everybody's heart beats in their chests like metronomes
until they stop, most things in nature seem symmetrical
inside their violent forces housing harmonious discord
as in an exploding volcano spewing lava is the seed for birthing land,
as a lioness runs down a wildebeest, killing it inside the serengeti
ngorongoro crater, a woman births a genius child somewhere in light
as an anaconda crushes then swallows a large dog in the amazon
& it all seems so asymmetrical until you consider
every living thing has to eat something for survival,
is perhaps an act of mercy rather than killing for malice,
revenge, or murder because of skin color, or something

equally stupid like torturing for worshipping different gods,
slaughtering entire families for fear of difference, anger,
with machine-gun fire

is different than flames devouring dream mansions
of those who live knowingly in danger zones,
where rivers flood, conflagrations rage through hot zones,
though pain is the same for these hearts who go back
to sift through ashes—their lives suddenly gone up in smoke,
swept away by surging rivers, tsunamis,
blown apart by hurricanes, tornado winds, earthquakes swallowing
lives cracked to smithereens by fear—as any other pain,
compassion is still here as an act of mercy when hearts embrace
the possibilities of love through healing

4.
during moments of deep pain some experience healing, resurrection,
perhaps feel them deeply in their hearts as a flash, like *duende*,
wisdom might pave the way to insight, beauty, a blessing, *duende*,
perhaps is a life-changing force as in the instant you know
death is truly possible, as daybreak will most certainly come
if there is no world-ending conflagration after darkness,
flowers at the bottom of the sky will bloom, *duende*,
in some place where two people will make love with their hearts,
children will be born, old enemies may embrace differences
& life will go on in harmonious discord until it ends

perhaps this is all we can dream of, hope for,
a few moments when there is clarity in our lives,
instances of mercy that reveal beauty, truth, as in watching

the mango tree growing outside my window beginning to ripen,
delicious fruit hanging like swollen breasts from its branches,
blocks my view of the sea—though eye know it's there anyway—
& eye can be thankful high up in those branches birds still sing

joyously every day, my heart sings with them
every time eye hear their music, the moment my eyes open wide,
eye breathe in whatever the day brings, time full of holy acts—

duende—profoundly impacts these sacred connections
we have one to another, each to each,
these blessed gifts we share as in breathing

SENTENCES

movement of time through the music of space,
eye hear a bell ringing blue in sentences

the language spoken in sleep becomes an echo here,
a translation when written down on white paper

in the air, when spoken, words seem like a dream
pulsating through ether in blue melodies of tongues

weaving inside sentences, saturated with local
idioms, carved from blues spaces by human breath

sounds rooted in voices here evoke metaphors
coursing blood-deep, form ancient tribal gestures

where words fixed in geographic locations repeat
through reverberating memory, bring recognition

ricocheting through a collective truth, perhaps
then language can evoke a shared history

when sentences might mirror rhythms of drums
& a rising sun could birth a circle of love

GHOST VOICES
A POEM IN PRAYER

GHOST VOICES

for Oliver Lee Jackson, Mildred Howard, Allison Hedge Coke, Margaret Porter Troupe,
and to the memory of my mother, Dorothy Smith Marshall

I.

CHORUS SONG OF CROSSING THE BIG SALT WATER

we are crossing, we are crossing, we are
crossing the big salt water of huge waves,
shipwrecks, monumental storms, we are crossing

we are crossing, we are crossing under a sky
with no guilt of what we are going through,
what we are suffering, why we have left our homes,
though we know we will go back there some day,
see people as we knew them,
we have left everything back behind there

now we are seeking new homes somewhere,
somehow, we are seeking to dream somewhere,
somehow; where? we don't know where, though
we know our dreams are out there somewhere

we are seeking to find a way, we are searching,
*we will look everywhere seeking **It**, though*
*we don't know where **It** is, but we will find **It***
*somewhere out there, we will look for **It***
wherever our journey takes us, we are going
wherever time takes us, we are going,
we are going somewhere; where?
we don't know where, but we are going,
*we are going wherever **It** beckons,*
*speaks to us, we are looking for **It***

everywhere, we are going where time
& this journey takes us, we are seeking,

*we are looking for **It** everywhere,*
*seeking to find **It** everywhere,*
*we are seeking, looking for **It** everywhere*

we are crossing, crossing the big salt water,
we are crossing under colossal waves
above us, ship loads of slaves, blood relatives
who survived our deaths but found another death
crossing through monumental storms
sardine-packed into stinking holds of ships

we are crossing over spirits beneath them
riding backs of african ghost crabs
under the mighty salt water, gray skies
with no remorse, no guilt of our suffering,
we are crossing, we are crossing over

together with relatives, though separated—
we are spirits down here, they are flesh up there,
sardine-packed into stinking ships—another death—
is why we follow ravenous packs of sharks
strung out for miles behind the ships we pursue
to rejoin them somewhere in the future,
fused to backs of african ghost crabs riding west,
on backs of humping, dipping dolphins bucking
waves rolling west from our lost homelands—
driven by churning, whiplashing winds—
like we used to ride bare-back back home
on galloping, snorting horses, we are goin;
where?, we don't know where but we know
we will find them somewhere out there
we have left our homes, memories,
ethos we carry with us where we are going,
after crossing we will fly back home again,
we will go back as shadows, not strangers

though we won't know what words to speak,
what language we hear, though we will know
sound, cadence, will recognize faces, certain
gestures, rhythmic ways of walking rolling hips,
but we will not know evolving local tongues,
secret codes hidden in everyday nuance,
though we will speak through eyes,
touch, speak through seeing, music
drumming language in our ears

we are crossing, we are crossing over,
& we will won't go home as we knew it,
we are crossing & when we go back we will go
as shadows, we are crossing,
we are going, where? we don't know where,
*but we are going & we are seeking **It***
where we are going; where? we don't know
where, but we are going, somewhere
*& we are going seeking **It**,*
we are going somewhere seeking,

going there looking to be reborn

II.

FIRST TAKE

from my terrace in goyave, guadeloupe, eye listen,
listen to sea waves washing in on shore,
whispering lullabies in low, hushed voices swirling
in whirlpools there, voices combing through sand, rocks,
salt water foaming, licking with lapping finger tongues
curling, then dredging as hissing syllables spray,
lisping in the wind roaring over the sea,
sound becomes a language scripting lost memory,

riffing through undertones of history
murmuring rumors, secret, coded utterances sigh

eye am hearing wailing journeys
crawling across time to guadeloupe,

                                   this volcanic butterfly island rising
from the dark, howling bottom of the atlantic ocean,
where flesh reduced over centuries to bone
scream as spirits, their gale-force presence now,
haunted voices climb on shore whistling
allegories, reveal treks, recollections,
terror of a middle-passage so deep & dark,
so terrible, translucent ghosts
covered their black holes for eyes with diffuse hands,
could not speak of what they saw,
blew out lights of their sights until now,

                                   400 years later

now you hear a few speaking, playing lost rhythms
scripted through skins of talking drums, raising voices
through sounds transferred inside blood recall
locked within african spiritual voices,
now, here, they evoke metaphors
lost in antiquity replays each time you hear them,
their antiphonal music recreated over time
through wooden sticks raising rhythms from drum
skins, rooted within a cultural DNA memory,
listen closely, you hear madness tempered there—
anger too from horrors they saw, listen closely,
you will catch survivors enrapturing us
with hypnotic wailing, caterwauling language spoken
through pulsating glissandos, vibrating,

                                   tuning-fork
tomes, cross-fertilized with mysterious reverence;
eye hear them now throbbing, calling through my dreams—

& you hear them calling out too, reader/listener,
listen closely, you hear them calling you too

across time & space their caterwauling voices
speaking directly to our hearts listen/hear

III.

THE ARRIVAL OF GHOST VOICES

in the dead of night ghost voices come, surround me
here in sleep, caressing spirit-lover, seduces me—
you also, reader/listener, if you are attentive—deep
in the dark, thoughts prowl outer limits of space, hover, cajole
inside dreams, hold nothing back from cocked ears that know
words sometimes are imprisoned inside—
correct speech lacerated with fawning taste—still there
are nuances, as the sharp blade of a knife reveals
hidden sweetness slicing through pink-green
blush of a mango's skin, reaches
the golden flesh of stringy nectar what
the palate sometimes evokes in complex similes,
metaphors, a rapier authority is unleashed
                                        inside moments of pleasure here

reading poetry finds meaning confused inside
pure wordplay, linguistic puzzles, hidden without sound,
voices can replicate themselves within effete circles,
severed tongues flap without surprise, song,
the words arrive in a whisper of strangled voices
close to being mute as castrated slaves singing about **It's**
power, reflection of choruses of fawning sycophants

                        so eye am hearing voices carrying true
measures of music identifying beauty here, ricocheting blues,

the terrible passage of pitched voices, haunting hoarseness
from swallowing salt water during the journey crossing
the atlantic, raises up, side-by-side glowing ghost-hyenas,
translucent piranhas searching for flesh somewhere
in fresh river water, in a green place full of blood-sucking flowers,
gigantic mosquitos carrying deadly diseases known
only to red-eyed pygmy alchemists—in my fevered dreams

eye am hearing sacred chants from dancing priests,
red-eyed witchdoctors, who know secrets
somewhere in the underworld of death
will grow into drooping white flowers known by voodoo
houngans, *loas*, who alchemize deadly potions,
serve this milk to disbelievers, turn them into zombies,
who slink around speaking rabid words,

          eating dirt, or clay

eye am hearing the arrival of those raised holy voices
climbing from the sea as african ghost spirit crabs
arriving in my dreams, eye am listening to their whispering songs,
melancholy winds bring siren calls, speak to me now/here
in this place of beautiful waters, in this night of seduction,
eye am hearing/listening for you to sing, old spirits,
so eye will recognize something old, something new—

            eye am listening,
listening to your whispering deep song arrival raising up,
seducing in the night, eye am listening, hearing your spirit

voices from the sea, arriving during this sacred night,
eye am dreaming while sitting on my terrace,
a wing of this beautiful butterfly shaped island

dreaming/hearing waves breathing life washing ashore,
whispering secrets ancestors kept

carried from africa, spawning in lullabies here,
living in low, hushed voices swirling in whirlpools eddying
there on beaches of goyave after flowing ashore
inside licking salt water curled like lovers shaped into intertwined fingers
playing syllabic sprays into songs, through vibrating tongues
winds blow in from mouths of saxophones, flutes,
where mystery whooshed lost scripts, premonitions,
undertones of history riffing in my heart

then eye heard them murmuring of journeys, of crossing
the atlantic, carrying them here to me now
ancestors reduced from time's ravenous hunger, from flesh
to bone to spirits, howling gale-force wind tongues
speaking to me like jet flames spitting,
searing my brain with parables of great-great-grandfathers,
great-great-grandmothers, those who went on to survive
became slaves in this tumultuous newborn america,
their spirits bathing me with sprays of revelations,
reincarnations inside spirits speaking to me
in this moment of history, scaffolding cadences
birthing words from skin-wombs of talking-drum
rhythms raised by flying hands, tribal memories
from st. louis, gorée, elmina, cape coast castle, anomabo,
slaves pushed out chained through doors of no return
from the gold coast—people from senegambia,
mali, mandingo, songhai, akan, ashanti nations—
transported here invisible after the reaper took them down
to swim inside battalions of atlantic waves, sweeping west,
crashing beaches of goyave, just below the terrace
where eye am lost in dreaming, now

they roar in foaming voices of african ghost crab
spirits, carrying their allegories transferred
via metamorphic memory totems in grips of pincer-claws,
a drummer's sense of time moved here via instinct,

metaphors created with drum sticks evoking speech,
rooted deep in complexity of ancient syllables,
accents, slipping clipped within a tonal language,
structured magic, mysterious flourishes, power,
inside audible multifarious systems,

                                listen, listen closely now

hear royalty passed down, transformed
through alchemy musical pitches unleash
cross-fertilized linguistic tones, secret codes, metaphors
these spirits kept locked inside melody, resurrected
african bolts of lightning flashes inside a secret
call & response oral rhythms, antiphonal
poetic forms, dreams, sluicing tempos, voices,
emerging from subterranean places, whispering,
flying on wings of tongues speaking run-on sentences
inside raging waves washing ashore foaming, breathing,
evoking spirits to rise—in me—from the wash—
sweeping syllables ashore seeking redemption,
a touch of sulfur in their primordial whispers, coalescing,
winding themselves around faith like octopus tentacles
spreading out, then coursing inside rivers of blood-fingers
reaching beyond death, informing voices to raise up
those who swam alongside fish, streaked silver flashes
of light streaming through currents holding ancient secrets,
full of miracles held one to another inside a confidential privilege,
a deep-song breathing, knowing, singing lineages
as abused african sensibilities are resurrected here
from primordial places—history living inside memories, ethos—
holding onto faith, these lullabies resonate again,
whisper through trees, conjugating, arriving
in this new world as powerful, original voices—evoking
change through reconciliation, admonitions,
vocalizing alchemy, refusing to go back through the swirling waves
gathering, listen to their undertones murmurings of **It**

like birds singing through vibrating reeds twisting—
tongues through foaming waves with rage after being chained
to death, starvation, unspeakable horror of a shark's open mouth,
its fearsome guillotine teeth clamping down on necks,
                              heads of beloved kinsmen

listen to these solos of salt waves foreshadowing
voices of john coltrane, jimi hendrix, albert ayler
roaring apoplectic, frothing love on shore
in a torrent of scalding notes, chords, screeching solos

listen to the caterwauling history in the scaffolding litany
of sacred voices beseeching sea waves thundering all the way
from africa—in gospels, in sermons, in speeches—
frederick douglas, martin luther king, jr., malcolm
stokeley carmichal—hear foaming voices cascading ashore,
spreading over this foreign, yet native, place
spraying droplets of rain riding on an eagle's wing,
soaring across the breath of this bold novel experiment
carrying new gospel fed an ancient manna

hear the voices swirling out of the atlantic,
listen, pay attention to what is being said

IV.

TRANSLATING THE DREAMS

each day the sun rises, ghost voices foaming wash in,
over sand, rocks, carrying primordial history to this place
                              of reinvention

soar through space whispering, spraying ancestral
evocations into the air, misting inside memory
constant linkages—language, culture transferred here—

over time embedded within sonic DNA rhythms,
music reborn here, now—
(can you see/hear shadows of tower clock hands tracking
backwards, recovering sacred voices hidden in time?)

witnesses carrying dreams anchored in history
of those who knew the beloved ancient spaces absent
in the west, who knew time is both enemy & giver of breath,
why artists try breaking through fear, create metaphors, evoke
sweet beauty, love, struggle each day the sun rises
bringing forward poetry, trumpet voices, guitars, saxophones, violins, bassoons,
pianos, oboes, harmonicas, a conductor's baton a symphony

every day blues singers, mezzo-sopranos raise their power,
move time, measures inside brushstrokes of painters
rhythms of music, poetry, the synchronicity of a dancer's movement,
joy in creativity shaping images, reminds us of the beauty
we all share, the same gift of breath on this planet
we cannot take for granted because survival is not guaranteed
here—any other space we know of—life breathes here/now,
speak to us ancient spirits, raise up your voices,

the truth of collective memory, why ghost voices fly
around the world as birds sing in springtime, summer wonder—
beauty can bloom, flower in people when they remember
mendacity can be overcome with faith,
when people dream, become agents of change,
beacons of light through acts of imagination, creativity,
forgiveness can anchor itself inside transformative love,
african ghost crabs can transmute their spirits,
metamorphose inside people in this new place,
fuse one to the other, breathe, create in them a new ethos,
endure slavery here and survive, transmogrify
into new spirits/bodies, sing, speak new
words rolling off tongues, neologisms as vessels, as rebirth,

create another language and thrive here,
                              birth fresh rhythms
when transferring the old to the new—like me, you too,
reader/listener—who were once blood kinsmen
who had to rename themselves as they recalled old histories,
had to relearn, reinvent themselves on this strange new soil
absent baobab trees, familiar villages, ancient rituals—everything
transfigured into new forms in a future coming around the corner,
somewhere in the ether—*where? no one knew where*—
something different was being created here/now
their spirits told them, they would find **It** somewhere—

where? we didn't know where, we only knew to keep on
going, keep on seeking ***It***, keep on *listening, looking, keep seeking* ***It***—

V.

THE NEW DREAM OF GHOST VOICES

where does life-force go after flesh falls away from bone,
does it evoke itself only in memory, metaphor, spirit,
recollection dissolving within disposition,
perhaps it's there in a tangle of disconnected wires,
loose ends prevailing in minds of those living in the fog of alzheimer's,
amnesia, the willful erasure of recall too difficult to digest,
so a counter argument is articulated

                              disrobing myth, history, religion,
events—real or imagined—a cover up for madness, murder,
plunder for chests of gold enslaving people to gain power,
we see beauty, karma slip away, greed washing through
weak minds, callous men love mammon, blinded by evil, malediction,
unable to feel the cleansing truth

spring rains heal earth's frozen skin after winter,

the rabid furnace rises all over the globe singeing hearts,
spirits of those lost, whose skin color, textured hair
triumph, creating lasting gifts of music, art

there is always the possibility of rebirth through imagination
struggle, reinvention of narratives, as voices sing themselves,
cradle wonder, joy, magical power (always the option),
voices swelling beyond boundaries rich with risk-taking,
love, cleansing, healing, something faith can embrace

beyond structure, religion, crosses personifying false myths,
tastes, invented legends, tongues recreate themselves,
fuse inside serendipity, differences embrace linguistic vortexes,
marry sound of local idioms to "high speech"
within cadences of poetry metaphor is fashioning
a new voice, marrying old images with the new,
the unexpected arrives in another space,
wandering comes dressed in amazement,
recognizing, blending cultures, changing time,
                                        creating new dialectics

suddenly clarity is raised, ethos reinvented in
clear, compelling rhythms evoked by drum masters' sticks,
raising fresh sounds through skins,
machine gun onomatopoeia ,vowels shot through space
exploding into shrapnel flying inside word
bombs blasting in choices people make
using language as syntactical force, a new,
pure form of communicating

                        the moon rises from its dark grave,
lingers mysteriously above the promise death keeps
locked inside tombs of atlantic salt water
down there in the darkness before healing
rays of the sun break through, bathing earth in light

healing songs of sunlight,

hear voices of the future arriving

VI.

CHORUS: AFRICAN GHOST SPIRIT CRABS CROSS KARUKERA (GUADELOUPE)

we arrived on this butterfly island of beautiful waters,
flying as mist through trees, as crab spirits
crawling sideways across this island,
we were invisible, shadows, flocks of flying ghost birds,
crawling sideways, as is our way over the ground,
we made our way through weeds, thickets of grass,
abandoned dirt roads, narrow paths snaking through
places where a few people with skins as white
as the moon glow in starlight gathered
we saw a few who looked the way we looked when
we were alive, with skins the color of midnight,
eyes soft as the love of mothers, aunts, grandmothers,
many looked bedraggled, were chained,
their eyes sad, heads hung low as beaten dogs
or birds with broken wings lying on the ground,
still some of us stayed because of the beauty of this place,
*others decided **It** was not here, so kept on searching for **It**;*
*where? they didn't know where, but they knew **It** wasn't here*
despite the beauty, so they left in a spray of mist
bursting through space, moving from tree to tree,
gathered in open meadows where some crawled sideways,
others made their way flying, moved across land—
forests, swamps, mountains—through air,
kept on crossing toward where? they didn't know where,
but they knew we were going, flying, crawling,
*moving toward somewhere, looking for **It***
somewhere out there; where? we didn't know

*where, but we were going, seeking **It** somewhere*
when we came upon another big salt water
though this water was warmer than the huge salt water
beneath the gray sky of no remorse, towering waves,
savage, relentless storms, shipwrecks, disjointed,
unhinged, leering skeletons peeking from silt,
gazillions of bug-eyed fish, streaming everywhere

we crawled sideways toward where? we didn't know where,
*but we were still looking for **It**, though we didn't know*
*where **It** was, nor where we were going, we just moved on,*
*crawling sideways, looking for the mysterious **It**,*
*that gift, searching everywhere seeking signs of **It** breathing*
until we came to be reborn

VII.

TRANSITION: GUADELOUPE (KARUKERA) TO THE GULF OF MEXICO

ghost voices left the north shores of the butterfly
island of beautiful waters, they rode crests of curling waves
shaped like curved fingers, rode ships crossing the caribbean sea,
blown north by blustery tonguing breath, riding wings of birds,
backs of dolphins, crawling sideways through silt, sand across
the bottom of the sea, swimming in salt water,
catching vortexes of spinning hurricane winds, rain storms,
day & night riding waves of howling demons,

                              lashing sprays of God's breath

whipped bitter voices of slaves—kinsmen—shipped north
chained to ships docking in the dominican republic, haiti, cuba—
by chance african ghost spirit crabs meet another spirit on the beach
at jérémie, where a wizened old black man called legba is sitting,
a small pipe drooping from his mouth, he tells them
he controls the crossing over from one world to the other
says he holds the keys to what the ghost crabs need,

tells them he can make a way for them to find **It,**
only if they listen, follow his directions, his commands,

waving pincer claws up & down in affirmation
                                    the african ghost spirits nod yes

they ask legba what must they do to find **It,**
he introduces them to a beautiful spirit named erzulie,
wearing three rings on three fingers of her three husbands
—agwe, damballah & ogun—
legba tells them she is the voodoo goddess of beauty,
                                    love, all things human

her first husband agwe is sovereign of the seas,
both are *loas*, like the african ghost crabs, so they are connected
metamorphosing, transmogrifying their shapes, forms, fusing
one into the other, part *loas*, part crabs—new entities altogether—
now the ghosts can go forward, they have become
                                    hoodoo spirit crabs

they go forward into the future transparent
seeking the promise of **It,**
they know is out there somewhere;
                                    where? they don't know where

they will follow black birds, storms, ships,
pass jamaica, cuba, enter the gulf of mexico searching for **It**
out there somewhere, northwest
in the direction are black birds are flying

VIII.

SONG OF THE HOODOO SPIRIT CRABS

we are crossing another big salt water
we are moving, going forward

after shedding our old shells, we have brand new pincer claws,
we can crawl sideways, backwards, go forward,
sometimes we can lift up from the bottom of the sea,
swim on top, later we will fly—some of us
already fly as mist—ike birds, but now we are crawling
northwest, following black birds;
where? we don't know where, but we are going
*searching for where we think **It** is,*

                                going where we think the promise is,
we are going forward with memories of the old mixed with the new,
we are looking to find another way, a third way,
leading us into the future
*where we will find **It**, the promise.*

                                where? we don't know where
but we are going, seeking the promise
that is our future out there somewhere,
                                where? we don't know where

*but we do know **It** is out there somewhere,*
we will find it, and we will be reborn

again & again, we will be reborn

IX.

THE NEW WORLD: MOVING NORTH

hoodoo crab spirits following wherever slave vessels take them
carrying kin folks sardine-packed in ships crossing the gulf of mexico
loaded with moaning black human cargo in dark stinking holds,
wasting away in wretched vessels
some leaped overboard dangling chains from their bodies,
sink to the bottom of the sea, become ghost spirit voices—
black men, women, children—gave up the living ghost,
joined translucent ones, who used to share

the same skin color as black birds—crows—

     free white humans traveled on these boats sailing

dark storm clouds cruising over blowing northwest were omens
predicting the future driven by waves almost tall as those
constantly rolling violently across the atlantic
were now thrashing warnings over the gulf of mexico,

& hoodoo spirit crabs howl deep inside themselves what
will become spirituals, yowling until they are weary,
they grow quiet, inaudible, when the gulf water calms,
they make their way forward towards where they think land might be,
where the promise might be found, where now they see black birds—
crows—flying northwest over the gulf, perhaps to rest,
where this mass of water begins to bleed, enter—
fuse into another entity of water
     a narrow slit of earth—an open mouth, a vagina
carved into the head of a body of land sprawling northward—
where a snaking tributary is flowing south,
emptying out into the gulf,
the snaking figure of muddy water—the misissippi river—
near the place where new orleans was raised,
birthing the mystery of congo square
where african drum rhythms roiled the air
& mardi gras carried cold-blooded voodoo
ceremonies from haiti, bringing marie laveau, rapture,
funerals to st. louis cemetery number one,

new orleans, rambunctious partying city

where in the electric air buddy bolden creates fusion
at storyville, spiritual-gospel, ragtime, blues birthing
jazz as he his cornet caressed libidos of panting ladies
who love him sassy, profane, the way he strokes their imaginations

in bedrooms, in their kitchens, his tongue probing
their fantasies in the midnight hours,
as louis armstrong spits out legendary
trumpet licks, solos so hot & brash he turns
daylight into midnight on saturday afternoons,
while jelly roll morton tickles magnificent piano runs,
& king oliver cooks gumbo in his creole band

so many hoodoo crab spirits evoke mystery, magic
here in the king of zulus marching funeral bands,
prancing voodoo rhythms of legba, erzulie, agwe, feeling **It**

but It isn't abundant enough here yet, so
kept moving north through silt, mud-covered graves
down deep in mississippi river bottom spirit, bloods
crawling sideways toward—
                              where? they don't know where
hooking their spirits onto underbellies of ships
heading north now underwater beneath skies
where black birds—crows—fly, the color of these birds
was once the shade of their own skins before they became life forces,
hoodoo spirit crabs—pink during day hours,
gray as time grew darker like african ghost spirit crabs
crossing the atlantic, caribbean—before time
draped a cape of twilight & the one-eyed cyclop
posing as the moon peeked down, before night spread
its immense winged garment of blackness across the sky—
a deep black expanse brilliant with stars embedded
                              like millions of brilliant diamonds

as wolves howled everywhere at this spectacular display,
hoodoo spirit crabs kept moving north, as crows flew towards—
where? they didn't know where, though they stopped
sometimes near river boats anchored at natchez,
and crawling sideways, wandered around looking for sovereignty

hoodoo crab spirits find spaces where blues music
can be born in the womb of the delta, where it flourishes
around greenwood, mississippi, here the rivers—
the tallahatchie, the Yalobusha—marry, becoming the yazoo river
here where cotton is king & the low down blues flower
in the field hollers of the delta and the cradling voices
of robert Johnson, before he dies at age 27—
hear-tell from a mysterious poisoning
by a jealous, jilted woman—answering his own
genius antiphonal guitar licks,

                                        just like back home in africa—
barking voice of sun house, black bottomed trills of ma rainey
the mother of the blues, the hot, saucy sounds of that
rambunctious lady, bessie smith, before she bleeds to death
her right arm nearly severed in a car wreck on route 61,
between memphis, tennessee & clarksdale, mississippi,
& every other mississippi blues singer, really—
willie dixon, leadbelly, blind lemon Jefferson—
                                        because death stops nothing—

these hoodoo spirit crabs kept moving north as crows fly—
their spirits searching for something out there, some-
where, though no one knows where **It** is
in this deadly place where cotton is king

& as is their custom, they crawl sideways back,
into the mississippi river, making their way again
through mud, silt & bones northward, to
                              where? they don't know where
following the flight of crows, they come to a space
where memphis is growing, raising up beale street, barbecue,
the blues, where b.b. king sang the blues
in his own unique style, playing his guitar named lucille—
                              call & response, antiphonal,

african, as elvis presley pickpocked his style to
becoming famous world-wide for "borrowing"
                                black music licks, wiggling his hips
like black musicians back in the day

some hoodoo crab spirits find homes in memphis,
root their spirits in that complex soil,
grow a culture full of moonshine, recipes full of ingredients
from africa transferred through osmosis
to the west, altered african ethos transforming music too,
rhythms, beats, the sliding style of singing notes, breaking,
bending chords, phrases, vocalized lines, rhymes
raised up from deep in the blood
marrow in bones, rooted in dues of the struggle
                                nothing would ever be the same again

changed by the power inside their distinct manna,
gut-bucket slurred tonguing syllables answering
themselves—again antiphonal—
changing everything here in this place called america—
body language altered, people now dipping their strides,
sly-cutting gestures shooting sideways from people's eyes
as they speak in slice & dice glances—everything changing
here in this evolving space of brutality, clashing ideals
in the new west, everything transformed here, now,
forever, during these violent, wrenching moments of rebirth

X.

GOING BACK TO GOYAVE, GUADELOUPE:
WHAT MY EARS NEEDED TO HEAR

now eye want to hear hoodoo spirit crabs speak
machine-gun words spitting onomatopoeia
bursts here in rapid fire vowels shooting through space,

language expanding without a trace of boundaries,
eye want to hear bombs exploding inside
choices hoodoo spirit crabs make as when murder flies
in the form of shrapnel-fragments during these times
when a thirst for power is laced inside rumor,
eye want to hold nothing back in reaching for **It**,
want to be surprised each time sunrise breaks tyranny,
reduces shadow to darkness when marshal music is heard
raising ugly clapping sounds of storm trooper jack boots
cracking the ground with steel tapping heel & toe echoing
uniformity, when simple truth abounds with evil

eye will hear muted voices murmuring in silence,
see severed tongues held up high on bloody sticks,
heads on poles, as witnesses see children murdered
in broad daylight, at the same time, flowers bloom
wondrous colors somewhere after the moon is
swallowed by rising sunlight, then eye hear
voices swelling, filling up hours with dazzling beauty
firing my imagination,

                                        dreaming

eye need light, probing laser beams pulsating through,
eye see hints of sunbeams blooming, daylight spreading
hints of rapture diffusing gloom
underwater where desiccated african ghost spirit crabs
crawled sideways through atlantic bottom silt,
over bones, rocks, leering skeletons peeking out of lost ships,
eye want to hear anthropomorphic connections sidewinding music
across holy floors of the caribbean sea, the gulf of mexico,
big muddy mississippi river, traveling incognito
beside bug-eyed cat fish, speaking through invisible
tongues of wind saying—though it might not be true—

we have arrived in this space after a life-time

crossing, from the east side of the big salt waves,
came dragging chains shackling our bony bodies
absent flesh, our terrible, long passage
metamorphosing us into spirits, breathing
voices full of mystery, songs, religious utterances,
amulets, tribal practices, accents anchored inside blood,
threading through languages no one here understands,
we have brought them—these foreign things—here
across foaming salt-waters to extend in prayer
our translucent hands seeking joy, love, **It**

eye hear voices stained with pillaged histories
bloody with pain—beauty too—bringing magic,
music, joy here too, telling me their full stories,
revealing themselves as truth carriers,
sweet manna coursing through their narratives
with octopus tentacles wrapping around them
as they swirl through my life, they are whirling dervishes
riding inside these crab spirit-voices swimming there
alongside fish, they have gathering seeds, rooting them
within their essence, secrets, cross-fertilizing lineages,
shared with miracles holding them—me—one
to another, anchored there within
the confidential privilege of knowing
the sweet song still sings in them, surging through
their symphonies, blood, knowing lullabies whispering still
inside wind music breathing, pulsating through trees
each day the sun rises, african ghost voices washing ashore
in foaming raucous waves of the Atlantic, climbing
over rocks, sand, carrying primordial history
to me here, now, bringing a constant reminder—

we all share breath on this planet
we cannot take anything for granted,
we have come to this butterfly island

with our whispering voices intact
we implore you in your dream state
to hear, listen, please, just listen

hearing their unleashed whisperings now
after locks of history were broken,

                                                  eye understand

their anthropomorphic language foaming
inside ghost voices of ancestral spirits,
housed inside spirit crabs moving slowly, resolutely
crossing over atlantic bottoms for centuries,
dragging themselves here, wailing sacred
utterances, carrying amulets, fragments,
recreating old practices, accents binding,
anchoring within blood song, call & response
recollections filled with aching madness,
ghost voices imitating the ocean's syncopated growl,
rolling now, rising up, spraying riddles, caterwauling,
emanating hoarsely from formations of spirit crab voices
climbing toward the surface of salt water, river water,
on-going symphonic voices roaring ancient secrets,
swept here through battalions of foaming waves
swept west carrying enigmas, sacred rituals—

can't you hear us howling to your hearts now,
we african ghost spirit crab wailers,
metamorphosed into hoodoo crab spirits,
who once rode the backs of bucking dolphins
dipping & diving through huge salt waves,
don't you recognize us rolling in snarling memories,
now, in wave after wave speaking of forgotten bones,
speaking now in unknown rhythmic tongues,
trooping forward now in wave after wave
rumbling toward the unknown world in the west,

can't you hear us now speaking to you
with hoarse voices howling like wolves

XI.

HOODOO CRAB SPIRITS FIND NEW HOMES

over time, all across the caribbean,
up & down the mississippi river,
the past turns on a dime toward the future,
when african ghost spirits metamorphosed,
becoming breathing, living people,
fused with spiritual children of ancestors
surviving the middle passage,
now howling sacred memories of hoodoo spirit crabs
creators of a new language here threading through
their music, poetry, dance, visual arts, full of mystery,
power, magic enchanting glimpses of nuance,
vamping fresh insights african
ghost spirit crabs metamorphosing here
as hoodoo spirit crabs in new orleans, finding a home,
fused & transmogrified & visible within me,
speaking through me, now to you, reader/listener,
the lineage breathing history inside metaphors,
inside my poetry, voodoo of their legacy,
their journey sewn into images of this poem,
cross-fertilizing with language empowering
all that has come before it now, rooted here
through acts of imagination, cadences
woven inside these syncopated sentences
carrying images witnessed by ghost crabs,
who crawling sideways across the atlantic
to guadeloupe, carried salted sea breath
sprayed through leaves—like dogs peeing on trees—
syllables blown by winds across land, swamps, dreams,

before entering the caribbean sea moving northward
passing hispaniola (now the dominican republic, haiti),
jamaica, cuba, were blown, crawling
across the gulf of mexico, entering the mouth
of the mississippi river as a song,
travel sideways upstream north following crows,
flying up the snaking river past birthplaces
of spirituals, field hollers, hambone, hand jive,
blues, jazz, rock 'n roll, gospel, new orleans,
natchez, greenwood, passing the tallahatchie, yalobusha
rivers forming the yazoo river, crawling upstream,
sideways, north, following crows to memphis,
on to st. louis, ragtime, crossing over the river
to illinois, to east st. louis, sacred mounds of cahokia,
finding in these places homes, forging a new culture,
cross-fertilizing with old africa, fusing now
the new—native americans, europeans—here
in the west, blackamoors speaking, evoking, transforming,
voices breathing anew in america now,
speaking this poem to you now, reader/listener,
this poem speaking to you, now, listen,

hear language forming in the sound of a baby
eagle's voice opening, closing its beaked-mouth
in a nest, hearing voices of hummingbird wings
blurring music of bees making honey,
an act of faith, processing love,
poetry heard under sun-rays knifing
through shadows as filigreeing light speckles
umbrella canopies of trees, death is heard
under the rattling breaths of gazelles
after their throats are caught in vice gripping jaws
of cheetahs, lions, leopards, imagining the terror
stirring in people before silt settles over their bodies
entombed, before flesh falls away from their bones

on the bottom of the atlantic, rivers, lakes,
history is a ticking time bomb
of human follies wheezing hard through centuries
sticky with close, furnace heat, incinerating
summers, leading to autumn's browning leaves,
before they start fluttering down like dead bees
when landscapes turn white as time, &
lungs gasp for air in sealed tombs of winter

there are moments we can look up, see open skies,
our imaginations spreading over meadows,
finding a path shooting straight up as an arrow
to enter mountains, clean air, then we might follow
a premonition to seek out a quiet place
a space to step into a dream, leading us to ponder
where we have come from—a terrible journey
filled with death deep in the dark atlantic salt water—
we might go carrying peace, love
in the words we speak as a love offering,
as we move stealthily as secrets crossing
this strange new land seeking the future,
we take one road that leading to another, perhaps
opening a place filled with exhortations of liberty,
spoken in a rainbow gathering of people singing
hand in hand under the sun in a moment
                                dazzling with clarity

now we might recognize **It** as a state
existing in hearts & minds, we might know
its gifts are sacred as beauty, as breath,   sacrosanct

now we might believe the invocation
of ghost spirit crabs was worth the journey here,
is essential to two different hands shaking,
sealing an idea, like wings connected to the body

of an eagle allowing it to soar—itself an ideal—
into space searching for a place to view the world,
is perhaps like us looking to launch ourselves—
blackamoors—into the sky, flying (soaring) all the way
back home to africa in our hearts & minds as an act
of discovery, then flying back to this space again
knowing our language is launched from here now

XII.

THINKING OF FUSING SPIRITUAL AND CULTURAL
    IDENTITIES NOT LOST

surviving in us are secrets, identity,
cultural glue locking us one to another,
spiritual essences, mysteries time cannot finger,
riddles, perhaps, the tuning forks of cadences
in speech, language, music, particular sounds,
timbres of voice, inflections, nuances,
the way vowels roll off tongues in rhythms
forming sentences, familiar or unfamiliar
is what courses through blood stone deep
in the marrow of bones sharing cultures fused
inside fingers playing harmony, melody
in certain songs ears know, recognize in hearts,
truth, as is the scaffolding architecture
language laces through lines of poetry,
evoking a sense of recognition,
something ears can pass on to hearts,
brains, echoing familiarity, foreign or local,
idioms anchored in geographic places
as seeds blooming in the ways people speak,
growing together, sharing ethos, values—
twin tuning forks serving as harmony,
locking into what eyes translate to hearts, brains,

visuals, outlines of faces, the shapes of eyes,
round with surprise, or oval with joy,
soft as flower petals—the breath from lips,
open or closed, fires the imagination
to feel desire, kiss the pillowing softness, licking,
engaging the tongue, sucking the fire passion
lying dormant in someone's heart,
pulled inside seduction of open lips
revealing pearls of white teeth, perfect
in their symmetry, cultural, as is
the resonant grace of a woman's feline
elegant stride, traces an antelope's
undulating rhythms in the sway of her hips,
is signaling hearts to beat wildly
for what is being promised here
in this moment of delirious fervor,
is remembrance, emanating from deep
inside cultural transferal, a secret,
knowable through rhythms music creates,
shoots arrows into hearts,
as brains comprehend hearing time
beating as hearts, thumping as one
in a bass line unifying the pulsating music,
fused inside a knowable feeling—a mystery
only disciples, initiates know the codes to

XIII.

THE ENLIGHTENED AWAKENING

"Should God die. I would die," an Akan Proverb

seven throw eleven wins
the game of dice, seven throw eleven, wins

eye am reaching back my fingers through these words
to touch your spirits, your heart's ancestors,
in this moment of reconciliation, joy,
before the obliterating journey,

                                     every indicator informing us
all was lost in the bones dissolving into silt,
before we knew ancestors could fly back
to the homeland, then wing forward through time
into the present, the future too,

                                     as the caressing spirit seducing me
through love as eye slept, dreaming during hours
after midnight, ghosts voices come serenading me here
inside memories, alchemy rooted inside blood—
DNA chromosones, where miracles anchor
inside mystery, magic rising here
sacred, in this moment eye feel your ancient spirit
fusing with mine through space, across time—
through the distorting of words, languages,

                                 syllables, sounds

sluicing from our tongues—to forming connecting tissues
infusing our languages rooted in blood,
no matter we have become strangers again—
as we were back then when tribalism, greed,

                                 the lust for power
separated our connection to each other—
were reasons my ancestors were thrown to sharks,
the horrible bloodletting passage through waters of the atlantic,
while yours, dear ancestors, stayed where you were,
living through other forms of bloodletting,
enslavement, in the space you banished me from,
now eye am telling you, you are forgiven
in this poem—now you must forgive yourself also,
love this stranger—myself, a blackamoor, before you now,
is your blood gene chromosome linking back

a rod-shaped arm, extending a handshake
across time, space, embracing you, ancient spirit,
here in this poem, eye give to you now
                              this provenance of unconditional love,

take it, embrace it—me—now, grasp my hand
extended here, in this moment of reconciliation,
receive my invitation, dear spirit,
                              brother, sister,

accept my love, forgiveness, now, recognize
this new language coursing through my poem,
speaking for us now, in my voice influenced by yours,
speaking in shared blood, scaffolded in shared horror
inflicted on both of us—my dreaming down through time—
knowing these crimes will be redressed through
reconciliation, knowing our metamorphosis is a gift,

a metaphor of sacred love

eye extend to you now through this poem, brother,
sister, knowing recompenses of this journey will be shared
as we move together into a future with our voices—
not theirs, not voices of our slavers—
                              writing histories of our own blood shed
throughout the length of this passage,
knowing we are recreating new history now—call it myth,
call it whatever, but it is our remembrance—
                              with our imaginations flying
as a breathing, living testimony, we are creating, evoking
in living language full of new metaphors
                              sluicing off our own tongues
in the musical jambalaya we are speaking now
in this poem breaking multilayered rhythms
filled with neologisms, the model we stand with here,

reborn, secure in this voice we are speaking now—
reader, listener—our multilingual poetic voices
deep in new world vocabularies

                    galvanizing power in invented forms

here, now, on display in the creative forces we move
as blackamoors forward into an unknown future renewing
through fecund imagination with an impregnating language
in our voices, we are breaking through linguistic paralysis,
raising up magic, mystery in this moment,
                    we create new poetic forms,

seven throw eleven wins
the game of dice, seven throw eleven, wins,

free of terror we are here
reborn, we breathe in the moment creating,
speaking the future in song
unafraid of madness of the past we are
syncopating duke's magic,
the train whistle rambunctious in basie's song
inventive, driving music,

the voodoo laced trumpet voice of shango riffs
nailing satchmo's gumbo voice,
the kansas city rooster sound of bird's hot
pepper soaring solo horn,
shooting white girl nodding sickness through his veins,
a sign of the times coming,
speaking through bud powell's catatonic words,
though one can see in his eyes
genius, slant of notes, riffs run off blurring wings
of his hummingbird fingers
flying over piano keys, tickling chords

seven throw eleven wins
the game of dice, seven throw eleven, wins

high priest of hipness, monk, block
chording mysterioso's black & white keys,
shuffling his feet back & forth
under the piano, the fleet, high-flying
rat-tat-tat speedo brash licks
dizzy blows spitting bebop with a cuban
flash up in his attitude

the president of hipness wearing a badge
saying ividivi sweet
jammin' soul bending syllables blown wailing
through saxophone speak bop cool
as the prince of darkness styled too hip for clues
to express through metaphors,
so he whispers muted kind of blue trumpet
licks creating new language
in music five times—so-called cool jazz, road-house
funk—rock 'n roll, bitches brew,
on the corner with them hip deep bass, drum grooves,

seven throw eleven wins
the game of life, seven throw eleven, wins

leontyne price, black diva
from mississippi, soaring sonic hoodoo
voice breaking through barriers
bringing ezulie to bach, beethoven, sounds
ella scatting way down deep
neologic word plays, ignoring dull ways
to phrase hoary song lyrics

new takes on black spinning vinyl lady day,
sarah, dinah, abby, bold

carmen slick styling mccrae, cold blooded vamp,
no nonsense nina simone
dropping spells on those who hear her voice phrase
her mysterious elan,
oral language word playing in blues poets
like muddy waters hoochie
coochie rollin', tumbling forty days, forty
nights stroking smoke stack lightnin'
got my mojo workin', cause my love strikes quick

seven throw eleven wins
the game of dice, seven throw eleven wins,

like lightning, howling wolf's song,
mr. highway man at your back door moanin'
for his baby, a spoonful
of evil going down slow built for comfort out
on the killin' floor, night
crawlin' king snake wang dang doodling, boogie-in'
chuck berry's song, maybelline

pulsing in the wee wee hours thirty days
you can't catch me, roll over
beethoven tell tchaikovsky the news, there's this
new music we call rhythm
& blues cause there's too much monkey
bizness reelin' and rockin',
little queenie, my ding a ling my own bizness,
johnny b good, sweet baby,
talkin' bout the queen of soul aretha's words
hey hey hey hallelujah
shoutin' inside fabric of gospel respect

seven throw eleven wins,
the game of dice, seven throw eleven wins,

in vowels, blind deep singing ray
charles stevie wonder took their voice gymnastics
way cross town where god-father
of funky soul was gettin' up on the good foot
of rhythmic black language
while the king of world music moon walked backwards
up on tippy toes waving

one sequined glove hat cocked breaking syllables
in a million different ways,
all handed down through african cultural
metamorphosis brought,
transmogrified in the west into sun ra's space
travels, voodoo child jimi
hendrix dropping bombs from his guitar blasting
at woodstock, thrilling millions,
whitney houston, living color, cameo
naughty by nature. fugees,
arrested development, a tribe called quest,

seven throw eleven, wins
the game of life, seven throw eleven wins,

rappers public enemy,
tupac & biggie, snoop doggie dogg, gangsters
rapping to the core, now comes
singers macy gray, beyoncé, new rappers
dr. dre, jz, kanye
west, kendrick lamar, j.cole, all this power,
transcendent human beauty—

adding mystery, ugliness to all of this—
after african ghost spirit crabs, transformed themselves
from voodoo spirit *loas*, legba, erzulie, agwe
on a beach in haiti, carried from guadeloupe,

their seduction of me in my sleep, dreaming, into hoodoo,
to harlem, where eye sit now in my study
writing it all down into this living, breathing poem
chronicling a long tortuous journey of miracles,
resurrection, redemptive legacy of blackamoors,
knowing you, reader/listener, are listening to me now,
knowing you do hear them speaking through this poem

seven throw eleven wins
the game of dice, seven throw eleven, wins,
seven throw eleven wins
the game of life, seven throw eleven, wins

love, holiness, *FREEDOM*, **It,**

seven throw eleven wins
the game of life,
seven throw eleven wins
games of life seven throw eleven
wins, **It**

from
SEDUCTION
NEW POEMS, 2013–2018

I.

GHOST VOICES WHISPERING FROM THE NEAR PAST

they call from the near past whispering
seducing through ether, they call

fragmented, disembodied, their meaning
climbing from silence, shapes emerge transparent,
seek a form to enter
silhouettes looking like amoebas

they float into our vision blooming flowers,
voices whispering at the edge of our ears

CATCHING SHADOWS

it was a simple wish to touch an elusive enigma—
a mysterious shadow crawling behind me
when a toddler, eye reached out my tiny fingers
to stroke the wavy figure, undulating wildly
across the concrete sidewalk, before it stamped
its inky paradox on my flummoxed eyeballs,

eye remember trying to figure out the mystery
the riddle imposed—like words my mother sought
to pull from her brain, or snatch from the air
when she vexed over the daily crossword puzzles
she was addicted to, before entering the looping,
cobwebbed mode of dementia—it was illusory

alluring, for a young boy like me to think through
where did the miracle of breathing came from,
or the weather, or if the sun, moon & stars were round
as marbles eye saw packed into drawn circles on dirt,
or concrete back when big boys shot steel shooters—
like lead entering bodies—into silhouetted rings,
looping cores, scattering them like roaches
fleeing for cover when hot lights came on
in empty kitchens, after white people sold their homes,
moved on after black folks bought into their leave it to beaver,
archie bunker neighborhoods, back in the day
& marbles scattered quick when hit —like white folks did—
or time, or birds flushed out of trees after hunters' shots
rang out sharp, cracking the chilled fall air, piercing
as bullets whistling sick past ears, winter slicing clean
came sharp as razor blades whipping around corners,
ripping through clothes, menacing as icicle daggers
hanging over heads so cold, made us lose our senses

as eye grew older my eyeballs popped bigger than
steel shooter marbles too, trying to catch the idea why
eye had to grow up around so many people—
black & white—who hated me for no reason
except difference—the way eye looked, talked, lived
the rhythm of music—blues, jazz—played in my house,
or the joy eye heard hearing people singing gospel
in black churches all day sundays, with hand-clapping
syncopation jack-legged preachers brought down
the house with shouting, raised the rooftops,
seducing, implanting into their holy-ghost sermons—

all of it infused a new hip dip into my fresh slick stride,
wicked, carrying uncertainty eye flew into a future echoing
with slippery meaning embedded into shiny words
politicians delivered—though they seemed elliptical,
elusive at the time of what the promised future would bring—

& as eye grew most people would become illusions,
like those wavy figures my fingers tried to touch
when eye was a toddler, were so elusive,

easy to see, plain as day—they were paradoxes, seducing
as they undulated widely through my life, like those shadows—
mysterious riddles, constantly flummoxing my eyeballs

SOON TO BE GHOST VOICES PLUNGING
THROUGH THE SKY

what was she thinking, the beautiful young dutch
scientist spiraling down through ukranian space,
what were her last thoughts looking around,
smoke rising in plumes from an already scorched earth
beneath her, where rockets had exploded leaving deep holes
where homes used to be, now full of mangled bodies
blown apart, like the plane she was flying in
on her way home to australia
         from amsterdam,
where she planned to be an astronaut,
     wanting to do something good for the world,

now she was flying to meet her maker,
like others who resembled small birds in the sky around her,
strapped in seats, secure as she was in hers, their wide-open
mouths sucking holes for air—like hers—screaming, perhaps, silent,
maybe, in dread—like hers—already sealed, with a muteness
embracing death, maybe not, though winds swirling
around them were whirlpools in a tidal wave of air screaming
louder as they plunged through space so high up in the light
burning from the sun, perhaps scorched them in a sky so blue
& clear it resembled a rare diamond, though the shining
metal shards of the plane—sharp as razors—falling
like glowing comets—flaming guillotines—all around them
sliced through birds before hitting the ground hard, exploding,
as their bodies did smashing into earth from such a great height

when everything—bodies, metal, dreams, engines full of flames—
hit the earth, fire was suddenly everywhere, then billowing
smoke rose in plumes, turned into dark curling clouds,
corkscrewing when the heartbreaking, terrified, anguished screams

evaporated, then everything became an eerie, smoldering stillness
in this scorched field, over where birds now flew, chirping,
as if nothing evil had happened here, though a once blue sky
suddenly turned gray in this moment filled with acrid smoke

eye think again now of the horror the passengers went through

& the young, beautiful dutch scientist, who wished to be
an astronaut, seduced by seeing herself flying through space
                    as she did in her dreams,
though not in the way she saw herself now soaring
before this horrific end to her moonbeaming ambitions

what were her last thoughts
before her screams evaporated so quickly
in the blink of an eye, in a sacred place
she longed to be in, high up in her cherished sky

GHOST WAVES

all around the north shore of hilo, hawaii, ghost waves
rise up scary from the bottom floor of the pacific

shaped like finger-tongues they snatch people sitting
unaware on cliffs, dreaming, kissing, living in the moment

then drag them down screaming into foaming ghost waves
drop their bodies into the raging deep blue water

some are never seen again, others are still there raging
their voices raised up in prayer, treaded through ether

breathing words, sentences, construct a memory of these
lost faces survivors throw back & forth across dinner tables

if the lost could speak of those now inside this poem,
how would they describe the terror suddenly upon them

premonitions all of us think of but never expect to see

MERCY

mercy for broken wing birds
young or old, sitting alone
pathetic on frozen ground,
looking, longing to fly up,
sing in green trees, warm blue skies

mercy for homeless people,
scavenging like hungry dogs
through garbage, sleeping on streets
in cold, remorseless cities,
with no love in their future

mercy for those killed in wars
for rich old men at death's door,
their young wives wearing jewelry,
bemused looks on their faces,
waiting for money to drop

mercy for cold assassins
killing for religion, gold,
dogma, beliefs of others
who walk around in shadows,
give orders to spineless men

mercy for plants, animals,
fish in seas suffocating
because of the greed of men,
their willful blindness to death
piling up all around them

mercy to sick predators
hunting young children, women
singled out for rape, murder,

who hate all without blue eyes,
people who don't think like them

mercy for those who refuse
to believe art is healing,
whether poetry, music,
dance, visual images,
the bonds of sweet human-hood

mercy for those who refuse
too know beauty is soothing
as love is pure energy,
beautiful beyond glory,
liberating hearts & souls

when it—love—is alchemy,
a driving force fusing me
& you—our bodies as one
another, heat rising hot,
aretha's echoing voice

is *mercy, mercy, mercy*

STRANGE INCIDENTS

eye read on yahoo one day of a very large bengal tiger,
somewhere in india, leaping out of a river,
after it had stealthily swam through towards a prey—
a fisherman quietly sitting there, fishing on the river
with his two children looking on—the big cat clamped
its jaws around the neck of the man, snatched him from the seat
of his boat, then dragged the kicking man screaming into bushes,
where eye guess it had him for lunch, or perhaps, dinner later,
depending what time of day the tiger wanted to eat

strange things are happening all over the world all the time
these days, you just got to be looking out for them,
like black people in mississippi voting republican for one
old white racist man over a younger white racist republican,
or weird clarence thomas might rule on the supreme court
for something—anything—to help poor black & white people—
though this possibility really stretches the imagination far out,
'cause it definitely won't happen any time soon for the reason
"tom *ass* clarence" hates himself too much to pull that trigger

did you hear about those innocent people going to watch
an action movie in a mall, then catching real bullets
in their own heads, at the precise moment they were cheering
for someone shooting somebody else in the film, think about it
for a second, because that's probably all the time you got
before something very weird will happen to you

like the fisherman in india in that river being snatched
out of his boat by a hungry tiger to fill its own stomach,
when he—the poor fisherman—was trying to catch a fish
to beat back his own hunger & wound up
being eaten for the exact same reason himself

strange, weird shit happening all over the world today,
all you have to do is step out of your own front door

& bam, thank you ma'am, it's right there in front of you

STRANGE HARLEM ENCOUNTER: A PORTRAIT

on 116th street & adam clayton powell jr. boulevard, in harlem,
eye encountered a strange young black man
blowing soap bubbles with a straw from a green can
he was doing a herky-jerky shuffle dance,
then he winked at me after he noticed a middle aged white man
wearing a white straw hat, then he said to me, "this ain't the south,
nobody's picking cotton up here, so why he got on that white hat?"
eye looked at him & said, "hey man that white hat is just a style
statement, you know, he's just trying to be hip on a sunny day"

the young black man looked at me
"naw, man, he just crazy, maybe he drunk, or high off something
we don't know nothing about," eye looked at him flummoxed,
shook my head, started walking in the other direction,
but he broke out laughing, stopped me in my tracks,
"now it's you who must be crazy, you better go get your head examined,"
then he laughed some more, kept blowing bubbles that rose
in the air, then popped, dissipated like black people's faith
in this country

the young black man continued his herky-jerky shuffle
dance, that's when eye looked at him & said, "did you know
thomas jefferson had a book that said the earth was oblong
instead of round, did you know that, bubble blowing man?"

the young man looked at me puzzled, without laughing, you know
i'll run for president, with you as my vice-president & we will win,
show the world what real crazy can be," then he danced away,
shaking his head from side to side, still blowing soapsuds,
laughing furiously as the spreading bubbles he was blowing
scattered, before popping in the hot, humid air, unmoored
as the skittering words the young black man was speaking
evaporated now, like the words he blew as he boogied away

HIGH NOON SHADOW

eye looked in wonder as my shadow inked concrete
behind me, it softened, then hardened its black shape
as if it were an amoeba trailing my footsteps
through the hot summer day filled with gaggles of people
at high noon in manhattan, eye listened to a sprinkling
of voices ricocheting around, airing intentions
murderous as mamba snakes, they troubled me deep down
inside my secret dreams, where eye often feel isolated
as my shadow snaking behind me, wavering over concrete

TWO NEW SEVEN-ELEVENS IN RHYME

SEVEN

train wheels spin over steel
tracks in voices of moaning deep blues wailing
through the air, you think you feel
paths of history as bad news carrying
tales of skulls crunched under heels,
when humans refuse to see greed as warning,
war is clues too kill with zeal

ELEVEN

In new york during winter, blanketing white
snow is transformed to dirt black
sorrow, when days carry blues into singing
plaintive through people who track
voices, like wheels spinning on ice are grinding
syllabic whine of rat packs
clawing nights through garbage cans, close air freezing
above it all, a man hacks,
spits out a trumpet blast from somewhere, cooing
sounds of love birds, in the sack
up in harlem, wind is a razor, slashing

QUESTION

an empty black shoe
left there on the sidewalk, where
did the lost foot go
looking for a replacement,
what does it wear now

A DIRGE FOR MICHAEL BROWN, TAMIR RICE & TRAYVON MARTIN

where does life-force of breath go after flesh falls away from bone,
does it rest in the womb of memory, raise up its spirit inside
ghost voices recognized once as bodies carrying names of michael,
tamir, trayvon, so many other young black boys & girls with bright eyes, looking
into a future of dreams before being cut down by spitting lead,
fired into their spirits carrying their names in ferguson, cleveland,
chicago, florida, where do their spirits go after breath leaves them
suddenly beyond hearing love from their mother's & father's voices,
brothers & sisters too quaking grief, close friends

do they hear music now, a trumpet lick sweet as a sad kiss,
wailing over piano keys tickling lyrical disbelief, rain falling
on days when mallet drum beats echo footsteps soft as memory
when a trumpet voice hauntingly pierces flights of mourning's
gloomy light, bird wings slicing through sadness of the day,
bass strings echoing echos, beneath dark aching words of a poet's voice raising up
names of so many robbed of futures by spitting bullets stamped with their names,
    spitting bullets
shrieking like hornets, stamped with their names,

where will all this death take us beyond tears, weeping music, poetry
moaning words of a st. louie woman, how long will memory remember this fear,
these lost names stamped on faces of paper posters
nailed to trees, walls in soiled rooms splattered with blood
inside mourning houses for years carrying memories of young black faces with
sweet smiles, eyes bright as suns staring into a future
once possible with dreams, lost in an instant after death
fired from demons walking still amongst us now enter their brains,
how long will we keep these spirits warm with love inside our hearts, before
amnesia's modern embrace obliterates time entombing
so many celebrated as martyrs now, yes, black lives do matter,
have always mattered here & now, each & every day,
every second, minute, every hour, yes, black lives do matter, alive

have always mattered, breathing, magical, beautiful, alive,
living does matter for those who know meaning lives here
when lungs take in breath, makes us whole, creative, does matter
when air is sweet beneath the sun, wondrous, magical as music, poetry,
yes, black lives do matter, all life matters every day light rises
with the sun, when we welcome the moon, shadows
wavering like wind-breath singing through leaves of trees swelling
with symphonies, voices, beautiful, powerful as choruses of blues tonguing
insinuation aching with puns, humor drawn
from black lives, inside songs, yes, black lives do matter
each day the sun blooms a trumpet voice within the coal skin of night,
where the moon shines in the eyes & mouth of a black child smiling
every moment in a trumpet voice piercing as the sun & moon
rising , breathing inside lungs inhaling, exhaling, the miracle

that is life, rising, falling, like pitches of music swelling with breath,
with beauty, black people breathing in the here & now every second,
every day, yes black lives do matter, living in a trumpet's voice,
will always matter, singing in the air, will always matter
beautiful as we are, will always matter, breathing in this life
will always matter, yes, always, always, always

II.

FRAGMENT

for Aretha Franklin

the pulsating bass beat threading through
the queen of soul's "rock steady"
remains wicked, scintillating, throbbing

aretha's voice right there in the mix
warms the heart, forces the feet to dance,
moves the body as it remembers old time

religion, when music was language, words
informing the pulse of our hearts with meaning
after we heard rhythms as one movement,

emanating from a single source, though mixing
in a jambalaya stew of impulses over time
moving people across geographic zones,

it is a wonder how memory secures, holds
cultural roots planted deep inside communities,
where seeds grow mighty baobab trees, sequoias

full of blooming flowers dazzling in their assortment,
colors when we hear the dazzling, clear, cutting-edge
voice aretha bellows, it reminds our ears

to listen to the power of nature's elastic breath,
its powerful thunder throbbing "rock steady,"
threading its bass song through leaves every day,

so is it any wonder "the queen of soul" refuses
to suffer fools when they enter her presence—aretha
knows she's the real deal, has always had it going on

JAZZ IMPROVISATION AS BLUEPRINT FOR LIVING

eye listen to jazz musicians improvising
road maps to living, blueprints, solos,
perhaps, lead to adjusting in a moment
to take flight to a space beyond sight, nuance,
quickly, in an instant, everything might change
in this music, faster than the blink of an eye
the rhythm is somewhere else seducing hearts
through beats, pulses entering our ears, music,
earthquakes of sound arriving in a split second,
before we know it's there—a tingling in the air,
just like when an animal, a bird knows it, leaves,
splits in the instant earth shakes, they are already
in flight—& it's already too late for us who are
too slow to react quickly in that precise moment,
but then we hear music trembling its voice,
making love to antennas in our ears,
its tongue probing our senses, caressing,
seducing the sound already formulated

in a musicians brain, rhythm has already been
launched into motion when we mere mortals
hear it touching us as spirit, movement, a flame,
improvisation, a solo launched as an arrow piercing
the moment, is real when it strikes the heart,
as genius music does in miles davis, jimmy cobb,
bill evans, cannonball adderley, john coltrane,
paul chambers on *kind of blue, all blue, blue in green,*

there too later—wayne shorter, herbie hancock,
ron carter, tony williams in the second great quintet—

all that shape-shifting, improvisational magic,
mystery created before we knew it was being played,

arrived here like an earthquake, changed the way
some of us listened to, heard music, altered the manner
many of us lived our lives in hermetic bubbles before
we followed heartbeats of improvisation switching
back & forth, the rhythms beyond normal
heartbeats, skipping to my loo, discovering new
shape-shifting solo modes, melodies created instantly
when we heard musical licks flying through
the eruption of space, earthquaking—in any place—
dipping & diving, then soaring like black birds,
doing whatever they have to too keep on keepin' on,
riding darts of notes in solos high up in space

EYE WANT TO GO TO BUCARAMANGA, COLOMBIA

on my way to cartagena, colombia, flying from panama
on copa airlines, the name of a city in the southern
region of that country catches my eye & ear when it pops
up on the screen in a TV map, on the back of the seat in front me,
the city was called bucaramanga & eye want to go there instantly,
want to visit bucaramanga, because eye love the music deep
in the word, how it rolls off my tongue like the thumping
in my own heart, reminds me of beats of hummingbird hands
flying over tightly strung skinheads of drums

eye want to go bear witness, see bucaramanga,
check it out for myself, find out what's happening there,
south of aracataca,—the birthplace of gabriel garcia marquez—
catagena, barranquilla, sincelejo, santa marta, cucuta, turbo,
all sounding rhythmic as sharply accented drumbeats
in caribbean spanish, echoing african mother tongues
eye want to go there to hear if bucaramanga people
speak caribbean rhythms, like the name of their city
is the musical language of african rooted indio
rooted mestizo sounds, eye want to roam the streets,
look into the eyes of the people, eat their food,
listen to whatever music is played there, want to go,
see for myself the architecture, whatever is up in the air,
eye want to go to bucaramanga, listen to the words,
syllables rolling off tongues of its people, want to know
if the sound of the language is the heart of the city's name
beating with rhythm, like that of hummingbird winged
hands flying over tightly strung skin-heads of drums

POEM FOR POETS HOUSE

for Jane Gregory Rubin, Stanley Kunitz, and Lee Briccetti

there are lines of words that stretch across white pages,
gather themselves into structures some call poetry,
from time to time the poetic sentences fly off pages into the air,
remind us of lines in the drawings of an architect
sketched onto another white page, spread out across a desk,
promising to become a building rising from a plot of land
near an historic river, where it will house books of poets,

sometimes the words blooming in these poetic lines
leap into space as songs, sprout wings after leaving poets'
mouths & people who hear them flying through space,
fall in love with rhythms breathing in some of these cadences,
like they do hearing notes of music in voices miles davis, mozart,
james brown, alanis morissette, aretha franklin, leontyne price,
michael jackson, youssou n'dour, salif keita & the beatles,

the music & words might become birds circling through
dreams, fly across the world to enter hearts of those dreaming
everywhere there are places for poetry to sing & bloom
like flowers in a garden surrounding a beautiful house,

like the glass & steel homes constructed from words of poets
reaching into the sky near the hudson river,
with windows wide open, clear, to allow the sky to sweep in,
is a metaphor celebrating the spiritual beauty of language,
the enduring wonder of poetry embracing us all

POEM FOR LOLA, ECHOING DEREK WALCOTT'S, "SIXTY YEARS AFTER"

for Lola Bluiett

eye remember long lines of boys snaking up greer avenue
circa the mid-1950's, back in st. louis, missouri,
when heat was scorching furnace flame in summer days,
when a fiery sun hammered high up in the blue looked down—
a golden coin, a cyclops eye—evoked in me
                               the legend of a dragon's lethal
tongue searing us young black bucks queued up back then,
one following the other, just to get a glimpse of the wondrously seductive,
beautiful lola bluiett, sitting up on her porch, a fabled queen to all of us,
across the street from my friend, donnell reid,
who never queued up to look at her
                               because he saw her most every day,

lola was an absolute temptress for all us young black studs queued up
like ducks in a row back then on greer avenue, she was the cat's meow
singeing our maddening, adolescent sexual desires, burning
like blowtorch dreams of plunging deep into lola's imagined sex
wet, though laced with fire inside our fevered imaginations,
she seared us all back then, each and every day
                           sweet lola did,

with the ancient fire most grown-up men knew
as rivers of lava coursing through bodies, causing our penises
to become blocks of wood in our pants each time we saw her—
a female enchanting as our blooming local flower
                           lola bluiett was back then—

that's when we knew the first pangs of puppy love welling up in us,
scorching as heat wrapped tightly around our new focus holding first love
we wore on dazed faces all during those years, it seemed so dangerous,

even then, these new throbbing, uncontrollable, sudden desires bulging
the front of our pants with an aching longing we could only soothe
with our hands wrapped tightly around our throbbing gristles
when we went home at night & caressed the fever away,
released ourselves from this strange new pain, this mysterious
aching we endured every single day, each time we saw lola
perched up on her porch, or moving her incredibly sensuous, body,
as she walked down some neighborhood street, beautiful,
seductive as any desire imaginable in our tortured imaginations

& when she deigned to look our way, licking her tongue across
her full, sweetly red, open wet lips, her wide, open large doe eyes
teasing under incredibly long lashes, we all could have rose up & flew
straight up to heaven in our imaginations, right then & there—

sweet lola bluiett, where did you go carrying all our puppy love,
where sweet fire of my young years, O where have you gone

A SINGER'S SIREN CALLING IN MARCUS GARVEY PARK: AUGUST 24, 2013

for Cecile McLorin Salvant

her voice reminds of a great dancer's body, supple
the way it bends itself into syllables, grace notes
extend into flight, phrases spin high during moments
her voice cruises light through space creating melodies,
improvising solos so stunningly elastic, so different,
though her voice echoes familiar clues—bessie, ella, billie, sarah,
abby—threads through our ears sassy as it eases sex into lyrics
wanting someone to be a lollypop she could suck & lick,

then she pulls back to naughty, french kisses—oo la la—
sounds of lascivious jelly rolls ala josephine baker,
then, for one so young, she turns on a dime,
becomes magical, changes again into a bright flower
blooming mysteriously right before our eyes,

suddenly her hypnotic light captures our attention,
won't let go when she soars, dips back down to earth, becomes
a spiritual song growling deep in the blues dark, she is a lover
moaning heat, trembling—soaked to the bone with sweat—
then passion leaps into the moment, flips her tongue risqué,
risky, elongates her vocal sounds into stretching possibilities
steep in a language of outrage, before switching quickly to tender,
love, we come to know now in her ancient voice
an urgent calling, a siren's song igniting cleansing flames,

it was a commanding performance, fierce, compelling,
unafraid, a searing light beckoning us hours after midnight

A BEAUTIFUL WOMAN PUTTING ON MAKEUP ON THE DOWNTOWN NUMBER 3 NEW YORK SUBWAY TRAIN

a woman dabs a little of this, a bit of that with a brush,
caresses her lovely face, smooth as any
                honey-brown female temptress's countenance

she holds a small jewel-encrusted mirror in her right hand
so as to see her best reflection in glass preening there

no matter her rapturous beauty, the woman isn't satisfied with what
her eyes decipher inside the reflecting glass, so
she applies a fresh coat of sweet candy-apple-red gloss to her lips,
purses them, sticks her tongue out as if about to lick
her splendor caught there as in a photograph,
                      still, she is not pleased yet

so she licks her left index finger lovingly, wipes it over her wet lips
until they glisten as if seducing desire
(as when a female movie star opens herself up
in a seductive scene when kissing a co-star with an open, damp mouth,
before their two pink tongues probe sensuously

              evocatively between two orifices wet with heat)

              now she is satisfied with her image in the glass,
so she rises alluringly, knowing all eyes are upon her in this moment,
smiles sweetly to herself, struts off the train when the doors open—
like the mouth of one of the lover's in the movie—

then she disappears, a dazzling illusion floating through the teeming
rush hour crowds gathered here, causing countless heads to turn—
swivel on shoulders like spinning tops—

our eyes following her now as if in a trance

HIGH UP IN MY IMAGINATION

For Margaret

high up in my imagination
eye am thinking of you
love, serene there in your space
filled with butterflies, luminous
hibiscus flowers, waving
when the wind tongues calm
through slats of blinds bringing light
with its companion of luminous gold
rays, bathing the moment with beauty
when our lips meet, soft, tender,
you are the warming sun
embracing my passion

SOMETIMES WHILE SITTING ON A BENCH
IN CENTRAL PARK

sometimes you sit here thinking of full-lipped
women strolling around naked inside
your active imagination, then you feel guilty
for even going there in your lascivious head
because you have a wonderful wife, margaret,
who looks at you, seems to know all you're thinking,
so you just drop the ball of that thought, since
you are afraid of getting caught with the lurid
droppings of this musing spotting the heap of pants
hanging down around your skinny ankles, because,
like miles once said, "margaret is a voodoo woman"
and she is, so with that thought scaring your mind
you go somewhere else inside your noggin,
like what do you think of when time strikes
the midnight hour, you hear sounds of bells ringing
in beautiful smiles, splendid as daybreak,
the arch of polished steel bending up over blue skies—
eye call it the upside down question mark—curving
above st. louis, missouri, the mississippi river
snaking muddy there, north or south, wherever
your voice takes you seeking poetry, it breaks
in all directions, long roads ahead following
clues, lengthening inside tongues seducing,
echoing blues—joy too—through new days,
voices whiplashing past you, squatting here
with words in your mouth you cannot speak
out loud sitting on this bench in central park,
because the man sitting next to you,
reading the wall street journal's conservative
editorial page, will surely think you are crazy

TELEPHONE CALL FROM SAMON FOR MILES DAVIS

the voice came in from nowhere over my telephone, it was samo,
the radiant black sorcerer of startling indelible images,
he came sluicing in on a scatological brush-stroke,
improvisational art-speak, risk-taking at its highest level,
an unconditional mack shot out into the dark
                              inside hip verbal word-play of street language

when the voice can be used as high-jinks rapology, cool jazz
scatting slick downtown riffs, harlem bebop, scag when it flew through
veins skipping signatures of white-girl time-changes, which was what
bebop lived through back in the day, is what samo needed now
to know as a key to unlock magical impulses of 1940's attitudes,
what mystery provided in surprise back then,
which is where all great music survives—
                        great visual art, poetry & dance too—

inside sequences of luminous metaphoric rhythms,
the happenstance of transcendent colors, images thrown together
on canvas, a sheet of paper—filled with notes, words, sentences flying
as bird wings—full of imagination, dancing into our lives as clues,
wake-up calls, signals fusing our attention, focuses it,
then wrapping everything all up within a rapturous moment of incandescent
                        beauty, like a yardbird, dizzy solo

now samo's voice was reaching out to me to meet miles davis,
"the prince of darkness," master of rhythmic nuance,
the golden trumpet voice of quicksilver mood changes,
unreconstructed black man not giving a fuck

what anyone thought was not inside his DNA
creating music there, with the power to move, innovate through
risk-taking rhythms dancing on the head of a needle, mystery ingrained
in his voice, magic was where he was, just like samo through brushstrokes,

images colliding with colors, his voice laid down with visuals depicting
a contemporary language of history through duende, like miles

hendrix, spoken through both these black sorcerers rooted in hoodoo

now, in this moment meeting miles was necessary for samo,
for his paintings to keep getting up on the magical one,
he had to know the spirits of hendrix, bird & dizzy—all dead now
but living in the disposition of the prince who knew their darkness & light,
because he held the key to unlocked secrets of the underworld,
where ancestors lived without flesh but flew as pure spirit matter
through that dark, unknowable space, bug-eyed,
their invisible arms beating wings without feathers, their breaths
as legacies still creating brilliant music full of colors in others,
swimming everywhere in the world, drenched in light

& this was what samo needed to know now, to transition to the ether
world he had so often dreamed of since he heard the calling of sorcery
pulsating through rhythms & colors he imagined in a long-gone dream,
where he collaborated with these radiant magical sorcerers,
with the prince of darkness whispering music in his ears

DEATH ALWAYS COMES

time always comes stealing breath as it blows
hot or cold across our nostrils, we smell
death there with the scent of decomposing flesh
wafting through breezes with putrid rumors
hanging around lunchtime at the beach, everyone there
talking shit about a dead whale washed up on the sand,
its rotten carcass smelling like holy hell
in the middle of august, when heat extracts drenching
sweat from everybody, it's like being in a sauna,
leaves the spirit wrung-out like a dishrag

it is nothing but time passing through sweating summer,
lovers remembering heat as passion lost,
wilted when temperature rose drenching in august,
while an old couple holding hands slouched toward winter,
their memory instructing them freezing cold is coming soon
ahead, right around the corner, they will find death
smiling in their faces—from a relative, friend—slyly
wearing a look they have long seen coming, known it
having worn it themselves all their long lives

A REMEMBRANCE FOR PRINCE (1958–2016)

eye met you a couple of times with miles davis,
you were quiet as a ball of dropped cotton
hitting a warm, slate floor, though you were alert,
your 500 watt lightbulb eyes glowing
                                 your creativity, shining through
the dark gloom of your time motivating the seductive music

you played all up in the innovation, packed deep down
in the rhythms absent a bass player,
always getting up on the one, raising the beat,
musical lines articulating your invention

you were curious, took in all ringtones
churning around your still, electric presence,
all things were like magnets attaching themselves
to the metal of your vibrating gift—
like miles—drew all attention your way—
again like miles—you were a rare piece of jewelry
everyone coveted, though you remained contained
somewhere inside your spirituality
deep as opaque depths of pools of still water

eye heard from miles you were a trickster too—
again like the prince of darkness , michael & sly—
who loved to make those who knew you best crack-up
in side-spitting laughter, like when you threw some
chicken bones—someone else's because you were a vegan—
at TV screens when someone said something stupid,
you were serious about living on this planet,
no nonsense, you didn't suffer fools lightly—
again like miles—because music was always there,
incubating inside your head every day, mysterious,
seductive as sunsets stevie wonder couldn't see

but heard in his heart in the birth of a song,
your purple rain mixed with cutting-edge creation,
hatched as a dove flying underneath an eagle's wing,
your language of funk echoing sly stone,
the guitar licks you strummed, prince, were dizzying

vibratos birthed in your studio-home in paisley park,
in chanhassen, minnesota, where you rooted your life
echoing african-american boogaloos, humor,
deep grooves, spiritual voices echoing funky news
of those who swam here from west african blues

ROMARE BEARDEN'S ART BETWEEN 1964 & 1985

I. LIVING IN HIS MEMORY

romare bearden rooted his artistic memory in mecklenburg county
surrounded by cotton & tobacco fields, when he was three
his parents moved north from charlotte, north carolina,
to harlem, new york, where he grew up—in pittsburgh, pennsylvania, too—
listening to parents telling tall tales of enchanting, wide-eyed obeah women
practicing mysterious african hoodoo rituals, he heard ancient practices—
conjure, spells, the power of the laying on of hands, bewitching forces
sluicing from people speaking in tongues—black voices gallivanting hallelujahs
all-day sunday morning—evening service too—church choirs booming come-to-
jesus magical call & response incantations, absorbed syncopated jazz rhythms
pulsating through summertime close heat in uptown harlem clubs—also
in pittsburgh—saw sardine-packed streets full of hipsters,
women of the night, lizard-eyed pimps slithering through the dusk's
evening shadows, "blues at the crossroads," humid with pungent voices,
singers moaning sweat & tears, dripping wet inside a slow drawling
speech old black southern people speak, a language wrapped loose
though tight with syllables twisting into sonic shapes bent like pretzels,
succulent words, original phrases heard flowing rich, tasty,
smelling of shredded meat of cows, pigs—north carolina style—cleaved
from scorched bones, came saturated with spicy aromas of barbecue sauce
tickling noses with hints of hot pepper, slathered over the marrow,
a slow heating simmering time & place, rooted in mecklenburgh county,
fast disappearing like breath into space with the swift march of modernity,
its massive sweep lathering an antiseptic culture of isolation,
created fragmentation, prisons buzzing through non-verbal modes,
now speech, communicated via internet, smart phones, communicates
through texting—even dates at restaurant tables quit each other
through text messages—after computers replaced pig-latin's mojo, juju,
the gullah geechee southern hand jive clapping hambone style linguistics
macking the juba hand-jive, greasy spoon gutter speech down to earth,
sweet home, original idiomatic secret ways of speaking through eye-to-eye
human contact, feelings, instinct, gestures, so absent in the new
generations homogenized grammar of politically correct speak,

in harlem, romy grew up picking up snatches of old word plays,
conversations overheard in his parents' boudoir, his grandparents' parlor
during time spent in pittsburgh, hearing tales describing the place where
he was born into stories he felt familiar with, as old black folks he met
& loved, so he pad-locked these folk images of a way of life
gobbled up by real-estate predators posing as friends, locked the old images away—
fading photographs in storage—inside the vault bank of his memory, to be used
later, when he began creating art, he privileged these recollections
(what bearden later called his "prevalence of ritual," a redefining metaphor
of who & what black people were), knew it was mythic memory echoing
gauzy images of what truth *really* was over *factual histories*

from here bearden created collages of maudell sleet, cut-outs of conjure
obeah women, from this idyllic magical space rooted inside his imagination
he evoked a dream-like visual language speaking directly to the spiritual
essence of black folks—other americans, too—of a time & place
connecting memories, their blood-deep longing to what they *knew* was true,
metaphors recognized, loved, celebrated, singing in their own hearts

2. RITUALS OF SACRAMENTS ROMARE SAW IN THE MIRROR
when romare looked into the mirror he saw other black folks' faces there too
in the image of himself staring back from the cut-glass, saw masks,
tricksters, profiles of people sitting on stumps, heard musicians innovating
music inside urban chaos—duke, count, louie, others—hip men getting down
with women doing the camel walk, walking the dog, the lindy hop, the turkey trot,
the cakewalk, trucking in the cotton club, jitterbugging, the black bottom
(a dance so nasty only initiates did it) singing wine-spodee-o-dee drinking wine,
he listened to blues guitars, read poetry of langston hughes, *cane*, by jean toomer
(later he read ralph waldo ellison, albert murray), though it was the brilliant colors
he saw on streets he absorbed everyday—bright reds, purples, blues,
oranges, greens, beiges up against browns, shades of black, whites, grays—
colors jumped out from everywhere, settled in his imagination,
then leaped onto his canvases, boards as dreams he saw in his sleep,
all was revelation for this former social worker, a gift of sacrament
he gave back in an unchanging pattern, a sacred rite he knew was resonant,

deeply rooted in mystery, echoes his eyes focused on (beauty, "joy, defeat, victory,
endurance" etched in those black faces staring back at him from his mirror),
the power of his own gaze underneath his ever present cap, or hat,
he looked like a kindly old buddha, nikita khrushchev, with his round bald head
he had the stoic look of a block of granite, though to black folks he was familiar
as a favorite uncle creating portraits celebrating their lives—to them
his paintings looked like snapshots gathered, pasted in old family photo albums
they saw themselves in his art as they really were—good or bad—
in images he created, based on his own face he saw each
& every morning staring back when he looked in his own mirror

3. CUTOUTS ROMARE SAW IN THE STREETS

when romy looked into his memory he saw bodies of black women
sometimes silhouetted in shadows, he portrayed them in cutouts
as if they were powerful, spontaneous improvisations heard in jazz rhythms—
fractured tempos pulled from traditional melodies—was what he imagined
when he ripped pages from magazines, papers, to create images,
splintered illusions laid down on boards, held together with glue,
cut up pages holding images of vanderzee's photos of sweet moments
in women's boudoirs, he scissored life magazine snapshots,
scenes from gordon parks photographs, witnessed zipping around
new york city streets in the wee wee hours, he saw finely decked ladies flashing
slanted eyes cutting back at him like razors, slicing through the dark, carving off
ends of slick conversations he rendered in collages slipping from lips notes
musicians cutting up on wailing solos of lady day, the president of pork-pie hats,
cut away to coalman hawking, sweet blowing johnny hodges's deep saxophone riffs,
wails moaning, driving music through chaos, cutting sessions in harlem,
loosey-goosey dap people hanging around outside clubs, listening to snapping counts
popped off, tap-tapping metal plates of baby lawrence—heel to toe, toe to heel—
out on sidewalks, 118th street, in front of minton's & the cecil hotel,
turn the clock back to the heyday of bebop, bird & diz, young miles, cutouts of duke
ellington's band stomping train whistles down steel tracks, head bopping
saxophones rode hip, dipping up & down between trumpet blasts, following
duke's piano runs jamming arpeggios, tickling ivory keys of who baby
don't you know the sweet keys, undertones of american music cutting solos,

fired back black through codes, in the wee inky hours of vanderzee's
harlem, night photos documenting spiritual denizens of the dark,
images snapped & clipped of a couple dancing, ripping rhythms
straight out of pages romy cut from a magazine, black & white images,
pasted together with glue, words, he saw himself in this mirror
reflecting snip snip images of night life swirling around him in a blizzard
of surrealistic images of black folks, with slanted wide-open eyes,
pork-pie hats slicing ace-deuce, cocked, couples out on dance floors cutting rugs
as music cooked, simmered, laid back, laid down, rose up again to rub up against
crescendo, cut-out rhythmic block-chords of thelonious sphere monk in minton's,
glittering piano runs of art tatum shimmering nights full of black folks
decked out, slithering reptilian across asphalt, like bud powell's tip-toeing notes,
high-stepping along lenox until the sun rose hot as great sex, ooh-la-la, get it
sweet mamas & papas in the darkness sent shadows scurrying back into corners,
where they slept until the parties started all over again around midnight

4. THE IMAGES ROMARE SAW IN ST. MAARTENS & THE CARIBBEAN
in st. maarten romy saw naked women in clear warm waters of the sea
inside his caribbean imagination, saw elliptical swirls of black angels
rising from blue green waters as he dreamed of mermaids
swimming in water colors he was painting, he looked at bucolic scenes,
striking pink bougainvillea bushes, the large blinding gold coin of the sun
rising with heat in february, vines snaking up outlining the painted yellow
body of a woman with bare nipples, a belly-button over a bush of brown hair
covering her sweet, moist vagina, laid up against a twisting mass of shrubbery,
weeds, close by at the shoreline two brown men wearing yellow straw hats
fished with nets, carried their catch from the clear-blue-green water,
the color of eyes of some of these mango-sweet caribbean women,
who lived nearby in the jumble of brown huts, surrounded by green
vegetation, replacing black & white cutouts romy created in harlem

women walked slowly here—instead of quickly—through verdant green
landscapes of his watercolors, surrounded by phosphorous blues, clear whites
muted browns, stick-figure palm trees rising up from light brown beaches,
a bulbous blue cloud hovering overhead instead of street lights,

with what at first glance looked to be an anteater's nose—
though it also resembles a crab's claw—what a miraculous change here,
a transformation where rollicking lenox becomes chaos of caribbean carnival
in romy's art, a wondrous celebration of stunning colors teeming with beauty,
a signature of his last witness & testament, a vision he saw
looking back into his eyes from his mirror down in st. maartens,
when daylight began fading into opaque moments of darkness

POEM FOR JACK WHITTEN
(DECEMBER 5, 1939–JANUARY 20, 2018)

PRELUDE TO A VISUAL INNOVATIVE LEGEND: ROOTS

you were born in bessemer, alabama, jack whitten—
like the baseball & football player, bo Jackson—
course he's younger than you, though both y'all legendary,
hunters too (bo kills bears & you octopuses, jack)—

what is it about bessemer it produces people like you two?

bessemer is an old 'bama steel town gone bust,
belly up like an old beached whale,
you—like bo—grew up brilliant there in america's segregation,
plantation system in the south, where white folks controlled everything
'cept your power to imagine yourself, jack, just like bo

you rode segregated buses with movable signs
when you were growing up here, jack, buses with bold letters
reading WHITE and COLORED sections,
then came a time when a "colored" army veteran came back home
to bessemer from a war to protect his country & moved the sign,
the white bus driver—who never went to war
to fight for america—shot him dead on the spot, just for moving the sign,
it was called insubordination to white folks' authority back then, jack,
you called it "America's apartheid" system, it's still around today

though times have changed for you, the past is still here
deep there inside the marvelous art you create today

in your memory of a swimming hole, "a car tire tied from a tree branch
to swing into the water" until some white men thought
you colored boys were just having too much fun, so they threw

"bushels of broken glass bottles into our swimming hole"
& a young black boy came out screaming "with bleeding feet,"
because white folks wouldn't let y'all swim in their swimming pools with slides,
floating platforms or use their beautiful westlake to fish
(it was *Reserved for Whites Only*), though you did risk sneaking in
from time to time, caught some of them many scaly critters breeding there,
heard sounds of real bullets zinging through the air overhead,
that was scary but y'all kept coming back, overcame fear
because of a need to catch those delicious fish, y'all didn't think it was fair
white folks kept all that great eating for themselves

this was one of the first signs you were a risk taker, jack,
so, you hung in there with these memories swimming in your head

your father was a coal miner, worked every day of his life,
you picked up the example of hard work from him, though the first
creative impulse came from your mother, Annie, a seamstress
who made "homemade clothes—shirts, pants, jackets, recycled clothing
from salvation army thrift shops and army surplus stores"
you & your brothers wore to school every day—your mother later opened
the annie b. whitten kindergarten—bo Jackson went there too—
she was the first creative person you ever knew—sparked an interest in art
deep down in your spirit (your younger brother billy, too,
who became a top fashion designer, created michael jackson's iconic
white sequined glove, worked with lionel richie, too)—
sunday morning black church services was a place of refuge for you,
jack, with all that great singing, preaching, down-home soul food—
fried chicken, pigs feet & chitlins—shielded you against the cold,
hostile, cruel world of alabama oppression,
instilled in you the will to survive absurd assaults
lurking everywhere in bessemer's racist world

you finished high school, was first in your family to go straight away
to college—because of good grades—entered tuskegee institute
as a pre-med student with a small scholarship from the national urban league—

you loved biology, botany, zoology, chemistry & math,
all these subjects you visualized later in your paintings—
& though you loved accomplishments of dr. george washington carver,
"felt something was transferred" to you being around his legacy,
tuskegee didn't have an art program, so you transferred to southern university
in baton rouge, louisiana, where you first encountered art history

then you got involved in 1960's protests (you had already met
dr. martin luther king in the montgomery, alabama protests),
marched on the louisiana state government office building in baton rouge,
the experience you encountered there changed you, you rode a greyhound
north to new york city, jack whitten, & you passed a test to enter cooper union
art School, the only black student in your class in 1960
& being from the deep south, spoke an oral hog-maw chitlin dripping black
alabama language dropping grease, none of your white classmates knew what
you were saying when you opened your mouth, 'cept your white figure
drawing professor, robert gwathmey—he was from rural virginia—
who understood your down-home southern black dialect,
"relished the rare presence of having a black art student" in his class,
his affirmation saved you from complete isolation at the school, then

everything changed for you again when you met visionary black print maker,
bob blackburn, teaching there too, he introduced you to romare bearden,
who called jacob lawrence, who took you up to harlem, hooked you up
with another great african-american painter, norman lewis—
all three of these very different visual innovators were very influential
on your budding visual work, though in very different ways,
bearden & lawrence gave you freedom to move away from narrative to collage,
lewis helped you move from painting figures of black people to what
they were feeling through abstraction—when you weren't in school or working,
you found your way to the cedar bar, met bill de kooning, franz kline, philip guston,
barnett newman, mark rothko, ad reinhardt, all prominent white painters

then you began hanging out with black painters bob thompson, emilio cruz,
joe overstreet, william white, bill rivers, bill hutson, met poets leroi jones

(amiri baraka), jack kerouac, allen ginsberg, ishmael reed, david henderson,
calvin hernton, musicians archie shepp, cecil taylor, john coltrane, marion brown,
albert ayler, eric dolphy, now you started hanging at the five spot—your all-time
favorite jazz club—on the bowery, where you met thelonious monk, miles davis,
kenny dorham, ornette coleman, jackie mclean, on monday nights you would
go up to birdland on broadway, listen to art blakey and the jazz messengers,
hearing all these great musicians convinced you to put away your long time
dream of playing jazz saxophone, it was replaced by manipulating
materials, making paintings, now this became your life's calling,
your dream of making music through the medium of sound in colors,
became the solos you would have played on your saxophone

when you had your first show in 1968 at the allan stone gallery,
your paintings were influenced by the surrealism of arshile gorky,
de kooning's control over your abstract expressionist gestures,
you realized after that first show your work had to shake off de kooning,
move another way to express your own changing vision of how
to make paintings, you built a 12 foot by 20 foot drawing board
on your studio floor, got rid of paint brushes, made a tool, you called
the developer, wrote on your wall "the image is photographic,
therefore, I must photograph my thoughts" and you did so by laying down
onto your studio floor "slabs of acrylic paint whose thickness" could be measured
"without emphasizing the psychological underpinnings of painting,"
you were interested in art going beyond the idea of self mirage designed
by nature, prevents—in your mind—artists from penetrating secrets,
"is why" you are still drawn to science to circumvent self, discover the root of being
in a creative solo, a visual metaphor leading to "illustrational fantasies," & you
are still there in this moment, pursuing visual dreams made manifest
in paintings you make, underpinned by music, metaphors

of stunning visual poetry—an art beyond narcissism

I: 1963 TO 1974
it has never been enough for you to just dream art, jack,
you had to see it in paint evolving, changing,

because time is a permanent state of obliterating everything
thought fixed yesterday, because seconds are constantly ticking,
moving ideas through space, as in your paintings,
jack, nothing stays the same,

                              as when, in 1963,
200,000 freedom marchers descended on washington d.c.,
as riots erupted in birmingham, alabama—close to bessemer, jack—
white policemen busted heads of countless people there,
arrested martin luther king jr.
president john kennedy called up 3,000 troops,
while in the same year sonny liston knocked out floyd patterson,
kept his world heavyweight boxing championship

you understood time, like events, is always changing, evolving,
nothing ever stays the same, so you created the painting, *the blacks*—
after seeing the play—a work with multiple mask-like black faces
against a white, anvil-shaped background, centered
in a black backdrop, the image is magical, haunting, brings to mind ancient
totems representing a cloak of evocative typography, conjures up a subversive
agenda hidden in mystery, power, there are a series of paintings
with strange looking amoeba-like faces floating up from below into view,
pulsating from dark canvas, based on your memory of being told
the tale of henry wells, a black renegade imprisoned on the second floor
of a courthouse, in carrollton, alabama, on february 6th, 1878

when wells' face was seen by a white mob gathered below, come
there to lynch him for burning down a church, when suddenly
a thunderstorm bloomed like a huge flower in the sky, a bolt of lightning
struck the courthouse, burned wells's image into the window
& after the storm passed the crazed mob broke the window, replaced it,
but wells's image came back the same as before,
stayed put, even after the mob shot & killed him

your series of paintings, jack—*head IV lynching, head VII, head XI,*
hide and seek, the gray void, christ, psychic eclipse—all

created in 1964, were symbols of process, paradox, your art reminded
of monk's piano notes on *misterioso*, the faces hovering in space, ancient as time,
contemporary as life breathing new, mysterious in this bizarre moment

then you left those dark images behind, found striking colors
in *ny battle ground* (1967), *martin luther king's garden* (1968),
garden in bessemer II (1968), *satori* (1969),
in 1970, your process, your application of paint changed once again
a gazillion colored straight lines streaked across your canvases,
from top to bottom—beige, gray, off green, white, black, brown—
line the surface of *untitled* (1970), blurred, diffused darker in *second testing
(slab)*, (1972), opaque, though brighter—a contradiction? —in *testing (slab)* (1972),
electric static, broken, diffuse, as in a sea of water reflecting black & blue
echoes in space, breaking lines up in *opos dipote* (1973), began disappearing,
smearing, blotted out, splotches of red, pinks, images trying to break through
a sea of shifting colors here, rising up, nudging the surface, the influence
coming from crete, where you spent summers now, experiencing
the morphology of the libyan Ssea bottom (called lyvikon pelagos in crete),
where you swam, went deep-sea diving to hunt octopus, saw mysterious shapes,
giant merou, sharks, silver flashes of sea bottom fish gliding through
ochre, green, dark blues, yellow, turquoise, pink colors, 100 feet down
in salt water, where jagged rocks sharp as razors loomed,
where octopuses hid in caves, flounder, all of these elements
began seeping into the hues of your paintings now, jack,
as in the cut acrylic series—the *pink psyche queen* (1973), *lapsang* (1974),
april's shark (1974), *prime mover* (1974), *chinese doorway, chinese sincerity*,
all finished in the same year, colors dredged up from the sea

process is important to you now, matters, you have become a sponge
absorbing culture, wringing out its moisture, essence, what you can use
to make your art, you would move forward from there

1975 TO 1985
now you switched the visual mapping of lines on your canvases, jack,
moved from horizontal to vertical, crisscross paintings with occasional lines
fracturing themselves as they sought stabilization in your evolving images,

you were trying to capture the evolution of symbols in each painting now—
very different from the ones preceding it—nothing formulaic for you,
who never respected "cookie-cutter painters, who always used the same method,
because painting for you is "creative flow as emotive response,"
a kind of improvisation pulled from a conceptual mind, like jazz music
riffing on an original creation in & from the moment it is forming
then pulled from the void—womb if you will—into birth

this process began a few years back with the faces in the window paintings,
now you moved full speed ahead, reversing line placement in paintings
from 1975 to 1985—*gamma group II, delta group II, sphinx alley III,*
kappa I, epsilon group I, sigma II, tuf I, tuf II, persian echo III, annunciation XV,
annunciation XIV, DNA II, holding pattern, dead reckoning I, norman lewis
triptych I—all these paintings broke pattern from mapping your improvised images
in the past, now you weren't interested in progression informed by modernity,
disagreed with the notion the avant-garde advanced time,
thought instead hands of human clocks spun backwards, like a cosmologist
you believed life was always out there in the world—like art—is essential,
spiritual, in understanding ancient civilizations as maps,
preludes to the present, analogies to work from, in your mind
painting is not metaphorical but analogous to the physical world
you live in every day, trying to understand it through creating art

1986 TO 1995

the *garden in bessemer* (1986) painting can be looked at from above as a map,
a city landscape—streets, parks, blocks of square structures—
with a rough, silver surface, glazed over layer upon layer of acrylic paint, blotches,
appear white & gray, textures like wire fences—some broken, some not—
jump into our eyeballs like an architectural drawing, without any bright colors,
this garden seems unrelentingly gloomy, washed out, though compelling,
as your painting *mask of god II: for joseph campbell* (1987) is also a map,
seen from above, perhaps an homage to the spirit of campbell's quest to excavate truth
in mythologies, history, psychology, anthropology, archaeology, cosmology,
in this painting you have fashioned a grid festooned with sudden bursts of colors—
red, orange, tans, blues, yellows, browns—inlaid into blotches—or splotches—
of gray, black & white areas, surrounded by what could be images of houses

your *spiral: a dedication to r. bearden* (1988) follows a similar structure,
feeling, only the structure of the painting evokes for me a circular movement,
though the colors here are more muted than in the painting for campbell
the energy of movement here sweeps viewers' eyes from left to right
as if we were experiencing a vortex of compelling jazz rhythms,
homecoming: for miles (1992), for the great trumpet player, miles davis,
who died the year before, is very dark—like his nickname, "the prince of darkness,"
the painting evokes a sky, speckled throughout with white lights—stars flashing
in a circle, crisscrossed with other lights, deep in a midnight, clear sweep of sky,
only now the viewers' eyes look upward toward a mythical heaven—where
miles's soul might rest—here we are struck, by *black monolith, II: homage*
to ralph ellison the invisible man (1994), for the great black novelist,
who died the same year this painting was made, it is striking work, a massive
black head—almost like a mountain—dotted with multicolored fragments,
the black figure is laid into a background of small white, pink & blue tile
squares surrounding the massive head with no discernible eyes,
mouth, ears or nose, just an impenetrable block of black granite
has risen there, suggesting it is immovable, a force of nature,
rising up from some mysterious place beyond our knowing,
carrying a mythical visual power that it would not be moved

these monolithic painted figures, begun in the 1980's, became
celebrations, homages, if you will, of genius human beings
who made remarkable contributions to american culture, art, these figures
are totemic in their presence, ancient lineage imbued with power, tribal
even, though these totems move beyond race, gender, cannot be pigeonholed,
are spiritual in what they bring to the table of what they do,
whether it be expressions of art, the tracing of mythology
through rivers of beauty, wisdom, these totems are conduits
through which history flows, is fashioned into languages—visual art,
music, poetry—are reminders of the past present here today,
connective tissue to ancestors, they are elixirs, tinctures,
carriers of miraculous substance, they evoke in us joy—fear too—
in their presence, we know magic is here, along with mystery,
add the transformative element—the essence of power

the *black monolith III: for barbara jordan* (1998) is strangely diffuse,
is it because she was a politician from texas in washington & it's hard
to feel the pulse, heart of a political figure, is it an elusive matter,
since many are all over the place, this scattershot painting with gray & black
small square tiles—though solid black in some spots in the lower middle—
still has power, exploding matter spreading out from the center,
brilliant corners: for thelonious "sphere" monk (1998)
reminds of the Jordan painting, only with more color—
red, orange, yellow, blue & green & white & grey tile squares,
surround an explosion of black paint spreading north to south
from the middle, then a smaller bursting thrust from right side to left side,
then the *flying high: betty carter* (1998) painting is a change up, improvising—
like Betty always did with her sweet jazz voice, wondrously sly & wicked,
sliding through notes & chords of any song she rendered—
bright colors—brown, mauves, tans, off maroon, green—
with blue lines outlining shapes of figures, with two dominant ones—
a big bold blotch of black—resembling a human figure, maybe a fish with fins,
or a jet plane with wings, about to take off—like Betty?—
separated from a smaller splotch of diffusing browns shaped like a head,
surrounded by brown & green lines forming another head, set against
a backdrop of small white & beige tile shaped squares—in all your work
from this time forward—improvised solos—leads to *vibrations*:
for milt "bags" jackson (1999), a very different painting in its composition,
the way it is laid out with bright circles—red, green, orange, blue, purple,
black, a yellow one cut in half at the edge of the picture, set against
a bed of white & beige square-shape small tiles—a signature now?—
the painting split right down the middle by a black straight line, bordered
all around by rectangular white-beige tiles is a departure for you, jack,
more childlike—the circles remind of lollipops for children—
it is stunning, beautiful, so different from *black monolith IV:*
for jacob lawrence (2001), a painting that returns to a powerful
massive image, exploding upwards from the bottom of the picture,
white, gray & silver small square tiles, outlined in red,
set against a back drop of small black tiles,
is a stunning totemic figure, a compelling avatar

leads to your *9. 11. 01* (2006) memorial painting,
after you saw those two planes hit the twin towers, jack, heard them strike,
plunge like swords into the bodies of those glinting silver buildings
when light glanced off the windows, you felt the plane's strike in your skin,
which moved, kind of rippled, like the building, then after the first plane struck,
you saw a burst of glass shoot out, a chandelier of glass hanging up there
in a clear blue sky, before it dropped in a shower of razor shards in a plume,
then after the second plane hit people started jumping from windows
doing grotesque dances of black ghost shapes, clothing flapping around them
as they fell like shot crows, then step-by-step the buildings began to fall,
crumple down & you saw in your mind the painting you would create later,
a black, bloody pyramid shape you lifted off the dollar bill, jack, blood money,
so you bought gallons of blood, splashed it all over your painting,
dropped bone fragments, silica, debris, rusted material into it,
brought a lifetime of creation to this massive, stunning painting & it shows,
9.11.01 is a monumental achievement, grotesque, with four large blades
thrusting upwards from the sides of a massive dark pyramid,
it is a work that will survive in its tragic power & beauty,
the calamitous political madness that led to its glorious birth

2008 TO 2015
the pulse of a comet streaking through the sky
between twilight & midnight, a whiplash
tail slicing red, yellow, pink, or grey, curving,
forming a woman's breast, thrusting a nipple
                              forward

before plunging off your canvas of waves,
                              echoes, jack whitten,

it was never enough for you to hope or dream,
you had to see hope or dream in the music of paint
birthed from your cutting up of acrylic colors, sweeping,
cutting across canvases or paper, echoing
                              whatever solo,

spectral flight you heard/saw in your fertile brain,
whiplashing through the way the day's flight sprung
light, sunk deep in the darkness of night,
perhaps glowing red as the passion of jayne cortez
you evoked in eight donut circles, one absent a hole
dark in the middle you dedicated to her,
again red, pink, blue, green, black against a sea—
a sky?—washed with waves of blood—mankind's?—
sluicing across the cosmos, a fiery glow after sunset,
what did those other 47 white spectral donut circles
represent in gray & black waves of cupcakes 1 & 2,
all those different colored circles of various impulses
breaking through the midnight canvas
as if they were there by remote control

again reminding of spectral probings from outer space,
echoing, replicating the same firmament underneath the libyan sea
where you were always diving, all of it now in your paintings,

then there is the shadowbox for children
from sandy hook elementary school, reminding of lollipops
pulsing various sweet colors of a child's appetite
the imagination wants to suck

these visuals of dreamscapes floating
at the very edge of the world,
the outer limits of space travelling through unusual
imaginary landscapes—real or imagined—
bordering on what dreams conjure up in sleep,
music pulsating, probing from the ether,
voices there throbbing, blooming from deep
inside the galaxy of the mind, space

artists like you, jack whitten, dream alive beauty
onto canvases from sleep, magical, mysterious flights

through paint, possibilities awakening power there
emanating from your art in waves washed in music—
monk, the "prince of darkness," john coltrane—
birthing beats, rhythms of the heart's voice speaking
a visualized language breathing onto your canvases,
you be flying through the process living with colors
in the whiplash tail-end wash of paint language
evolving through premonitions, of rhythms
mirroring what's up ahead deep in the matrix,
riding musical syncopations whirling from monk's world,
coltrane's spiritual voice, the prince of darkness up in your head
alongside ornette coleman's harmolodic music, scats, colors,
ideas whiplashing spilling out in vivid hues, some muted,
emerging from edges of cut up paint skins
forever evolving in moments of creation, the cutting
edge of a cleaver chop chopping shredded skins of paint,
reborn in your art again & again on surfaces of number 10 cotton
canvases, you are remaking in paint on a *soul map* (2015) image,
a photograph in your head, you are mapping a spiritual metaphor,
a terrain of humans here on earth, galvanizing now as a creation,
birthed out of black & white shards of chopped up acrylic,
evolving inside your ever changing imagination, chop chopping
every day through reinvention, chop chopping, chop, chop,
every day you rise, jack whitten, go inhabit your studio to work

LUSTING AFTER MANGOES NUMBER 3

for Margaret

eye wake up before the sun becomes a burst of fire
high above my house up on a hill in lush goyave,
guadeloupe, overlooking the caribbean sea
full of curling foam washed waves carrying histories
whispering memories of the transatlantic slave trade
& the devil's eye above casts off towering orange flames,
ignites huge explosions of cascading tongues of light,
sweeps all wavering shadows into deep secret corners,
where bright finger-glows burn but cannot go
because of the opaque darkness blooming there,
despite the luminous light surrounding me here

everywhere, it must be—as miles davis once told me—
all about timing, which leads me to know to arrive
precisely behind my house, in the yard, under the blooming
haloed trees full of ripe mangoes dangling seduction there,
a split second before the rooster arrives leading his posse
of hungry hens followed by cute little voracious chickadees,
right after flinty-eyed rats have abandoned the feeding table—
which is my abundant, sprawling, tropical backyard—
where fresh mangoes fall onto in season, succulent,
fragrant beyond belief, they remind me of alluring breasts
swollen with sweetness, plump lips, soft, inviting, luscious
when opening to kiss, suck sugar from the tongue inside
swelling in the mouth of someone you love, deeply

it's a race against time to win the day in my backyard,
soon after field rats take their fill, nature swarms the prizes—
those mouthwatering, delectable griffy mangoes
lying there on the moist ground—eye must get to before
tiny sharp teeth bite, pointed beaks peck, then penetrate the hard
green skin brushed with rose & yellow blush of the mangoes

lying there, coveted on feeding grounds, they are scrumptious
prizes eye must get to after rats take their healthy bites,
the rooster & his brood peck holes in skins ants can stream through
en masse, wherever they find openings, then surge, advance
like a well-trained army, swarm all over the yellow
stringy flesh sweet with nectar in a frenzy, then gobble up
the treasure, leave behind only dried up leather-brown husks
resembling corpses on battlefields all over the earth

so eye must be there on time, as the prince of darkness
told me, because who gets there first enjoys the fruits of their labor,
the sweet golden nectar of a mango's ripe flesh, succulent,
beyond belief—to gather up all that saccharine fruit,
taste those wondrously lush mangoes when they fall right after
the sun's first light explodes through yawning darkness,
the sky opens up everything it sees with its can opener laser beams,
offers in my yard a splendid spread of delectable fruit—
not only mangoes, but papayas, bananas, *maracujas*—called
passion fruit too in new york city—for me to feast on, fresh
here, everyday, where most things pop on my taste buds,
open them up, it seems so new when eye wake up, find this
radiant beauty surrounding me, love breathing there
so warm, softly next to me, ripe & succulently sweet
as a fresh griffy mango eye am just about to eat

LESSONS IN SEDUCTION

in a blink extreme tropes can be embraced, measures,
language filled with scherzos, seemingly alluring

images, metaphors blooming loose as muumuu skirts,
or dresses wrapped around hour-glass bodies of young women
in hawaii, these moments can be as sweet as honey at first glance,
the attraction might tempt you with outrageous acts of flim flam,
chiaroscuro dreams languishing inside
gripping intoxicating schemes caused by wordplays,
fears, delusional performances, some spoken, others

unspoken gestures of rolling hips reminding of sea waves

mascaraed eyelashes batting sideways after
creating tears that snake black down cheeks after winking,
fluttering bold promises of sex after midnight

secrets can reveal profound unknown mysteries
like a tendency to fully embrace lust, strip off
all pretense in the act of feverish copulation,
when trembling sounds woo male or female transgender
suitors who know what's up with all these locked up,
hidden secrets with the key of a probing tongue,
but eye tell you now, reader, it's about seduction
when you think of the push & pull of carnal desires

it's enticing to wrap your tongue around words
ravenous as plums bursting through sentences, they can be
sometimes bittersweet as broken love affairs are, though
vexing when someone you love deeply drifts away like a leaf
blown airborne across a beautiful blue summer day,
when a breeze can elicit memory, arouse deep passion

then love's seducing tongue can lick across your face,
wondrous as that moment remembered, exploding—
then & now—in a climax together, your faces
flush, beautiful as a sentence of garcía márquez

PASSING BY LA CASA OF "GABO" MARCH 7TH, 2014

(Gabriel García Márquez died April 17, 2014 in Mexico City, Mexico)

the sienna colored terra-cotta house of gabriel garcía márquez
jumped into my eyeballs like a dolphin in the act of leaping
out of the sea, into my sight, it looked out over the ancient stone wall
wrapped around old cartagena, northwest over the caribbean sea
towards kingston, havana, miami, the house sat in front
of the legendary, magnificently appointed santa clara hotel—once a convent—
where the rich come to gather (mostly white, baby whales fat cigars stuck
in their mouths, goofy caricatures of what they think rich
manhood should be, look like, draped on their arms lissome trophies,
well-endowed mulatto latin beauties, long silky black hair cascading
down their backs, while other trophies—mostly american
or european ladies—with bleached blond hair shaking from side to side,
strutted around—slender, too—haughty
                          as well-kept bejeweled mascots)

it is beautiful, "gabo's" house, walled away from prying eyes—
like mine—who would drop by just to look at the man who wrote
                          One Hundred Years of Solitude

now the great man, once full of words flooding out in conversations
with friends through his great books, is said to be silent on his 87th birthday—celebrated
yesterday—& all eye can do is have photographs of me
taken standing in front of his wondrous sanctuary,
                          terraces jutting out
for him to see the sea better, a birdhouse like a retreat
                          perched on top—

at the highest point of "gabo's" casa—surrounded with fresh blooming
flowers bobbing their perfumed bouquets in the air—in the front yard too—
where he used to go too think, write, meditate,
looking at his beloved sea, watching all the rainbow people passing by—
some of them waving when they saw him sitting there
when they strolled the old stone walkway topping the wall—

the walkway here reminds me of havana's malecon—it protects the city
from onslaughts of the sea, conquering armies too in the past,
perhaps is where "gabo" hatched the idea for the worn out palace full of goats
chewing the curtains, where the 200 year-old tyrant in *Autumn of the Patriarch* lived with
his double in absolute sloth, looking out to sea,
saw his enemies approaching with an armageddon of ships

now the mind of "gabo" is said to be empty—he has written this
himself, though he still is the trickster supreme, might have
another sleight of hand wizardry up his sleeve,
                            though eye doubt it—

friends say he cannot understand words of love from his admirers,
cannot read the eyes of sacred alchemists, who evoked
the acrid smell of african sorcerers, witch-doctors who could cure the vacant
look of those suffering from deep hallucinations, self-hatred, sleep deprivation,
who made love to pit bulls in their own backyard with people
watching in horror, they say he cannot smell the sweet seductive odor of women
who eat dirt jam-packed with feces of wild boars & panthers, who drive men
crazy with lust, say he cannot recognize blood flowing through streets
in gutters next to curbs of sidewalks, duplicating the river of blood
he created once in macondo, after its owner had been shot,
before the blood climbed up steps like a snake to enter the house
where he was born, ran across the floor terrified of the death he saw coming,
screamed under the woman's chair, who birthed him into this hellhole
without a future, in the last seconds of his life

                        they say "gabo" cannot hear
the words of his great friend, fidel castro, he only knows gestures,
showing kindness, a macaw's squawking talk, a bird singing
at sunrise of joy, when light & a breeze caress the feathers of its wings
when it lifts off in flight, after the sun breaks through night's sleep,
rumor has it "gabo" still knows the scent of rain tickling his nostrils,
in the knowable, eternal language history speaks through language
winds speak when the tongue of a storm approaches from the east,
carrying jagged swords of lightning thunder-clapping within the immense

dark clouds carrying the source of calamitous storms—hurricanes,
cyclones, tornadoes, furious rainstorms full of kettle-drum languages,
howling high-pitched voices, deep-down moaning of tribal women
mourning the loss of loved ones, culture, their homelands—

                    then rumor has it
"gabo" will perk up, rise up from his muteness recognizing his own life
in this language full of fierce, awesome storms, then a smile might break
briefly across his lips, his eyes flashing recognition one more time
before darkness comes, when he remembers familiar voices
from long ago in his head filled with cobwebs & they speak to him in a familiar
tongue—before media speak, the internet, iphones, ipads, computers, corporate
sanitized bullshit dominating the airwaves with false creativity & intelligence—
in this moment he might recognize echoes breaking through cobwebs—
like his old friend, the columbian painter, alejandro obregón—
rising from the past again, a place of blood-deep friendship
& he might speak to them in silence without even moving his lips, then
perhaps "gabo"will drift away again, enter the realm of joyous oblivion
as it embraces him in silence, forever, leaving us
with all these wondrous words & books he created

BLUE MANDALA

for Xenobia Bailey

you can catch a clean number 7 subway train from 42nd street,
times square, head south, arrive at a gleaming bright stop
in new york city, get off at the 34th street/hudson yards station,
walk through turnstiles, see people craning necks upwards to snatch
a glimpse of a miraculous marvel—a wondrously blue mandala
embedded in the roof above their heads, translucent,
take in how the healing powers of light in this new creation dance here,
magical, circles spin, radiate through prismatic flight, pool inside spirits,
the beauty of this blue-tiled multicolored mandala locked in place
above the subway entrance, where people riding up or down the long
crawling escalator, remind of those conveying metro passengers
underground in paris, france, to believe inspiration lives
somewhere in a promised future, if only for a moment, now

this blue miracle hatched, born, flew from the imaginative brain nest
of xenobia bailey, like an eagle soaring like dr. j flying through space
for one of his eye-popping windmill, tomahawk dunks—making a statement—
uptown in harlem at rucker's legendary basketball court
back in the day when huge afros & short basketball trunks were the rage,
& you, xenobia bailey, a genius throwback too, weave your artistry clear,
here mirroring the mysterious power of sun ra,
one of his little beany caps emblazoned with secret codes,
helicopter blades, otherworldly objects, perched atop his head,
over gold lamé robes, mysterious as african hoodoo expressions,
created to bewilder anyone stuck in the prevailing status quo

we see in your blue mandala, xenobia, riddles spinning throughout
your creation full of planets cruising intergalactic galaxies
carrying beauty through your rainbow universe, you create space
inside a cosmic language your art renders, secrets deepen,
you are an echo in the night, a blooming, cerium flower on rare earth
in the light, when the blue moment seeps bright into a sky

tinged with wonder, when the sun rises with a blazing smile full of joy
inside a *kind of blue* sweeping musical moment, your cobalt wing
fixed high overhead is a round kite of music, a signature solo,
like one by john coltrane, jimi hendrix, or john gilmore

your blue mandala circling through space above our heads
full of miracles—rotating bicycle wheels, their spokes glittering
like rays, lances of light gyrating throughout the sighting

WHAT IF TRUTH CAN'T SEDUCE

what if truth can't seduce with rare beauty
a wondrous sunset in the west glowing,
pulsating with golden waves washing through
the misting day hours, darkening now
with regret, swollen as booming, passing clouds,
when moments of wonder fade in an instant,
become faces once beautiful, now old,
wrinkled with the aging skin of discourse—
like apples fallen from branches rot on the ground—

truth can be questions swelling upwards, climbing
through clear, blue skies each morning the sun rises
above clouds, over mountain peaks breaking through
a moment beneath storms thunder clapping
with lightning—sword blades flashing in bloody hands
of ancient warriors—reveals a truth as well as hails
mysterious glory pelting in ringing words of poets
mapping out a sacred music in sentences—
beneath a language of sky-breaking dazzling colors

truth there seducing full of rare wondrous beauty,
a moment in time frozen in a loving smile
when teardrops flash in eyes because deep love is lost
in a time of silent death stalking crowds of people
mowed down as a lawnmower would a field of grass—
& a human mind can be the most lethal instrument,
a machine of mass destruction, the deadliest ever seen—
as in a church in charleston, sorth carolina, a club
in orlando, florida, the bataclan hall in paris, france

a bomb raining death in an airport in bruxelles, belgian,
a speeding, large container truck cutting down people
on a street by the beach in idyllic nice, france,
all of this madness seduced by a poisonous truth

A DOUBLE RAINBOW ARCH

for Stanley Cohen

a double rainbow arch up in copake new york—
remind of the steel one flashing silver under
a bright sun there on the Mississippi River
fronting the city where eye was born—St. Louis,
Missouri—but these multicolored ones evoke
in my poet's mind entwined twin Coral snakes
anchoring their tails in green hills rolling across
my shocked eyeballs in front of a friend's stately house,
as white clouds cruised through a blue sky laid out
like a dinner table clothed in the same color
filled with food activating my appetite, eye ran
wild as my imagination writing poetry, me

always amused at why people's heads crane, then
swivel on necks imitate spinning tops when they see
flames, a different touch in a world filled with spectral,
polychromatic people, who swirl pain in rich hues—
kaleidoscopic—eye have always clued into whirling
colors, various in paintings, language smacking
idioms inside syllables, architectonic games,

sounds sluicing through words poets speak in tongues,
rain down through rhythms, fame, seduce our senses
with music, games, serenade our love through phrases
titillating our eardrums, receptacles
as vaginas are when stroked by probing desire's
erect pleasure, some bodies quiver, trembling
tame flesh erupting now like voices of great singers

hallelujahs in the nights filled with seduction
in a rare moment that invites glory, beauty
here in a metaphor spreading its wings

SEDUCTION

I.

it is the transmission of language through air, eased from lips,
thrown into space—guttural, or beautiful, mundane,
transferred to a miracle—that brings us to reexamine
the vast silence of skies full of planets we thought were diamonds,
when we look down into a deep dark chasm plunging below us,
we thought we might face a pregnant moment full of possibilities
echoing up to us, holding out mystery, wonder,
thought we might find ourselves enchanted by seduction,
when our minds trapped listening to those pulsating echoes
throbbing up from the dark like strobe lights, carrying feelings
we did not recognize or know but felt them as invitations,
was it then we thought of stepping into space, saw ourselves dropping
in a dream, our arms flailing cartwheels, eyes fixated somewhere
beyond sleep, we were sleeping deep inside a moment,
where we found what we thought we had been searching for so long—
to meet a sacred promise we thought of keeping—
on the other side of sleep, a doorway leading to death

now that we find ourselves here carrying so much baggage—
weight from the journey—we may reconsider what faith taught us
we might discover if all the stars lined up in the dark sky
in the shape of an arrow cocked in a bow, pulled back

                              aimed at a target
before the taut string broke, snapped in this dream
when belief misfired, devotion wavered, a kernel of doubt flared,
then flickered (like a candle flame there by an open window

                              shimmying light,

when a tonguing breath of wind switched back & forth
between a gentle breeze & a fierce tongue-lashing

an angry jilted lover popping a whip, snaking through space
when she ran the hoodoo down to a shocked, cowering lover)

then the sacred vow we swore to keep might shilly-shally,
falter, torn between philosophy, religion, need, shaken by greed,
money, trinkets, the lure of sparkling diamonds on fingers,
necklaces around necks reminding of nooses—a hangman's glory—
the allure of wonder in the swaying back & forth dance of a cobra
flicking its tongue of invitation, balancing beauty & horror—
could be a perfect metaphor of contemporary seduction
framed in this slender body housing life & death—
might tempt us like so many lovers who once felt
the exhilaration of language coursing sensuously,
magically through every touch, their eyes always on each other,
the heat of lips pillowing deep in soft flesh, pressing imprints,
tongues entwined inside bellowing furnaces of their mouths,
their lovemaking sizzling with aching heat,
lust, craving to please, then too feel all this appetite
dissolve, dissipate, suddenly gone like the candle's flame
snuffed out when an icy wind knifed through the open window,
like a guillotine dropping its sentence of death on a neck

2.
what is it then we thought we saw or knew in an instant blessed
with ricocheting syllables, echoing language, reverberating, breathing
inventive through a poetic line, shimmering in space in the cat eyes
a sweet woman holds shining golden in the darkness,
was it music you knew you heard playing so wondrously in her
dancer's body, moving hypnotically with pulsating rhythms,
scintillating control, evoking the lover you wished for in your dreams,
her honey-heated vagina sweet as an open mouth sucking you deep
inside her luscious twin gifts—the lure, sweetness of it all—the heat
bringing you here seeking consummation
before your imagination exploded with the miracle
you deeply felt when release coursed through your body,

your spirit opened as a flower, as when great music is made
then heard in space, the beauty & power of words
when poetry suffuses with dreams, a suite of longing

3.
it is time you look deeply into moments when events come
surprising you with wonder, what did miles say, "play above
everything you know," you might enter a sacred zone
where creation becomes improvisational, necessary

you can enter space inside yourself where magic soars,
risk-taking is imbued with mysterious powers,
you might not recognize the allure seduction brings to the table,
after all the failures, struggles, love involved in great invention,
even when surrounded by silence of the deep dark hole,
the invitation where you might be standing over, even now,
you hear something calling, seducing your spirit—some call it suicide,
others call it life, art—something on the other side of what you know

perhaps there is a new music in the vast silence of black skies
full of planets we thought were diamonds brings to our ears,

what is heard in the cat eyes of that wondrous woman
you have been dreaming of forever, know as a poem, beckoning you
with a language beyond literary metaphor,
a visual rendering full of inventive new rhythms
your imagination has never heard, nor your ears recognize the sounds
inside the colors of vivid paint strokes, stevie wonder's music of plants,
voices pure with mystery, magical—duende?
beyond seduction, yet seducing you anyway, in this moment,
your eyes, ears informing your heart what beauty to love

USAIN BOLT'S FINAL 2016 OLYMPICS

I.

a lightning bolt unzips the black night sky, looking
like a miracle zigzagging through space
inside ether, flying at an otherworldly pace we can't imagine,
in dream, a human zipping past our eyes this fast,
but there went usain bolt seducing us with sheer propulsion,
urging his body forward to reach immortality through speed,
drew our attraction to him—metal to magnet, bees to honey—
locked our eyeballs onto his every high-stepping move

whatever bolt did from this moment on, running track
was special, despite his playfulness, serious aura, the chameleon,
mysterious, deep magic of his nature pulled us to gawk whenever
he put on display his prowess, otherworldly dominance,
exuding complete control over incredible power,
the bullet-like thrust powering this lean, tall jamaican's
roadrunner body, long legs wheeling as he sprinted, leaned,
dipped into curves, piston legs pumping hard & fast down a track,
while the other hapless racers—also known as speed-demons—
strained to catch him, flailing arms in futile desperation,
faces grimacing whenever he bolted by them,
left them all feeling his gusts brushing their skin like a tonguing

wind, he was a lightning strike, when it was all over after
he crossed the finish line first again, flashed a 1000-watt smile,
struck his cocksure signature pose resembling a lightning bolt—
one arm cocked at the elbow, the other stretched out
as if he were shooting an arrow from a bow up to god—
it is the trademark victory stance worn on his apparel—

perhaps he thought of himself as of a lightning bolt too up in the sky,
flashes we all viewed in our lifetime, he seduced us,
all those shutterbugs popping camera lights up in massive crowds

packed in like sardines inside huge stadiums, cheering him on,
it's crazy to witness all this adoration—women twerking, others looking on
in awe, wonder, perhaps a touch of jealousy, envy—men mostly—
in all this devotion, delirium bordering on worship, cult

everyone hoped he would see them, acknowledge all that love
streaming tears down multitudes of faces in all this bedlam, clapping
thunderous approval, showering applause of what they saw
each & every time he set golden shoes encasing his feet
on any cinder track all over the world, when he bowed in a swoop
while receiving their affection, he smiled, then waved back,
his long, sinewy, sleek muscular arms shining with sweat,
when he rose up his glory beyond all those who came before him—
winning triple-triple olympic gold, three straight games, without one loss—
his legacy was cemented forever, exploded into myth, legend

2.
in august 2016, when he reached almost god-like reverence,
a level of holiness that symbolized the ultimate glory
for bulletlike speed-demons—with him being the fastest of any time,
because no other had ever reached this glorious height—
bestowed in these haloed games, stretching all the way back
to ancient greece, this sleek black jamaican man sprinted into history,
then he said he had run his last olympic race, so perhaps
we will never see him run again, except in our dreams, perhaps not,
maybe we will not see his likeness again, perhaps so,
but this eye know each time eye look up & see a flashing
lightning bolt ripping jaggedly bright across a black night sky

then eye will always think of him smiling, will think of usain bolt
zigzagging through darkness, sprinting his way to glory

HINTS OF SEDUCTION

seduction is sex, passion,
the allure of temptation
driving hot fast flashy cars,
swooning as sunrays slice through
a muckrake of pure darkness,
seduction is lust, kisses,
fixated on love, fashion,
a chain of sweet encounters,
probing soft lips of the mouth,
grooves entwining, sweet, sucking
tongues of candy, slippery,
phallic, probing vaginas
swamped with soupy saliva

seduction is the pursuit
when mystery is thrilling
deep suction of a wet kiss
caressing tongues of language
oscillating back & forth
feeling a body moving
swept up in perfect rhythm,
a great dancer's sculpting art,
a supple invitation
pursues what is magical
as the elixir of breath
sings pulsating poetry
caressing hearts bring voices
lyrical as spring winds, birds
trilling, trebling violins,
feasting, eating, godiva
chocolate smearing fused mouths,
oscillating tuning forks

electrical connections
arouse primal desires,
seduction is a lit bomb,
pursuing war for money,
greed, insatiable drug, pooh,
people seeking attention,
power, another venus
flytrap ensnaring, craving—
again—desires, longing,
addiction to language, sounds,
watching basketball games, dunks,
swishing jump shots, cross-over
dribbles, addicted to faith,
truth, however you see it
looking at a man, woman,
the color of their skin, eyes,
texture of hair—locks—silky,
waves back to you when breezes
become caressing hands, make
strands of mops lift into dance,
kinky naps lie flat as rugs,
sporting shapes of quo vadis
before seduced by afros,
greasy, oily jheri curls,
then false wigs waved once again
from halloween bobble heads
perched atop robot bodies

seduction is sleeping late,
a fabulous plate of food,
eating ice cream on hot days,
con men & women macking
silver tongues slicing clean through
words—knives through butter—create
new neologic phrases

like "bomb cyclones," meaning cold
"bombogenesis" weather—
words never heard before now—
brings attitudes of terror
to dress up like eskimos
the pursuit of composing
poems, music, painting, acting,
science, politics—good, bad—
reading a great book, walking
to "get out of your own way"
like bono sang, be seduced
by fragrance of fresh flowers,
lovers walking hand in hand
searching for sweetness in eyes
in central park in springtime
in all that deliciousness

EACH OF US HERE

for Beata, David and Wieslawa

each of us here for a moment in time, dances
in the air, the smell of love, beautiful people,
those who are ghastly occupying the same place

earth spins through light towards darkness
time moves leaves on trees, stevie wonder's voice,
tomasz stanko's spare trumpet licks echo miles
davis' choices in krakow, poland, where footsteps

ricocheting history over cobblestone streets,
carry voices of szymborska, milosz,
vodka-laced phrases of herbert, komeda here,
swelling through billowing gray fog of november

yet mystery is here too, real as time is
as each of us moves through it,
through space with superstition, wonder, we
humans do, holding fast to life

they can be seen as birds
soaring with music, as poetry sometimes does
when carving bllerinas' bodies into shapes

they dance in gaps, while others flying through
space jack-knife, double-pump into the galaxy,
their torsos break-dancing up in the air before
tomahawking basketball dunks to riotous cheers
we are here, erupting through brief moments
on this planet of rock & water, spinning
indecipherable, the road ahead full, packed
tight with illusions, they surprise us jumping out

from hidden, secret places, love can reveal
itself as a paradox here, in each of us,
a flower growing in a war-ravaged space
where hatred abounds, despite tendernesses

LYRIC STILL LIFE

once again for Margaret

love, hand me flower petals of your laughter
shimmering as a school of silver fish
swimming fast just beneath the clear surface
in an ice-cold lake, somewhere deep in memory,
during the thaw of springtime, early morning
rinse, where no waves moved across the surface
but the silent air hung inside a misting veil
full of fragile dewdrops, just before the sun rises
splendid over the rims of mountain tops
fencing in the lake, trees sprouting in the east,
your face appeared wondrous as a sunrise
in the image of a photo above your name

NEW
POEMS
2019–2020

DUENDE

for Garcia Lorca and Miles Davis

it's in the bottomless power, magic of duende
climbing stealthily from earth, wrapped inside
secrets, mystery infused in black magic
that enters bodies in the form of music, art,
poetry imbuing language with sovereignty,
in blood spooling back through violent centuries,
voices echoing ancient Africa, rise, thread

from skins of blessed, sacred rituals, people
emerge from drums as heartbeats in time
where memory is revived here now through metaphor
when olden voices find their way vibrating into song,
rhythms stitch forgotten sounds into language
beat out of them by whips on slave ships,
bring back wonder of feet pounding, dance

the holy ghost lost in bloody homelands,
now souls underneath, rise up through bodies,
spool back with talismans, hypnotic, pull ancient
voodoo up in buckets filled with holy water,
evoke memories drinking from whodunit secrets
awakened in poetry of Garcia Lorca,
Andalusian dues heard in Miles Davis' clues

vibrating anew in *Sketches of Spain,* andante blues

SEARCHING

eye am searching for a quick way to redeem myself,
searching through bold forms of art—paintings,
the shapes of Melvin Edwards' sculpture, the poetry
that fired the imaginations of Pablo Neruda, Aimé Césaire,
César Vallejo, Jean Joseph Rabearivello, the sacred prayers
witch doctors, shamans, and voodoo priests chant,
who absorbed the magical holy mantras wise men
raise up to their Gods when evoking power of ancestors,
who leap up on licking tips of flames as dancing figures,
during twilight hours, their eyes red from traveling
the great journey from the long lost past carrying words
that need translators here, which is the holy task of poets,
painters, dancers and musicians who speak history
through riddles, metaphors locked in rhythms and time,
and women evoke the twin magic too raised up through
the very same gods but have different body shapes,
and whose sagacity far exceeds the wisdom of men

so eye have tried to reinvent through language a music
laced and stitched with echoes that speak of the past though
anchored in the present and seeking a voice that will evoke
the future, carried there as if shot from the lost brain
of a legendary madman electrocuted for burning dictionaries
that only carried words of 5th rate plagiarists of placebos,
who rejected the magical words of great poets, substituting
in his dictionaries instead the doggerel of fake priests
who only prayed for the living dead and only after
they were paid with the flowing blood of masses
with their severed bloody heads nailed up on pikes,
surrounded by laughing fools pointing small bejeweled
fingers up at the heads while vultures circle
as a chorus erupts from giddy fools: "we want more,
we want more heads, we want more, more, more, more!"

eye think of the fact no one pleaded guilty for the murder
of Spanish poet Federico Garcia Lorca, shot down for being
a homosexual, a poet, in 1936, in Grande Fuente, Granada, Spain,
where his bones are buried somewhere still unknown
in an unmarked grave, his voice still resonates here
today, lives strong in the poetry of poets everywhere, so

what is it evil people search for forever throughout time,
wedded through holes refusing to carry magical words
in their sentences, some poets pass themselves off as fake
priests who only pray for the living or dead when they get paid,
what is the poisonous need—dream?—keeps them up
needing blood to drink when the sun rises each morning,
when werewolves and vampires stalk for blood when moons
shine bright as pearls or rise red or white with their mythical
voices howling in the dead of night, can you hear them
baying at the moon from somewhere in trump's White
House, needing to see severed bloody heads up on spikes,
his legions of mindless fools screaming: "we want more,
give us more, we want more, more, more, more, more . . ."

A POEM FOR AN OLD MAN WALKING
AN EQUALLY OLD DOG

an old man is walking
an equally old dog
or is it the other
way around, no matter,
they both look down, weary
is the word written here,
a description of them
the man & his stick cane,
the dog held by a leash
though it might be something
close—a rope, a thin chain,
a line, or a tether
because it's cold outside
today, the sun is out,
shining through doubt because
clouds cruising through the blue
above it all reminds
memory of large ships,
or gray-white schools of whales
thundering through the waves
down here in the soaping
foam, boiling in voices
above these old spirits
looking not left or right
but down, moving forward,
attached to each other
by hook or crook, they know
trust over the long years
earned sweetness of friendship,
love even, despite fights,
a fresh bone in the mouth

of the very old dog
lodged in the memory,
something mysterious
like that, perhaps, will turn
the trick, a switch hidden
inside their brains will do,
can see it in their eyes,
the love in their sweet smiles
looking at each other
& this poem is a leash
in six syllable lines
connecting them to you
reader, connecting me
to you through these skinny
six syllable lines, stacked
to resemble this stick
the old man is holding
like faith in his gnarled hand,
will keep his dearest friend
walking there beside him
there is nothing else now
in their lives but this love
they hold for each other

A TANKA FOR STANLEY MOSS AT AGE 95

Stanley Moss fights death
with hundreds of poems he writes
every breath spoken
constructs defensive armor
from every word he breathes now

A WANDERING 7–11

for my mother, Dorothy Smith Marshall, 1917 to 2018

today the sky is gray black,
dark as clouds sweeping death through my memory
stamped on faces of friends lost
fighting great storms of raging life—chickadees
beat tiny wings like dots there,
periods—their faces—like kites—once loved, float
like soiled pages torn from books

serve as brakes on dialogue, my mother's face
up there grieving with the rest,
floating cold in blue ether, her doe eyes those
wearing masks of confusion
like these phantoms surrounding her, lips frozen—
like hers—set in stone, silence,
cast in memory these inaudible ghosts,
without even a gesture—
only when we recall them—their love, sorrow,
whatever tales they left us—
perhaps some hip words in a deep poem, colors

brushstrokes of a painting, food,
tasty as wet, soft smooches, my mother's smile—
warms me now in looping dreams,
blooming sweet as her perfume seduced male hearts,
beating drumming metronomes
beckoning breath, metaphors swimming around
all of us—sky blue ether

from where my mother's arms reach out, surround me
in laughter from the misty
beyond, that is what haunts me here now, over
questions—where does breath go when

it flies beating feathered wings, carrying clefs—
like birds—splitting up in space
deep as jazz solos creating diverse breaths,
improvising off one beat
as they dance like twin notes inside the music,
do they descend down steep stairs
leading to where neither comes back, though both run

to catch the black, smoking train
choo-chewing through space, where no one keeps return
tickets, though now they still go,
quiet as it's kept, no one has a choice in this,
no one ever gets to vote—
not even the women who birthed—brought—all us
here, we're on our own to dance

this bloody tango with faith—a skunk spraying
funk over us—you reader
there, feeling cold as winds cut through like razors
where you live now alone, cold,
carrying words icy as assassins eyes,
you feel a deep need to be
rescued here, because you read poems laced with ripe
new metaphors stitched throughout
with bold language bursting inside sentences
laced with sweet mangoes—replete
with premonitions, you want to hold on to

what to do when everything
switches in this whirling change, all the faces,
colors, shapes, hair, informs us
different narratives rule situations,
leaves us—perhaps with some words
mirrors deep poems in my mother's smile, warms me
here in looping dreams blooming

sweet as her perfumed laughter reaching me now
from the misty beyond—still
what haunts me here is wondering where breath goes
when it sucks inward, whooshing
breath blowing hard beneath gray black high clouds, rain
brooms sweeping cold through—cobwebs—
memory echoing colors of music
ricocheting from steel plates
beneath shoes of bojangles tapping rhythms
through champagne nights of harlem
back in the day, still hanging around today

so is it any wonder
these seven-eleven stanzas are chasing
a strict, slick style of being
in the moment now, instead of combing through
reruns of slavery's lore—
chains hanging off our ankles, nails in our tongues,
eye mean already been there

done that song & dance, now we're moving beyond
hip hop, rap, whatever comes
shaping language, after that will turn into
a crap shoot—don't mention new
forms—sort of like wearing contemporary
fashions—skinny stovepipe pants
the color of scarlet cherries, blood orange,
shirts wide open at the neck,
black & white, pointy, checkerboard shoes made from
leopard skin, suede, blue laces
criss-crossing, like X's stitching bullet wounds—

eye tell you now the sky turns
black at midnight, rises bright—sometimes—when light
comes as a gift from the sun

rising like faith, can be a beautiful thing
if people could synchronize,
turn their collective heartbeats into pulsing
beehives breathing above us

AFTER READING A HIROSHIMA NUCLEAR BULLETIN ON YAHOO
ANOTHER 7–11

the yellow tongue flame spit out
from the blistered lips of Hiroshima, spreads
full of radionuclides, a torch of poisons
streaking through fire across Pacific blue water,
though naked eye can't see it unless flying above
as an astronaut high in space
with superman's x-ray vision

then you might see this dart plume of poison
aiming its green tip lurking beneath blue waves,
shot east toward—hollyweird—
but, of course, no one will believe the words of this
poem can be pushed aside lacking scientific proof
because how does a poet sing anything of worth
except words of truth deeply felt,
singing songs of love this poem is telling you
now life & death comes no matter
whether you believe it or not it will arrive,
you can take that to the bank & cash it

ALL OF MY GOOD OLD FRIENDS

all of my good old friends are dropping,
dying flowers all around me,
leaving as birds in the night suddenly fly away
never to be seen again, they become ghosts
eye see in other faces suddenly their smile
plastered on heads of total strangers
as we glide by each other, they are memories
fading like old photographs we collect
inside worn old picture albums we store away,
like old songs we used to dance to when young
before we knew death was surely coming our way

CORONAVIRUS REDIAL

a blooming fear wakes you
envelopes your body,
inside your mind, fear
    of touching there is no
place to hide, as the silence
of death sweeps like a poisoned
broom through our lives, creeps
a stealthy killer stalking
through cities we adore,
live in, an invisible
plague with no smell or shape
stalking death could be on
lips of ones we kiss, love,
there are no words to describe
macabre scenes of bodies
stacked, piled high in trucks
refrigerated,make-shift morgues,
mass graves on Hart Island,
in retirement homes
decaying, on parking lots,
in dark streets in Guayaquil,
Ecuador a bonfire of corpses,
a crackling stench nauseating
the sky blackened by vultures
like a million fireflies,
the wailing music
of stunned relatives—
mourning prayers
incinerated flesh—spewing death.

DARK CLOUDS BLOOMING UP AHEAD

dark clouds blooming up ahead over a small town
in heartland America, blocks out the sun as lightning cracks,
booms across space, red maga-cap-wearing bucks gather
white, circle around a car menacing a Black family anywhere
in rural USA, beneath the sky a symphony of thunder
midday claps of slashing swords—flash jagged fields,
aqua-green summer grass crisscrossing highways *ever-which-away,*
how some ever you look in front of you out here where
grass has flattened like manes atop lions' heads,
right before their golden eyes blaze,
their nostrils flare and history pulls the trigger
of primordial instinct & they attack without remorse
far away from asphalt, a warning sign,
a metaphor if you wish—of what this poem searches for,
a clue, a predilection of what's ahead, as it winds
its way through curving questions—hooked and
sprouting tails, at the bottom of human savagery
a hunger so deep in the psyche of human darkness,
aggravating—mysterious impulses beneath
spinning wheels of speeding automobiles,
trucks circling in a funereal light, omens bright
as a flashlight—perhaps, a philosophy of coffins
heading west a procession of hearses snaking like ants,
then quicker than quick or the blink of an eye—
a swirling, black dervish resembling an elephant trunk
drops down, howling out of the sky in front of you,
is a surprise, much louder than the last scream you feared
you heard before it quickly thrashed around you,
like what you thought death might be in the center of truth,
like life you no longer recognized, coming straight at you,
bleeding, pleading once again to your maker
to please let you survive this moment of peril, this madness,
this roll of seven, this middle finger, in the dice game of life

spared you once again, dealt you a winning hand, so
you thank God—the Creator—for the umpteenth time
in your, up & down stock market roller coaster life,
just as sin creeps back into your brain once again

BLOOD

there is blood shed through voices
blood inking red finger maps
snaking across concrete gaps, blood
blooming petals of bright red roses
blood seducing madness in brains

HURRICANE MARIA, 2017

watching hurricane maria hit guadeloupe
a category five wind & rain monster
in september 2017, an evil, violet eye
in the calm center of this massive storm
churning up, frothing sea waves,
prowling like a black panther
we noticed the cold-blooded clouds
staring down—margaret & me—
our lovely, small house
filled with sweet memories creativity
dreams, love, & we wondered if
it would still be there the morning after

THREE WASPS IN JUAN DOLIO, SANTO DOMINGO

for José Bedia and Margaret Porter Troupe

four wasps flew into José's condo
in Juan Dolio, Santo Domingo,
flew in through the open sliding doors
looking for whatever it was only they knew,
but they didn't seem to find whatever it was,
so they started terrorizing me, buzzing
all around, dive-bombing over my head
like hornets, while eye was eating breakfast,
swooping down, making me flail my arms
like wind-mills, Margaret just sat there, still
as silence, ignoring those wasps, hailing
from backwoods Gloster, Mississippi, she
was raised with them, but being from asphalt
streets of St. Louis, Missouri, eye kept on
swatting at those buzzing little bugaboos,
trying to kill them, but failing at that
eye got me a broom to smash the tiresome
little annoyances, when one got stuck up
in the sticky glue of a spider's web
up on the ceiling, hanging upside down
from a light bulb fixture, it started wiggling,
spinning wildly around, but couldn't get loose,
so it hung up there like a lynched black man,
or a woman, buffeted by winds blowing
through open doors like a probing tongue, it—
the breeze—kept the thing spinning around
until it just died, before the other
three wasps came back to rescue their friend—
lover? who knows—it was too late anyway,
so they just kept buzzing around, up close,
sniffing at the dangling dead one—for what?
though careful not to get too close themselves,

to stick onto the deadly spider's gossamer
glue—which meant certain death for them too—so
then the three seemed to go into deep mourning
while flying around, they reminded me
of stumbling drunk people, thumping hard
against the ceiling, then they flew back down,
looked again at their fallen comrade
up there just spinning, no movement, except
the fluttering, from time to time, of its
frail, transparent wings, and Margaret said,
"wasps must have emotions too," made me feel
sorry for the dead wasp, for its three friends,
seemingly so inconsolable now
in their mourning, bumping like crazy up
on the ceiling, that's when eye put down my broom,
vowed never to kill another wasp again
unless they were trying to sting me,
then all bets will be off, eye told myself,
because in a blink eye would go back to
killing all them buzzing little bugaboos,
in droves, just like the deranged, wild swinging
American fool eye truly am at my core

SONIC FIREFLIES

the beauty of voices of jazz & blues,
syncopation of syllables flowing
free form through improvising sentences
sluicing, embracing, metaphors glowing
eyes in the dark like words imitating
fireflies pulsating bright in a black sky
when gleaming eyes of a prowling black panther
suddenly clicks on bright as flashlight beams
under moon rays probing into hidden
isolated mysterious places
somewhere deep in the buzzing countryside

WATCHING SEAGULLS HUNT FOR
FISH IN SINES, PORTUGAL

for David Murray

seagulls perched high on gabled rooftops
in Sines, Portugal, search the sparkling
sea waves below brimming with fish, then
they squak, extend their wide, razor blade wings,
before diving, like released Peregrine Falcons
slicing down through a clear blue sky
stretching due west from my view—then

they become silhouettes, screaming,
searching for food, their tiny heads
revolving on necks—perusing devices—
scan foaming waves with laser beam eyes,
zeroing in on delectable fish before
transforming themselves into assassins,
avenging angels when their radar gaze
spots supper in the frothing salt water
churning with schools of all kinds of fish, then

they dive straight down, snatch a few
from waves boiling with plenty for these
avenging angels with hooked, geiger counter beaks
cutting through wind currents,
slicing through shimmering scales of fish
like killers do every night anywhere in America
on Saturday nights during killing frenzies

then eye watch the seagulls shoot straight up
like missiles shot from canons through clouds
the fish wiggling desperately in their hooked mouths
look like worms on fishing hooks all over the world

then the gulls become silhouettes again
shot look like black arrows shot towards the sun

SPRING TIME MOVING TOWARD SUMMER: A CRAP SHOOT

at the edge of green springtime
voices sprout wings, pursed lips explode ruby red,
pucker up kisses blooming
open wet petals plump as rain drops jelly
bean size splashes down from clouds, then
eye hear choirs of birds singing sweetly now, feel
a deep peacefulness soothing

cruising beneath blue(s) swelling up—a solo
blown here by marauding winds—
changes faster than humans see, deeper still
than all religious fervor
probes carrying words light as feathers floating
beneath zigzagging lightning
strikes, rambunctious spring's blustering wind tongues
lift saxophone licks moaning slick
as "who do you love" bop solos rapping hip,
sliding off chord changes, beats
flicking behind time, cuts through clutter like sharp

knives slice through butter—"brother
can you spare a dime"—because it's a crap shoot
when you roll them bones across
light green cloths spread out across tables real quick,
or throw them up against walls,
out in the public, watch them hucka-buckin'
when kites shimmy, flip through spring's

warm air, summers just around crowded corners,
people dressed to the nines bet
those black dots looking up from them small white squares
like cold snake eyes of gangsters
when they throw them bones real hard, they will roll true
herky-jerky 'cross bad luck,

leap to paradise when those dice stop prancing,
and money drops down, then luck
definitely matters who wins or loses
because the game changes now
is all about whatever language is used

to tap down pain, hurt feelings
after green backs money meant for roofs over
losers' heads flew, plunged like rocks
through wind swept skies—many became suicides—
paid for winners' heartfelt joy
when they shot themselves as arrows from bent back
bows—sheets of words built bridges

into metaphors there—converted deep poems
to drum sounds, constructed songs,
sluiced images zinging through spoken rhythms
flung into space, threw up smack
as language mirroring place, echoing roots
geography remembers
race mirroring faces, memory, music,
speech rooted, gestures—ham bone
slaps thighs—clucking tongues, bass grooving love,
deep beats in this moment, poetry
deep in word plays original bag, sings verbs

sweeter than chocolate cake
eye remember melting in mother's red mouth
when she clamped down, smacked her lips
on all those saccharine portions piled high there,
dripping bonbon brown icing,
then she would look at me with authority,
as she ate every slice

with greedy satisfaction she winked at me,
coolly, like the queen she was,

dabbed a napkin to touch up corners of her
full mouth smeared with bonbon brown
icing smeared, looking like a striking painting
echoing one of Romare
Bearden's majestic ladies of Harlem nights,
decked out in beautiful silk,
eye remembered this memory at her wake
when eye saw her nestled there
in her coffin at rest in all that white silk

smiling as if she had eaten
plenty of those sweet brown chocolate bonbons

WATTS 1965

eye came in the dead of night broke to watts
looking for whatever was there to pick up,
since my pockets were empty, had holes in my shoes,
nothing in the refrigerator to eat or drink, though
eye had poems in my imagination, though
eye couldn't make a meal out of those words

FLOWERS BLOOMING IN CENTRAL PARK

for Margaret

the sun god climbs the sky between her ripe plump breasts—
a promise? they remind me of two melons, new sunrises
would bring into our lives—a mirage of the past? swollen, erect
nipples! but then again this could be a dream teasing my aging
longing, when grey clouds bloom, drop rain, it's April, spring
time, and the sun washes over, cleans again my cobwebbed desire
and eye find myself thinking of flowers beginning to flourish
in Central Park, their multicolored buds like heads swaying
atop slender stems when a gentle breeze sashays through—
like a tongue—in the park, alluring me, like a female dancer
blowing caressing kisses in my fevered imagination

in the first place, we all live alone—like these flowers—yearning
throughout our own lives to grow—inside our own bodies—flesh,
death lives there too, so does life—no matter what, people,
dogs, cats, rats, insects, fools, all kinds of creepy things, vibrant things
     also—live here too, everywhere, carrying whatever, voices, poetry
hanging in the breeze, breathing—cold, warm in the air,
to speak truth, if at all possible, is the way to go, now in this weird,
destructive period—time frame—we walk through now—crawl,
perhaps stand up straight if our backbones permit
laddering up our spines—but we know time is always
moving like weather—a tornado there, a day of sun

here, today is what it is, with or without our approval—
then, sometimes we run across an old feeble dog, alone,
dragging its ass through a park, living fire gone from its eyes
tired now—which reminded me suddenly of the sweet
heat of a beautiful love affair eye had once and my memory
plunged deep into an equally passionate woman, whose tongue,
a lance of fire, lit my fuse, as did her burning cinder eyes,
sucked me down into her sweet-honey passion and we rode,

the volcanic crater of her vice-like, welcoming vagina grip
was bucking heat, flesh to flesh, until collapsing, trembling,
wet with sweat as daybreak broke outside our window

that was then, this is now, eye have spent 80 years roaming,
different streets of cities around this spinning globe
revolving around the sun & moon, bright eyes of stars watching
people down here doing terrible things, with no place to go
to escape what we have done, surrounded by all this damage
people have inflicted on each other, on this planet
when there is no place to run, hide from all this avarice
we have indulged in, all this ugliness full of evil contempt
and now the bill is coming due with the deadly arrival
of a novel coronavirus, the white nationalism of Trumpism,
which has erased the concept of "United" in the states of America

A HAIKU AND A TANKA

A QUICK SNACK HAIKU

yellow banana
rests like a dream on my plate
for a brief moment

SOME COLORS IN FRUIT

my watermelon
is green on the outside, red,
sweet on the inside,
juicy as ripe tomatoes,
plums & cherries in my mouth

GLOSTER, MISSISSIPPI: TANKAS & HAIKUS SUITE

kids rapping bebop
out on the block in gloster,
mississippi, hot
as a skillet full of grease
cookin pork bacon

kids creating words
here like razzamatazz, zeebop,
then a bossman come,
his nickname smelly fool, dude
had a cool sidekick,

diddy-wah-diddy
was his name, tall & skinny
as a lean lamp-post
or an exclamation mark,
mouth shaped like a fish

when he opened it
words flew out like silver fish
flashing in the sun,

he rapped like jay-z,
faster than 2 chainz poems,
slick as rihanna,
quicker than a ferrari
race car, faster than rap-poems

sweet as mother's love
these words silver moon faces
up in a dark sky

a cold drink at noon

in the mississippi sun,
the love of gloster

in beautiful young
faces beaming from children
here, deep as pure song,

music in heart beats
sweet in blues rhythms, gospel,
voices in the air,

blooming like flowers
bright as children's deep set eyes
shining rare diamonds

THE HAITIAN DRUM HAMMERERS OF
JUAN DOLIO, SANTA DOMINGO

for José Bedia

they start early in the morning, rain or shine
hitting with their tiny pointy hammers,

they create a sound-rhythm these drummers do
sometimes four-four, six-eight rhythms, but then

they go off these sound-tracks, create voodoo,
ra ra rhythms of their own, accented

drumming voices shouting, *yemaya, damballah,*
come here, sing with me, help me set a rhythm

to complete my healing work, it's kongo time
in the spiritual world of juan dolio, santa domingo,

listen to the haitian drum workers speak through
musical cadences of their pick a pick,

knock knock drumming chorus hammers, up under
their chanting work songs, led by their leader,

listen to their consonants, vowels clashing off key,
picking moments to come together in one voice,

then slide off separately—slippery as eels
wiggling in different voices—African,

Haitian, Dominican, Puerto Rican, Cuban
pitched through tight, hip group improvisations

changing course in a moment of pure genius,
evoked by love of simply playing music together

TRYING TO FIND MY WAY INTO A POEM IN 14 LINES

eye was looking for a way into some poems
forming in the kettle drum of my brain when
eye thought of kernels of popcorn simmering—
one of my very favorite snacks eye pop myself—
deep in oil, just about to flash boil in a steel pot
over blue flames on a stove, reminding me of lovers
licking heat between each other, or hungry demons
watching this spectacle, and it reminded me then
of water boiling in huge cauldrons slave masters
used to throw unruly slaves into, then high five
themselves when flesh of slaves burned off,
that's when eye looked closely at the sizzling oil,
eye thought of people being shoveled into
garbage disposals chewing up everything there

TRUMP'S RESPONSE ON HEARING
THE NEWS OF COVID-19

when he first received the news
trump hesitated, then said
"why don't we just let this wash
all over the country," then
see what happens after that

TRUMP IS AMERICA'S WATERLOO

the reason America got
Trump as president
is because they wanted
a white man there
in that office, no matter what,
how stupid, corrupt he was,
they yearned for a mirror
pale reflection of themselves
after the 8 year reign
of a brilliant black president,
Barack Hussein Obama,
so many white folks needed
to see a two watt on a dimmer
switch—someone uniformed,
without a hint of what
the country actually was—as they
were, most people in the world
knew they were clueless—
in a multicultural world
all around their self-imposed
isolation, an act of selfish
hubris and racism here,
coming due as eye write
this poem with no solution

TRUMP'S LEGACY TO BLACK AMERICANS

first of all he lied about how rich he was,
lied about his fake teeth, fake hair,
lied about how great a job he was doing
lied about almost everything, yet many people
refused to believe he was lying when he was
lying on camera in front of their eyes,
in the recording booth of their ears
and videos of their camera eyes, yet many
still believed him, no matter what proof
truth was told them, shown them, that
he is a **cockwomble**—a Scottish noun meaning
a "male, prone to making outrageously stupid
statements and/or inappropriate behavior
while generally having a very high opinion
of their own wisdom and importance"
with being a fact then the question is why
did so many fall so completely for the con job
he was selling, when all proof ruled against
believing his duplicitous fabrications?—
plus this *fake* man is totally insecure?

was it because millions of white folks wanted
a white man—no matter how avarice, corrupt—
to replace Barack Obama in the White House—
a Black man—as President in this yet to be united
states of America? is it because he was a *mack* man
pimping racism so deep here white folks could
settle—and they did—for incompetence,
stupidity over the history of a smart Black
man—and woman—who did the job with elan,
creative elegance, fairness without scandal?
what do Black people have to do to prove
their beauty, worth, contributions to this nation?

THERE IS ALWAYS SOME THING

there is always some thing we need to know now,
some thing beyond fear of anything, even death,
something human, perhaps, a gesture, like love
extended to a homeless dog swarming with vermin,
a homeless shadow of a man lying there now
mirroring someone's former self,
lying there now in a pile of garbage, in front of you,
dead to the world with hunger for what they used to be,
back when a fading photograph they carry tucked away
in a wallet, in a torn pants pocket, fraying, around edges,
was proof then reflecting brighter, better days ahead
opposed to this moment this man faces now
a sneering Doberman Pincer flashing fangs at the end
of a lease, taunting in hands of contemptuous policemen,
armed to the teeth, eyes cold with official arrogance,
reminding of modern day Hitlerian storm troopers

so what is it some Americans refuse to believe
when they see, boot stomping red-capped fascists
spreading like wild-fires sweeping across the nation
their faces lit up with generational hatred,
marching, chanting, their voices distorted carry,
like coiled cobra snakes, reciting verses
from the King James Bible, denying climate change
spit out venous streams of poison, hissing
"Jews will not replace us, Jews will not replace us."

THIS ONE IS FOR THE BLACK MAMBA

for Kobe Bryant—1978 to 2020

I.

quiet as it's kept, Kobe, you were a once in a lifetime shake
& bake round ball phenom way back in high school,
you could do anything with a basketball in your hands,
so fierce you were, driven to the point where many loved,
hated you in almost equal measure, but that was small stuff,
none of it fazed you, Kobe, because you never cared what others
thought of you, you already knew who you were, and
where you were going, like the lyrics in U2's song, "Lights of Home,"
when Bono sings "Hey, now, do you know my name . . . Hey, now
do you know where I'm going? . . . I can see the lights
in front of me," and you saw "the lights in front of" you, Kobe,
and you knew exactly where you were going and how and

what you had to do each & every moment of your life to get there,
when you planted your spirit, feet firmly down on the court,
so focused you were on being the very best out there, Kobe
nothing else mattered but playing the game hard to win,
to do whatever possible to outshine all others who stood there
in front of you, was your hold card, your go-to position
from jump, to take no prisoners, so intense, relentlessly fierce

Kobe, you were totally locked in, even way back then, when
you were in high school, you bit all opponents in their jugular veins,
flicked off all foes like they were bothersome flies or mosquitos,
gnats buzzing around in your space, annoying you—even
spectators could tell this by the exasperated, concentrated
death stare screwed into your intensely, focused face
whenever anyone got close—so you beat them down, you know,
like stomping worrisome roaches trying to escape
your size thirteen basketball tennis shoes encasing your feet
and you left their corpses mangled there on the floor

2.

but now in order to go forward with this poem
eye have to turn back the clock, Kobe, spin
the clock's hands back towards Italy, when you were different
though a curious kind of cat, a curious innocent young boy
growing into yourself, before you became
the deadly basketball hitman, an assassin-in-waiting,
intensity deep down inside your ruthless self,
then the baby tree limbs sprouted up in height—
living with your father, Joe "Jellybean" Bryant,
a 6 feet 9 inch basketball star himself, balling overseas
for AMG Sebastiani, the Italian pro team based in Rieti,
Italy—reached out, stretching to feel the sun and rain
nourishing your baby limbs suddenly grown into branches
sprouting into your new, deadly self, now you begin
to know yourself better—no toady now—Kobe,
you learn to speak Italian, obsessed with the game—
European style—study it like a mad scientist watching
your father and others—six years later, in 1990, when
you were 12 years old, started playing for a youth team,
also in Reggio Emilia, then in 1991, when you were 13,
your father moved back to the United States
to Lower Marion, Pennsylvania, the place of your birth—
a suburb outside of Philadelphia, where soon—rapidly—
you grew into your insanely competitive self

your dominating game in high school escalated when
you started incorporating things you picked up from pros
like the wizard, Earl "The Pearl" Monroe, a friend of your father's,
who taught you a few basketball tricks—sleight of hand moves,
slick fakes, wicked crossover dribbles, innovative,
cold-blooded jazz solo licks, quick, black cunning Philadelphia
playground moves, deceptive trick-nology, infused with deep,
slick, breathtaking wah-wah Jimi Hendrix guitar blues
flourishes you began loading all this up into your hoodoo,

Houdini mack, and rap, hip hop linguistic game phrasing
your evolving, magical switcheroo, shape-shifting spin
around screen and pick blow past game, then you stole
some old changes laid down from the "Big O"—Oscar Robertson's
deft pump and fake, then shoot off the dribble with a quick
Jerry West release, then slide off another screen and drain a jump shot,
you took Elgin Baylor's footwork and uploaded it into your Dr. J-like arsenal
though you couldn't quite lock down Michael Jordan's fade away
jumper that caused many round ball players deep blues back in the day—
though that too would come your way after you mastered it later

over time, with a whole lot of practice—you soon became
a bigger version of Allen Iverson's wicked stop, then go,
hesitation moves, with all "The Answer's" slick deceptions, you
locked that too into your game, leading Lower Marion to a 1996
Pennsylvania State championship and became a high school
All-American superstar, averaging 30.8 points per game

3.
from jump street you had this deep need to play against
the best who happened to land there in front of you,
because you always saw yourself apart from the rest, always the best
that's just how you were wired, who you were, totally deadly, so
you turned down Duke, Kobe, after they offered a full ride,
because you saw them as less than what your ambition needed,
so instead, supremely confident as you were—bad ass, cocky even—
you took your game with its god-given otherworldly talent
to the pros, where you became the youngest ever
to compete up there against those bad-ass "big boys"
in that elite group of ego-driven ballers, Kobe, like you, but
some toadies too—though not as gifted, cocky as you

4.
your single-minded, steely desire to conquer whoever was there
in front of you with a basketball in their hands, was a challenge

for you, caused you to fiercely catapult your body quickly up in the air
as if it were a rocket lifting off into space, to zoom up, throw down
thunderous, rim shaking slamming dunks, body twisting, mind-blowing
     layups with either hand, now you score almost at will, drop, draining
30 foot rainbowing or clotheslining game-winning jump shots,
defenders waving hands futilely in your face, hanging on your arms,
you stare them all down, killing them with your lethal game, Kobe,
earning you the nickname "Black Mamba," because your scoring binges
were so deadly, on the spot, so true to your attitude, character,
the way you played the game out there on the court you were there
to destroy anyone you played against, to kill all comers,
you were, your gangly limbs, legs gyrating, long arms waving
ever-which-away—a gigantic black widow spider about to attack
a helpless prey in its web, futilely trying to find a way to escape
your furious fight to the death onslaught, because as soon
as they came out there on the court they were your mortal enemies,
Kobe, so you quickly turned into a lethal, venous mamba snake,
attacked all comers as if there were never a tomorrow,
housed the same character as the venomous bite of that legendary
Black African serpent, so you sneered at those you defeated,
laughed in their faces, savaged their spirits, ripped their hearts
from their chests, left gaping bleeding holes in their confidence,

Kobe, that was not enough for you because then you stepped back,
figuratively threw their beating hearts down on the floor,
then stomped them as you kept on steppin,' thrusting your middle finger
like a dagger up into the air as if you were stabbing that enemy to death
the invisible one you always kept deep in your mind

5.
then, in 1996 the Charlotte Hornets drafted you straight
from Lower Marion High with the 13th pick and traded you
to the Los Angeles Lakers for Vlade Divac—a huge mistake for Charlotte,
one of the biggest in pro basketball history but a great gift for the Lakers—
now, out in LA, you find yourself living in the fast lane

in the "City of Lights," find yourself with all the "tinsel town" denizens,
Hollywood movie stars, and you fast becoming the brightest bona fide
superstar in that glittering city of fast cars and even faster lives

you take the young Black pop singing star, Brandy, to your 1998 prom,
then in August, 1999, you meet Vanessa Laine, a knock down beautiful,
17-year-old Mexican-American model, dancer and cheerleader—you are
21 years old now and a rising megastar in the NBA—and Vanessa
knocks you completely off your feet—and you marry her in April 2001,
causing an earthquake split between you and your parents, which grows
wider & wider into a chasm over the years—but your basketball career
and exploits only explode as your skills grow into championships
and the rest, as they say, will go down in basketball history
though there are rough patches along the way, like in your
first game, coming off the bench you didn't score one point after
taking one single shot in the six minutes they gave you, but
in your second season, in 1998, things turn around when
you are selected to play in the NBA All-Star game, where you score
17 points, then Shaquille O' Neal joins you and together, in 2000
you win your first of three straight NBA championships, but in 2003
in Vail, Colorado, recuperating from knee surgery, a young
white woman accuses you of rape, which you deny, and in fall 2004
the civil suit is dropped, in 2005 you settle with your accuser
out of court, around this time, you begin calling yourself
"the Black Mamba" after the assassin in the movie "Kill Bill"

Kobe, you always lived your life dangerously close to the edge,
always took chances in the way you played the game of life,
the way you played the game of basketball was no different, because
in both you were always in the attack mode—even in practice
with teammates, you never took your foot off the gas pedal,
you hit them with elbows because you were always about winning,
you once called yourself "a little psychopath . . . a scary type"
because you were always about dominating, just like "MJ"

in all you will win five rings, two without "Big Shaq"
who was traded to the Miami Heat in 2004, now you are crowned
"The King of LA," with your last title being in 2010 with a rematch
seven-game win over your archrival Boston Celtics, you collect
your second straight finals MVP award, cementing your legend
as one of the very best to ever play the game of basketball,
but that wasn't the end because in 2012 you would lead Team
USA to the gold medal—your second—with a win over Spain

6.
Kobe, you Xeroxed your game after Michael Jordan
your childhood idol, though you evolved your own warrior game
as an assassin, created your own brutal, take-no-prisoner style,
because in your mind you were no copycat
like Miles Davis in the end wasn't Dizzy Gillespie, though
the "Prince of Darkness" borrowed some of Dizzy's licks,
altered a few solos played by the slanted-up trumpet king
wearing a tam on his head, cocked ace deuce,
hailing from South Carolina—Miles was from East Saint Louis,
Illinois, when he played hard bebop uptown Harlem
with "Bird" jammin' at Minton's on 118th Street, like Miles, you
quickly became your own spirit force pursuing perfection, you
won five NBA championship rings, (but fell short of the sixth
won by your mentor, "Air Jordan," whose game and attitude you
Xeroxed as if it were the poem you read every night before you
went to sleep), you won a scoring title, appeared in your 18th straight
All-Star game, scored 81 points in a single game, second only to Wilt's
100 point game—he was also from Philadelphia—and eye will always
remember that photo image of you, snapped by Andrew D. Bernstein—
flying, both legs and feet tucked up under the purple, white and gold
Laker uniform, your arms straight out, both hands cupping the ball,
in front of your coiled body, head turned to the right, eyes on the rim,
mouth open, before you tomahawk a slam-dunk that must have
shaken the rim, left the packed crowd screaming at The Great Western
Forum in awe, now that move reminds me of your friend Michael

Jackson's moon walk or a Jimi Hendrix or John Coltrane solo,
breathtaking, and in April 2016, after tearing your Achilles in 2013,
and tearing your rotator cuff making a two-handed dunk
in 2015, you announced that the next season would be your last
and it was, but in your last game in April 2018 at the Staples Center,
you dropped 60 points, taking 50 shots—like the ball hog you were—
to get there—but no one cared because it was your last game,
Kobe, and everyone loved you, hated to see you go
then you retired as the first player to ever play 20 years wearing
the same team's jersey, then you dropped the microphone
on the floor, saying those now memorable words, "Mamba out!"
a big smile spread over your face as thunderous applause washed you
in thunderous adoration, it was an unforgettable night for a forever
star, and now all that is left is to compare you and your friend
Lebron James ("Bron-Bron," also called "King James") as to
who is the best after "MJ," though that too is being hotly disputed
now amongst many white critics, though as some Black playground
fans say everyday—"What do those white boys know about this?!"

7.

when you retired from the game, the Lakers hung both
your numbers—24 and 8—from the rafters at Staples Center,
but you never looked back—didn't let no grass grow under
your feet—went down another path, started writing books
for children and one of them became a short film, winning you
a golden statue Academy Award in 2018, you stopped
going to Laker home games until your daughter, Gianna—"Gigi"—
became a basketball player who wanted to go so she could
watch, learn from the best, so you, like a father took her and all
the LA Staple Center fans were happy again to embrace you

8.

and so, it was a very terrible way for you to go to the other side,
terrible to fall from the sky through wet gray day fog in January,
in Calabasas, California, in 2020, right above the Steeplechase community,

(

at 9:45 AM, where you, Kobe Bryant, your 13-year old daughter, Gianna,
on your way to a tournament featuring Gianna's team named Mambas
lost your lives with seven others in a mangled Sikorsky S-76B helicopter
with the wreckage strewn over a rocky area the size of a football field,
on a hillside buttressing a small scruffy mountain they found you
after the flames with your long arms wrapped around Gigi
trying to protect her from the impact of the unmovable mountain

what were you thinking, Kobe, as the helicopter kept circling,
seeming to wander around up there in all those blinding,
billowing clouds so thick the pilot didn't know which way was up
or down, were you talking basketball with Gigi, the other six passengers?
you once told someone you wanted to be immortal, now, today
you have ascended to the spiritual realm, Kobe, not only as a legendary
basketball icon—one of the greatest ever—but also as a human being
you had learned the gift of sharing with others, growing into a spiritual
father, on the road to developing even greater things, you changed,

at the end of your life, you became a better, softer person,
who smiled easier, didn't seem so competitive, because—though
we will never know this, it is only my speculation—your death,
Gigi's and the seven others, was truly a great loss for legions
all over the world who will scream your name as long as the game,
basketball, is played and eye can hear this chant swelling up and down
from crowds in arenas as long as hoops are played

"Kobe, Kobe, Kobe Bryant, Black Mamba" making a house call!

THINK OF IT

think of frogs boiling in hot water when
watching people sweat in hot spaces
while walking through blow torch streets
in concrete cities all over the globe
because head in the sand climate deniers exist

you might wonder what it is all about
burning to death while sleeping, or swimming
in lakes, or oceans where there are no fish
or making love with windows thrown open
& hear no singing birds when climaxes come

causing men & women to scream with joy
or caught singing somewhere out in a meadow
trembling, removed from sizzling asphalt & bricks,
people dozing here in quiet, saccharine moods,
trees fluttering green heads above, kissing sweet

wind tongues licking honeyed flesh, lathering
scorched cheeks—this can be rare because many
only think of stashing blood money away
because life is beating hearts—not gizzards—
it means loving trees, flowers, animals trapped

in forest fires, tribal people, birds, saving fish
baking in deep hot lake polluted cauldrons
filled with skulls, teeth, bones, fingers, arms & legs
littered over these unreal lunar moonscapes,
graveyard sea bottoms holding unforgiving

memories in pits of our human depravity revealed,
signals no remorse here in empty holes of eye sockets
looking up into space through clouds of dust

after volcanic eruptions shook worlds
when skies clouded over with cinders of ash

falling stones splashing into lakes race toward
boats fleeing whirl-pooling waves full of screaming
survivors, all of this carries unanswered questions—
is this the reckoning we all must face now,
when thinking of how our bones will reveal

themselves in the future, inside texts of history
books where metaphors are created from bullet holes,
armies marching to war because of religious faith,
when the choices are whether to write sentences
evoking poetry filled with music, love

dreaded voices of sacred spirits, voodoo priests,
musicians creating holy rhythms we dance to—
what are the questions we must raise now, are they
washed in genius colors from brushstrokes of painters,
portraits of what our bones will reveal in the future?

think of them now, those bone chilling questions,
when you look out across the world, bend your vision
& look around mountains curving through space,
with your lens wide open, holding no malice, then
pray for clarity, dream, hope you see beauty there

TIME

time will bring us shining blue
skies in time blazing up suns
above us in time moments
will transform gray clouds to black
people will rejoice in nights
with music songs in night clubs
flight in time will lift sadness
horror will transform faces
bring back life with light beneath
masks wearing beyond carnage
break out joy and laughter
be reborn with metaphors
laced with new tongues in language
American beyond race
in time we will breath again
in that which grows here today
though rooted in history
sprouting new tribes of flowers
in seven throw eleven
roll of tumbling dice of life
though here in this slender poem
only seven syllables
structure the lines of this poem
about time and poetry

SOME THINK

some think it is the long, short road we travel over,
people we encounter, what their spirits reveal
flashed through lens of their eyes—warm, cold, or bright,
perhaps dull in those of killers searching for victims, though
whatever is run into by happenstance, or choice
the destination could be as important as the route taken,
might be a lodestone—magnet—pulling us to take one step
after another, as luscious lips of a magnificent woman—
a beautiful spirit draws us closer to a kiss
when her sweet breath blooms, perfume, swells,
lingers on her bonbon tongue, probing, delicious, deep
in a lover's mouth, reveals what we think love
in our libidinous imagination could be, what
holds us fast in that hot space of slippery seduction,
takes breath away, is full of pure, enchanting beauty

like when a journey is breathtaking enough to teach
in moments that can lead to pure transcendence, is what
might pull this poem through madness to mango metaphors
sweet with childhood memories, striking images
encountered on desolate roads cutting through corn fields,
& you saw black clouds drop a howling tornado funnel
that wiped out a small sleeping town somewhere in Kansas,
out there on the plains with your family, ran into stupid men
looking to murder just for thrills because you were black,
so they could lift their heavy balls up out of quicksand—
do they bust their nuts, pop orgasms doing this,
watching blood flow like rivers from screaming mouths after
machete slashes rip red lines across necks, open up floodgates
so life can enter death slowly, but now eye digress

because being an old man now, who has watched these same
scenarios happen so many times before, after looking at beauty

on a promising day, hoping creativity would flow my way,
perhaps, soar as eagles do when their wings spread feathers,
open up, ride the wind slicing through light, become spirits
we poets wish we could become searching for the right words
to write in a poem that will speak truthfully of freedom
in any space, eye am bored with it all now,
but then there comes this clear, chilling moment
pulling me back to face the treacheries of earth,
when some think it's alright for a man to slaughter
his stunned wife to death in broad daylight, hacking her
through blood-curdling screams, in front of their children,
as a foghorn blows mournfully in the harbor,
a gray fogbow bends into an arc somewhere over Scotland
majestic as the silver one shining when there's sun
arching above the Mississippi River, fronting my hometown,
St. Louis, Missouri, that some of us call "sad louis,"
some think it prophetic watching an "ice finger" of death
birthing in an underwater cave, a blue hole forming a sinkhole,
a cat's eye off the coast of Belize—so what is it we don't know
but think we definitely know when it comes to everything
swilling around our lives ugly every day—
though we do know this—a dead fish never smells better after
laid out on a table in the sun seven days later
& you can take that to the bank from an old man who still thinks
he is young in his heart, though knows his body is weakening
as he walks up steep stairs, a hard knot of a "charley horse"
ambushes him over & over again & again in very real time

NANCY PELOSI

what can be said of this petite
Italian woman from Baltimore,
who steps up to the plate,
accepts the big call, backs down to no one,
a warrior with a very sharp blade
she knows how to swing
a modern day Joan of Arc
down in the cesspool of Washington, DC
where she's defeating men
every single day

HOMAGE TO ELIJAH EUGENE CUMMINGS

eye never pressed flesh with you but heard, knew you
through your booming, prophetic voice, your noble,
caring heart, saturated with love, forgiveness, a warrior's
temperament ready for battle when that was needed,
so this is a tribute poem for elijah eugene cummings,
remembered after poet e. e. cummings—kind of—
though the quiet, booming voice of the politician hailing
from baltimore via "souse kalinah" was a poetic voice too—
though not the same as the taciturn, modernist, experimental
voice from cambridge, massachusetts—yet each of you
e.e.'s. shared a plain spoken, "lyrical directness" that carried
a sense of playful humor, a kind of metaphysical
rambunctiousness saturated both of your egalitarian genius
delivery of language, rooted in the good soil you grew from,
grounded in a place where prophecy rose through poetry,
politics, prayer, to do the right thing, the righteous thing

FOR HUGH

for Hugh Ramapolo Masekela, 1939–2018

my dear brother, we once told each other
we would go to the other side together
though eye couldn't imagine how we would do this
since death has always been an individual act
the place where rumor has it—though no one,
spirit or human has ever come back to tell
the truth of what it's like to be there with all those
bones & maggots, so that veracity, that fact, reality test
is thrown open to doubt, to mystery,
hearsay, so to speak—& what you have then
beyond this dilemma is the flat footed question, fact
that darkness looms forever over us all in skies
with eyes staring down we believe are ancient stars
above our beating hearts, waiting, pulsating
rhythms in sync, that light up the night, as we learn
or figured out somehow the mystery, creative
mastery of living in corrupted space
everyday keeps our heads above the flooding
waters we swim through disguised as sharks

so what is it about danger we have come to
understand, figured out from both our hard
scrabbled lives drenched in spilled blood of close
friends & beauty, both reverberating inside our lives,
was it the truth of music driving us through those
Frankenstein moments, Dracula miscreants
who haunted our streets & dreams with evil—for me
in St. Louis, Missouri, you in Johannesburg, South Africa,
both cities so different, but so alike in senseless slaughter
where we grew with wide open eyes serving as radar

was it the magical, healing power of love

that so convinced you & me despite cold-blooded
whacks of "two-by-four" pieces of solid wood
upside people's foreheads we knew, when we lost close
sandlot baseball games for me, soccer for you
scary in neighborhoods of blood letting, for me in "Sad
Louis, Missouri, down the street from rock n roll legend,
Chuck Berry, while you in South Africa was helping
create & shape music of kwela, penny whistle jive,
mahtathini, mbaqanga & black american doowop
with Jonas Gwangwa, Miriam Makeba, Caiphus Semanya
& so many other great musicians sprouting trees
down there at the cobra poisonous fang of South Africa

but then the jazz trumpet, vocalized styling
of Louis Armstrong, Dizzy Gillespie caught your attention,
then came the prince of darkness' hip, cool music,
that turned your head & trumpet licks around
like a spinning top when you came to new york city
& met miles himself, who also loved what you were
playing on your flugel horn, it transformed you
& now you are a bona fide legend with a musical voice
shaped into an original instrument of beauty all your own,
a voice eye hear constantly echoing, threading music
through my head full of beautiful memories of you

SPACE TRAVELS

space travels around the world through wind storms
licking tongues blowing fiercely over mountaintops,
air crisscrossing city streets fluting there inside
sounds, chutes conveying voices of tribes sluicing news
clashing with other tribes, who have different hues and
cries because of skin color, though their thoughts might be
the same song and dance to the same music, speak the same
language though jitterbugging syllables might seem foreign—
to you due to the soil your blues rose from—though who
do you love in the region echoing memory of you
rooted in recognized drum beats, harmony, songs you heard
transporting melody inside ears back through time, resonant
as spheres heard in tears of Miles Davis' trumpet spears

stabbing words of poets riffing deep blue notes, sluiced
through sentences, cascading murmurs, clues unmasking
metaphors of choo-chooing train whistles, wooing hoodoo
Black Mississippi gospel, guitar lyrics reverberating,
infused with electric ghosts throughout Delta shadows,
who plunge through mysterious, fluttering silk curtains—
primordial senses—that wave, enveloping around
enchanting hours after midnight, when haints come out
and small birds flying with eagles like dots across white—
or red eyes—of moons stare down like a one-eyed cyclop
that always bewitches all doubters with questions

plunging through the mysterious curtain enveloping
senses, around the bewitching hour of midnight,
obscure flights of bats, soaring eagles, small birds remind
of zig-zagging dots zooming across perceptions of eyeballs
transmitting back to brains, signals whether feathers
lifting wings of eagles spread as if they were giant wings—
arms—of airplanes slicing through ether up there

in space, sharp as razor blades editing breath of rappers,
blues singers, or words—metaphors—paint brushing
strokes locking in sentences of modern day poets

down here on earth, men, women lacing transfixing
spells love infuses into their poetry when deep feeling is
scatting there, electric in the moment, in memory,
words cannot replace the beauty of soft lips cushioning
a haunting kiss with a probing tongue charging bodies
connected, as if wired with electricity around the globe,
great poets speak too as if they were live-wire bodies
and people know music of shaped expression deep
in their bodies, rhythms inside language there recognized
through tongues transporting folks back through time
to when and where questions are rooted in the soil,
where shared culture through a common verbal dialect
is heard in local songs music stitches through memory,
and echoed inside idioms, patois, licks trumpet riffs caress,
saxophone wails, guitars translate through plucking strings
that tremble, quiver over hammering ivory keys of pianos
block chording scherzos heard through cascading voices
people inside music know, hear language of tears
murmuring in the air mimicking flags fluttering foreign
dialects unmasking lewd secrets here beneath blues,
singing of the deep hoodoo lyrics of John Lee Hooker

underneath southern American skies filled with birds
washed with all colors and heard all around the world
casting spells of musical witch doctors and wired
deep into the voices of great American poets, whose
haunting metaphors slice through space and time
like a honed razor blade editing, and will live forever
in songs of troubadours singing around the globe,
beauty of poets space traveling through their poems
all over the interconnected globe of language love

brings a voice of redemption whispering a song
probing deep like a echoing sentence into our ears

A POEM FOR DEREK WALCOTT

like a bullet fired through space from the other side,
between light & darkness you came with a poem
sluicing from your lips, came with words constructing images
sharp as dagger points penetrating our bodies, brains
& ears like singing birds do in blushing green mid-morning
light, you came into my world like Neruda' s poem full gallop,
riding a lopping horse with a satchel filled with metaphors,
packed with original sly word plays & tricks,
your accented St. Lucian patois, switching back & forth
between proper—the Queen's English—& colloquial—Creole—
expressions, both ruminating in your poetic language,

now eye hear your foaming sea wave lines flow in here
hissing, in Juan Dolio, Santo Domingo, with accents
clipping, chopping, speeding through African influenced Spanish
full of salsa rooted in merengue, sluicing voodoo through French
laced with Spanglish, the many Haitians here who come to work,
speak, marinated in their *grio, lambi* based patois, laced
inside a kind of African based French-Spanglish—

it is remarkable how black folks everywhere shape, create language!

so eye listen to find your voice, Derek, in the salty sea speech
rolling in from the Caribbean, then roiling south, thundering,
hissing, foaming towards St. Lucia, where your spirit now rests,
facing your beloved sea, then eye hear your raspy voice
calling out to me from where you sleep, "don't fuck up this
tribute poem, Quincy, because you know I'm a Nobel Prize-winning
poet and you're not, motherfucker, & don't ever forget that!"
then eye hear that sneaky voice of yours break into a gaggle
of raspy giggles—almost a rush of chuckles, a lark—
cracking your small little mound of a stomach, shaking it
with side-splitting laughter, your sea green eyes laughing

so very hard it causes rivers of tears to burst, run down
splashing your ruddy, light brown face in rushing torrents

ANOTHER VIEW FROM SINES, PORTUGAL

for David Murray and Valerie

in Sines, Portugal, in David Murray's and Valerie's lovely house,
we rose each morning to a wondrous sweeping view,
of the Atlantic stretching west, no borders, no limits,
no boundaries holding it back, save wondrous expanses
our cruising minds sought to carry inside a profound beauty holding
this rich moment, a compulsive nature full of voices rising up
day, or night, Muslim, Christian exaltations,
intercourse with lovers in space mixed inside sounds of cars
passing barking dogs, sea waves voyaging in frothing as they eat
sandy shores like sharks chomping breakfast, lunch, dinner,
a dialog with white seagulls slicing over it all,
their bladed wings slicing through darkening skies
reminded of cleavers dripping red blood in a butcher's shop
as the sun sets in the west, outside my window here

looking northwest, eye see a grafitti covered wall swarming
with hip-hop scrawl echoing imagistic language of Jean Michel Basquiat's
paintings of horned skulls leering out from canvases
                                    shocking the world,
with an artistic handshake welcoming me to Sines,
whoever drew these images held a philosophy close to Basquiat's—
even mine is an affirmation, recognition, a handshake
shout out from Sines to New York city, that eye recognize here

CHASING WORDS IN LINES

for Toni Morrison; 1931–2019

eye am dreaming, thinking of sluicing words
structured into lines stretching across pages,
they remind of newborn bloody babies
pulled from wombs of fecund imaginations
when poets chase metaphors as painters, birth,
translate colors into rhythms of musicians, voices—
plucked from grapes clustered in vines, find
their places in fine wines on dinner tables—

shaped into contours of the world, they are echoes,
seeds popping from the ground as flowers, memories
stitched through poems as words—lyrics,
songs of bono—are leaps of faith, as in soul deep narratives
sewn into our lives inside Toni Morrison's books,
her sentences are blues underlining broken shards,
razor sharp as jazz they will cut you badly
if you're not ready to hear the sho nuff truth

but there is sweetness here too, in Toni's blues,
her vision full of grace beyond happenstance,
is a fertile place tracing america's history
shaped by bloodletting firing squads of race
to lay one's head down onto a pillow
& listen to the truth defining falsehoods
some historians serve up on forked tongues
laced with cyanide in race baiting narratives

but Toni cut through all duplicitous bullshit
with a voice clear as a sword's beheading fools
in her works of fiction, essays & public speeches,
she once said "art is dangerous" & left no doubt
who she was listening to—Miles Davis, Angela Davis,

John Coltrane, William Faulkner, Gabriel Garcia
Marquez, Lucile Clifton, Toni Cade Bambara, Ella

Fitzgerald, Jimmy Baldwin, Amiri Baraka, the silver
gloved wizard, Henry Dumas, Sonia Sanchez, street voices
she grew up listening to in Lorain, Ohio, the down-home
language of black women fixing hair in their kitchens,
black beauty parlor saturdays, sunday mornin' go to church
hand clappin' rituals shoutin' out the gospel of layin' on
of hands in sacred river baptismal ceremonies
serving as doorways for initiates to pass through

to kiss & greet spiritual ancestors in white robes,
it's where your spirit Toni Morrison just flew to
accompanied by hand clapping, singing black choirs
belting out hallelujahs & praise be to your name,
while cooing birds trilled lines of your prose,
flapping wings, we heard the word "excelsior"

PICKING A DANDELION

for Joe and Jill Biden, Cheryl and Charles Ward, and for Margaret

walking along together
in the nation's capitol
Joe stopped, stooped, picked a flower—
a dandelion to be exact—
then he handed it to Jill—
who smiled in her white summer,
dress full of pretty flowers,
and someone snapped a picture
of this sweet, simple gesture,
it revealed something deeper,
profound, beautiful about
their love for each other here,
that taught all of us watching,
how to reach across time, space,
with a tender touch, a kiss
for one another here, now
in this moment of hatred
before time on earth runs out

INDEX OF TITLES AND FIRST LINES

TITLES

FIRST LINES